1912
FACTS ABOUT TITANIC

Lee William Merideth

[signature]
APRIL 15, 2001

Historical Indexes Publishing Company
P. O. Box 64142
Sunnyvale, California 94088

Manufactured in the United States of America

1912 Facts About Titanic
by Lee W. Merideth

© 1999 Lee W. Merideth

Includes bibliographic references

Printing Number
10 9 8 7 6 5

ISBN 0-9626237-4-1 (paper)
ISBN 0-9626237-6-8 (cloth)

Historical Indexes Publishing Co.
P. O. Box 64142
Sunnyvale, California 94088

(408) 944-0352 (editorial and distribution)
(408) 944-0835 (fax)

Email: historyindex@earthlink.net
Visit us online at www.factsabouttitanic.com

This book is printed on 50-lb. acid free paper. It meets or exceeds the guidelines for permanence and durability of the Committee on Production Guidelines for Book Longevity of the Council on Library Resources.

For Eleanore, my mother, who will read this,
and for Edward, my late father, who won't.

It's not the great American Novel,
but it's a start.

TABLE OF CONTENTS

PHOTOGRAPHS

PHOTOGRAPHS

"...whatever fate had in store for them."

PREFACE

On April 11, 1912, many of the over 2,200 people on board watched the green hills of Ireland slowly disappear from view as the RMS *Titanic* steamed into the western sunset and into history.

Three and one half days later, two thirds of these people would be dead, most of them having frozen to death while bobbing in the dark and frigid waters of the North Atlantic Ocean, screaming for help that never arrived. Each suffered a horrible fate that few of us can even imagine.

The passengers on the *Titanic* were as diverse a group of individuals as you will find anywhere: some of the richest and most prominent people on two continents, traveling for business or pleasure, shared the same ship as some of the poorest European emigrants traveling to America to start a new life. During the first half of their voyage class distinction kept them apart, but then disaster struck and class distinction disappeared. The survivors all shared the same lifeboats, waiting for whatever fate had in store for them.

We have always been fascinated by the *Titanic* disaster. The world's largest and most luxurious passenger liner–the jewel of the premier steamship company–setting out on its maiden voyage and then, in the middle of the night, striking an iceberg and sinking. A creative fiction writer could not have generated a greater cast of characters or more unusual set of circumstances. There are so many "what ifs" in this story that a whole book could be written just about them: What if *Titanic's* officers had heeded ice warnings and slowed down? What if it had rammed the iceberg head-on? What if the water had not been so calm? What if the water had been warmer? What if there had been more lifeboats?

Titanic's sinking has been the subject of hundreds of articles, books, movies and videos. It is perhaps no surprise, then, that James Cameron's *Titanic* was the largest grossing movie of this century.

One feature of this tragedy is the nature of the people themselves. The calamity is filled with endless tales of strength in adversity, courage, honor, and remarkably few examples of cowardice. While their wives, sweethearts and children boarded the lifeboats and rowed away in the night, the men stood back, knowing they soon would die from the sub-freezing water. Then there was the crew who, given the opportunity to rush the lifeboats, didn't. And there were the engineers who must have known they were giving up their lives as they maintained the generators to keep the lights on for as long as possible.

One thing to keep in mind when you read about the *Titanic* disaster is that in the context of the early twentieth century, these things were the accepted norm. We cannot judge nor condemn what they did or didn't do because, eighty-five years from now, our descendants will be asking why we did some of the things we have done.

1912 Facts about the Titanic presents a collection of little-known facts and stories about the ship itself, the people who experienced her, and the tragic events of April 15, 1912. It is not intended as a definitive history of the ship and its brief life. Instead, this book is a collection of some of the most interesting information about the doomed liner. I chose not to specifically number each "fact," opting instead to simply set them forth for the reader to study and ponder. The "1912" in the title symbolizes the year in which the disaster occurred, not the specific number of facts contained in this book. In fact, there are far more "facts" than the title implies.

I would like to thank Jerry Russell of Civil War Round Table Associates, Little Rock, Arkansas, for developing the concept for this series, of which *1912* is but the first book of many to follow; my publisher, Theodore P. Savas, of Mason City, Iowa, for giving me the impetus to get it done (the threat of bodily harm has a wonderful way of focusing the mind); and most importantly David Lang, of San Jose, California, who helped with the editing of this book.

Finally, and most importantly, I want to thank my mother, Eleanore Merideth, who gently reminded me on a regular basis, as only a *mother* can, that if I didn't stop procrastinating I would never finish this effort. I heard the same arguments all through high school and college.

Mothers never change.

Lee W. Merideth
Sunnyvale, California
November, 1998

ti'tan'ic: a. Having great stature or enormous strength; huge; colossal. b. Of enormous scope, power or influence. *(Webster's Illustrated Encyclopedic Dictionary, 1990. Tormont Publications, Inc.)*

RMS TITANIC:

When she steamed out of the harbor at Southampton, England on her maiden voyage at noon on April 10, 1912, RMS Titanic was the largest movable object ever built. She was the engineering marvel of her time.

Titanic was state-of-the-art manufacturing, the crowning achievement of the industrial revolution, and the pride of a nation. The mammoth liner was the final word in Victorian luxury and opulence. Her construction was one of the monumental engineering feats of the century, and her sheer size bespoke safety and strength. Indeed no one could even conceive of anything that could cause it to sink. "Titanic," proclaimed a leading engineering journal, "is practically unsinkable."

Among her First Class passengers were some of the wealthiest and most famous men and women of the age, while Third Class accommodations held hundreds of the world's poorest emigrants, most traveling with everything they owned in the hope of starting a new life in America.

At 2:20 a.m. on April 15, 1912, just over one hundred and eight hours after leaving the dock at Southampton, the stern of the Titanic plunged into the icy waters of the North Atlantic Ocean beginning her two mile descent to the dark bottom of the sea. She took with her more than 1,500 souls in what was the worst peacetime sea disaster in history. Her loss stands as a grim reminder that man, despite his abilities to produce grand engineering accomplishments, cannot overcome nature.

The story of the RMS *Titanic* begins a half century before her launch. . .

"...practically unsinkable..."

CHAPTER 1

BIRTH OF A DREAM

In 1867 British shipping line owner Thomas H. Ismay purchased the White Star Line, a fleet of sailing vessels providing service to the Australian emigrant trade. Ismay felt that there were better profits to be made by servicing the business and emigrant trade from Europe to North America after the American Civil War.

Financing for Ismay's plans was guaranteed by financier Gustav Schwabe, whose nephew, Gustav Wolff, was part owner of a shipbuilding company. Ismay would have his money as long as his ships would be built at Schwabe's nephew's company.

■ Beginning in the mid 1860's, transatlantic passenger requirements were burgeoning because the United States government was offering unlimited freedom to immigrate due to the westward expansion into the Great Plains.

In order to escape war, poverty and religious persecution, well over one million immigrants were entering the United States every year from European countries.

■ Thomas Ismay reorganized the White Star Line into a new company called the Oceanic Steam Navigation Company but he retained the White Star Line name.

The only practical way to cross the North Atlantic before the invention of the airplane was to travel by steamship and there were really only three considerations a passenger had to make in deciding which ship to take: cost, speed or luxury and sometimes a combination of all.

There were dozens of steamship lines providing transatlantic passenger service and each steamship company had its own marketing angle. The White Star Line's boast was that their ships would be very fast and even more luxurious than any other ship in service. In balancing the two demands, White Star Line would always build their ships designed for luxury over speed.

■ The average transatlantic voyage took just under seven days to complete at 22 knots. If a ship could steam at 25 knots, the trip could be reduced by several hours, which allowed for a faster turnaround and ultimately more trips. But seven days, or even six and one-half days, was still a lot of time to spend on a liner. Thus, if you were planning on attracting the wealthy traveler, then you needed something better than your competition: unsurpassed luxury and service.

■ Steamship companies carrying First Class passengers catered to them to make their voyage worth the cost, but it was the Third Class passengers who actually generated the revenue to keep most of the liners running. In theory, steamship companies wanted to carry a good mix of First and Second Class passengers and plenty of Third Class passengers to make a profit.

■ In 1870 Ismay asked his friend William Imrie to join the company, and a new management company, Ismay, Imrie and Company was formed to manage the White Star Line.

■ In 1840 Hickson and Company, Ltd. was organized as a shipbuilding company on the River Lagan in Belfast, Ireland. In 1854 Edward J. Harland became general manager and then in 1859 he bought the company.
Harland was an engineer who made several significant contributions to the art of shipbuilding, primarily the replacement of wooden decks with iron decks. This method of construction made ships much stronger structurally and allowed for the building of even larger ships with more decks.
In 1861 Gustav Wolff joined up with Edward J. Harland and in 1862 the company was renamed Harland and Wolff. Fifteen year-old William Pirrie also joined Harland and Wolff in 1862 as a draftsman and by 1902 was the managing director of the company
With the purchase of the White Star Line by Thomas H. Ismay in 1867 and because of Ismay's agreement to have ships built at Gustav Wolff's company, Harland and Wolff became the sole provider of ships for the White Star Line.

■ In August 1870, *Oceanic*, the first ship built by Harland and Wolff for the White Star Line, was launched in Belfast, Ireland. Additional ships joined *Oceanic*, including *Atlantic, Baltic, Republic, Celtic* and *Adriatic*. (Most

White Star Line ships had names ending with -ic, including *Olympic* and *Titanic.*)

As the White Star Line grew, Harland and Wolff agreed not to build any ships for White Star Line competitors.

Harland and Wolff was considered to be the best and highest priced shipbuilding company in Europe. All work done for White Star Line was done on a cost-plus basis and no expenses were spared. The two companies worked so closely that Harland and Wolff invoices were paid without question.

■ Joseph Bruce Ismay, eldest son of Thomas H. Ismay, joined the White Star Line and in 1892 Thomas Ismay retired. The son, known by his middle name, became infamous when *Titanic* sank twenty years later.

In 1892 White Star announced that a ship named *Gigantic* would be built and launched in 1894, but the ship was never built.

By 1910 the White Star Lines owned and Harland and Wolff built the most modern and luxurious fleet of all North Atlantic liners.

■ The first large, modern steamship built for White Star Line was *Oceanic II*, completed in 1899. This ship was the first attempt by White Star to provide quality service, luxury and comfort instead of trying to compete with its competitors for speed.

■ American millionaire and financier J. Pierpont Morgan created the International Navigation Company of New Jersey in 1893 with the purchase of several smaller shipping lines and in 1902 changed the name to the International Mercantile Marine Company.

In 1902, the stockholders of White Star Line approved the sale of the company to the International Mercantile Marine Company (IMM). Although the sale was opposed by Bruce Ismay, the stockholders, with some influence from William Pirrie of Harland and Wolff, approved the sale and ownership of the White Star Line passed to the IMM on the last day of 1902.

Bruce Ismay was offered and he accepted the job as president and managing director of the IMM by J.P. Morgan in 1904, giving him unlimited control of the IMM.

Although the IMM was an American owned company, any ship owned or managed by the White Star Line would continue to have its home port in Britain, carry the British flag, be served by British crewmen and follow the shipbuilding guidelines and be governed by the regulations of the British Board of Trade.

By 1912 the IMM owned 120 ships with a total gross tonnage of over 1.1 million tons.

■ Because of the 1902 sale of the White Star Line to the IMM, the British government decided to subsidize rival Cunard Line to insure that Cunard would not also be sold. This support was seen as a potential military necessity because companies supported by the British government would have to allow their ships to revert to government service in the event of war, and any new Cunard ships would be part of the Reserve Fleet.

Passenger ships kept getting larger and in 1906 the two largest, fastest and most luxurious ships that had ever been built were launched: Cunard's 30,000 ton ships *Lusitania* and *Mauretania*. These ships culminated Cunard's attempt to regain their superiority in both size and speed.

■ In 1906 William Pirrie, now Lord Pirrie, started a major two-year modernization program at Harland and Wolff.

Three existing building slips were demolished and two huge building slips were created in their place.

A huge 240 foot by 840 foot steel gantry was built and it towered 214 feet over the building slips. The world's largest floating crane was built to assist in the construction of ships to be built in the new slips.

■ The safety record for the White Star Line was about average for most steamship companies of the time and in the forty years prior to 1912, White Star had survived some significant disasters.

In 1873 the *Atlantic*, sister ship to *Oceanic* ran aground off Halifax, Nova Scotia, only fifteen miles from its destination. Some 546 people, including many children, drowned in the worst *non-military* related maritime disaster in history up to that time.

(It should be noted that the worst disaster ever involving an American owned vessel was the 1865 sinking of the steamboat *Sultana* on the Mississippi River, where over 1,800 former US Army prisoners released from southern prisons after the Civil War were killed when *Sultana* blew up due to faulty steam boilers.)

In 1883 the *Noronic*, the largest livestock carrier in the world, was lost without a trace.

In 1893 the *Germanic* capsized in New York harbor due to an accumulation of ice on its upper decks. There was no loss of life and the ship was eventually salvaged and put back into service.

In 1907 the *Suevic* ran aground and lost 200 feet of its bow.

In 1909 the *Republic* sank after a collision with the Italian liner *Florida*. *Republic* took so long to sink that everyone on board was saved except two passengers killed in the initial collision. All of the passengers and crew were transported by lifeboats to *Florida* and other ships that were summoned by wireless.

Overall, in the thirty-nine years after *Atlantic* sank in 1873 until 1912, only four passengers of the millions who made the trip were lost on transatlantic voyages. This gave passenger travel on the new, modern steamships an excellent safety record. In fact, in the ten years ending in 1912, over two million passengers had crossed the Atlantic Ocean on White Star Line ships and there had only been two fatalities.

■ The quest to build larger, faster and more luxurious ships continued. By 1914, just in time to be affected by the outbreak of World War I, the German owned Hamburg America and North German Lloyd companies would own the largest passenger ships weighing in at 50,000 tons and the Hamburg America would be the largest owner of ships in the world. Most of these ships would be sunk, scrapped, or commandeered by England and her allies during or after the war.

The British government, in order to maintain its superiority in shipbuilding, contracted with Cunard to build *Lusitania* and *Mauretania*, which weighed in at 30,000 tons each. *Mauretania* set a speed record in 1909, crossing the Atlantic at an average of 26.6 knots, a record not broken until 1929.

Not wanting to be outdone, White Star Line would have to figure out how improve on the design of the Cunard ships. If they couldn't beat Cunard with speed, then they would overwhelm them with size, luxury and service.

■ In early 1907, Bruce Ismay and his wife were the dinner guests of Mr. and Mrs. William Pirrie. After dinner, Ismay and Pirrie retired to the study for coffee. During that time, while sketching ideas on a napkin, they developed the concept to build three mammoth ships to compete with all of their rivals. These ships would be so large they could carry more people than any other, ships so luxurious that even the Third Class passengers would be treated better than First Class passengers on other ships, ships so well built that they would be the last word in safety. One of these huge ships would eventually be named *Titanic*.

Titanic fitting out. The A deck Promenade has not been enclosed. National Archives

CHAPTER 2

THE WONDER SHIP

The concept behind the construction of *Titanic* and its two sister ships that night in Lord Pirrie's study was the latest step in the evolution of steamship construction. In the forty or so years ending in the early 1900's, ship construction had made the complete transformation from the age of sail and wooden ships to the enormous ships being turned out in several of the major countries around the world.

■ The reciprocating steam engine, turning one or more propellers and fueled by coal, had replaced the sail, the paddle wheel and the wood fired steam pressure cylinders of earlier ships. Shipbuilding technology had advanced in the previous forty years pretty much like aircraft technology would advance in the next forty. When Bruce Ismay and Lord Pirrie sketched out the design for their new ships in 1907, it had only been four years since the Wright brothers had made their first airplane solo in North Carolina.

Consequently, by looking at the history of change in just their lifetime, Ismay and Pirrie planned to take a major leap in construction of their ships, knowing full well that whatever they did would be superseded in the future.

■ The Cunard Lines' two masterpiece ships *Lusitania* and *Mauretania* had been in service over a year when Ismay and Pirrie had their meeting. Both ships had broken the transatlantic speed records, they were the two largest ships afloat, and they were by far the most luxurious. The rich-and-famous traveled by these two ships whenever possible. Ismay and Pirrie knew exactly what they had to produce in order to regain the prestige lost to Cunard. White Star Line had made it a business practice to place luxury over speed, and Ismay and Pirrie went into the planning phase for their new ships knowing that they could not, and would not, attempt to match the speed of the Cunard liners.

To keep it from being sold to foreign investors, Cunard was heavily subsidized by the British government. Cunard and the Royal Navy worked together to develop a new type of reciprocating engine and they jointly held the patent on the design. White Star and Harland and Wolff didn't have the development funds to design their own engines to match these, so didn't even try. They knew that the few extra hours that passengers would spend on their three ships would be offset by the luxury and innovations they would incorporate into them.

■ It was a given fact that White Star Lines and Harland and Wolff would collaborate on the design and construction of the ships on the usual cost plus basis. No expense would be spared in the building of them and the latest technology would be used. If the technology didn't exist, then it would be developed. Harland and Wolff would build to White Star specifications and Harland and Wolff would be responsible for building every part of these ships with very little of the work being subcontracted out.

Three ships would be built of this, the *Olympic* class passenger liners. With the turnaround time of three weeks to New York City and back plus port time to load and unload, (seven days out, three days in New York, seven days back and four days in Southampton) it was planned that once all three were completed, there would be a departure from Southampton every Wednesday at noon.

■ Two of the three ships would be built almost simultaneously at the two newly enlarged slipways at the Harland and Wolff shipyard on the River Lagan in Belfast, Ireland. Approval to build the ships was given by White Star Line in April 1907 and preliminary work was begun immediately. On December 16, 1908 the keel for the first ship, hull number 400 was laid down and on and on March 31, 1909 hull number 401 was begun next to its sister ship. The keel for the third ship was laid down in 1911. In keeping with the White Star Line tradition, the names of the ships would end in -ic, and to convey their size, White Star would name them, in the order they were built, *Olympic, Titanic* and *Gigantic*. (In response to the loss of *Titanic, Gigantic* was renamed *Britannic* before it was completed).

Harland and Wolff's hull number 401 would become RMS *Titanic*. It would be a truly magnificent ship.

CONSTRUCTION SPECIFICATIONS

The two liners *Olympic* and *Titanic* were built from the same plans, however changes made to *Titanic* before it entered service would make it larger and heavier than its sister ship. Here are the specifications for *Titanic*:

Approval for Construction:	April 1907
Keel laid down:	March 31, 1909
Launched:	May 31, 1911
Maiden Voyage:	April 10, 1912
Length:	882 feet, 9 inches
Beam (width):	92 feet, 6 inches
Height, keel to bridge	104 feet
Height, keel to top of funnels:	175 feet
Decks:	10
Weight:	46,328 tons
Displacement:	66,000 tons
Service speed:	21 knots
Maximum speed:	24-25 knots
Primary designer:	Alexander Carlisle, brother-in-law of Lord Pirrie.
Supervisor of Construction:	Thomas Andrews, nephew of Lord Pirrie.
Cost, 1912 dollars:	$7.5 million
Cost, 1998 dollars:	$126 million

(The value of a 1912 dollar is worth about $16.80 in 1998.)

EQUIPMENT

Anchors: Two at 7.5 tons each (located port and starboard) and one at 15.5 tons (center), kept on the forecastle deck. The center anchor took a team of 20 horses to move it to the construction site.

Anchor cables: Two at 96 tons each and one for the center anchor at 101 tons. The anchor chain for the center anchor was 1050 feet long.

Rivets: Three million, weighing a total of 1,200 tons.

Engines: Two four cylinder, triple expansion reciprocating engines. The pistons on each engine were eight feet in diameter and the engines themselves weighed 1,000 tons each and were four stories tall, still the largest ever built. There was also one 420 ton steam turbine engine.

Horsepower: Each reciprocating engine produced 15,000 horsepower and the turbine engine generated 16,000 horsepower. The port and starboard reciprocating engines were powered by steam directly from the boilers. The excess steam, instead of being vented into the air, was used to power the center turbine engine.

Boilers: There were 24 double-ended boilers (could be fed from both ends), 20 feet long and 15 feet 9 inches in diameter with six furnaces. These boilers weighed 100 tons each. There were also five single ended boilers, 11 feet 9 inches long, 15 feet 9 inches in diameter with 3 furnaces.

Furnaces: There were 159 coal fired furnaces, shoveled by hand from coal bunkers.

Coal capacity: 8,000 tons. When steaming, the ship would consume 650 tons of coal per day. Coal bunkers were located close to the furnaces, but even then over four tons of coal had to be shoveled into each furnace every day by the stokers whose job it was to feed the fires.

Propellers: Two three-bladed wing propellers, each 23.5 feet in diameter. These were counter-rotating (turned toward each other), which was a new design concept that allowed for a much smoother ride for the passengers. These propellers could also be reversed to allow the ship to back up or stop in an emergency. There was also one four-bladed propeller in the center and it was 16.5 feet in diameter. This was powered by the steam turbine and could not be reversed.

Rudder: 78 feet high, weighing 101 tons.

Funnels: There were four funnels, each 60 feet high, 22 feet wide and large enough to drive 2 locomotives through side-by-side.

Number 1: (closest to the bow), vented boiler rooms 5 and 6
Number 2: vented boiler rooms 3 and 4
Number 3: vented boiler rooms 1 and 2
Number 4: (closest to the stern) a dummy funnel added to help with the aesthetic design of the ship, this funnel was used to vent the engine rooms and the galleys (kitchens).

Mast, forward: 101 feet high, made of steel except the top 15 feet which was made of teak wood. Contained inside the mast was a 50 foot ladder the lookouts used to climb into the crow's nest. The mast was raked (tilted) 2 inches per foot.

Mast, aft: 97 feet high, with a teak top and raked 2 inches per foot. This mast did not have a ladder inside or a crow's nest.

Marconi antenna: What we would now call the radio antenna was stretched between the two masts.

Whistle: Triple valve, so large that when blown it would rattle windows for miles around.

Structure, frame: Steel frames three feet apart, except for the bow where they were two feet apart and the stern at two feet five inches apart. The bow was built stronger to reduce damage in case the ship ever ran into anything, such as another ship or maybe even an iceberg.

Structure, bottom: There was a double bottom which was a series of sealed compartments seven feet high across the entire bottom of the ship.

Structure, plates: The ship was built with one inch thick steel plates, triple riveted with hydraulic rams. The plates were then sealed to prevent leakage.

Electrical supply: Four 400-kilowatt steam-powered generators with an output of 16,000 amperes provided electricity to power:

150 motors (76 used to run the ventilation fans)
10,000 light bulbs
A 50-line internal telephone system
48 clocks
1,500 push buttons to call for attendants
dozens of electric signs
520 portable heaters and fans
Marconi wireless system
Eight 2-1/2 ton cargo cranes
the huge whistle
four elevators
15 watertight doors
and hundreds of lessor electrical items such as: kitchen machinery (mixers, mincers, potato-peelers, roasters, ovens, stoves and hot plates); passenger services (fans, lamps, electrical requirements) and ship operations (winches, ships elevators, work shop tools, water heaters and refrigeration).

THE SAFEST SHIP AFLOAT

■ *Titanic* was designed to be watertight and the builders achieved that expectation.

The hull was divided into 16 watertight compartments by 15 transverse (meaning going across the hull from port to starboard) watertight bulkheads.

■ The purpose of the watertight bulkheads was to prevent the ship from sinking in case of a collision.

The design allowed the ship to float if any two amidships compartments or the first four compartments flooded. *Titanic* would also float long enough to rescue the passengers and crew if any three amidship compartments or the first five compartments were flooded, assuming that help would be available within a few hours.

The first two bulkheads extended up to D deck, the next eight up to E deck and the last five up to D deck. (Generally, on a ship the lowest deck—nearest to the keel—has the highest letter assignment. Thus, the A deck is often the highest deck on a ship. On *Titanic*, the A deck was the second highest; the Boat deck was the highest.) Unfortunately, some of those bulkheads that only went up to D deck extended just a few feet above the waterline. Due to the slant of the decks, raising higher toward the bow and stern, even E deck amidships was only fifteen feet above the waterline.

Three of the bulkheads near the bow of the were fairly close together to reduce the amount of potential damage if the ship rammed another object.

■ There were three major design flaws in the construction of the watertight compartments:

First, the decks themselves weren't watertight due to the many openings for stairs, ladders, elevators, etc. Because the bulkheads did not extend above E deck, (or D deck in many instances), if the bow of the ship was flooded the weight of the water would pull the ship downward and eventually the water would overflow the top of the bulkheads and spill into the adjacent compartment even if it hadn't been breached.

Second, the watertight bulkheads were transverse, but there weren't any longitudinal bulkheads running the *length* of the compartments. Thus, if water entered through a hole in the side of the ship, it would fill the entire compartment and could cause the ship to list (tilt) to one side or the other, which then could cause it to capsize.

Finally, there was a 12 foot wide corridor that ran almost the entire length of E deck that was used by the crew to move around the ship. It was also the only way Third Class passengers could move from the bow to stern. This corridor was an open channel for water to travel the length of the ship.

■ Connecting the watertight compartments were huge watertight doors.

Only 14 of the watertight doors on the lowest deck could be closed from the bridge. There were, however, three ways to close those doors:

1) Electrically, all doors from the bridge of the ship.

2) Manually, all doors by a member of the crew.

3) Automatically, by a unique float device located next to each door that would close the door if there were more than six inches of water in the compartment.

All remaining watertight doors on the other decks had to be closed by a crewmember with a special key and only upon receiving orders from a ship's officer.

■   An innovation hailed as an important safety feature was the double bottom which was tall enough for a man to stand in. The inner set of plates were 3/4 inch thick steel and the compartments inside were sealed. The double bottom was designed to provide an extra method of protection. If the outer plates were pierced, the water would be prevented from flooding the ship by the inner plates.

Unfortunately, the double bottom did not extend up the sides of the ship. Since it did not extend past the water line it was only effective if something pierced the bottom of the ship and not the sides.

■   In spite of all of its flaws, *Titanic* was designed and built to be the safest ship afloat. Because of its size, there was absolutely nothing the designers or builders could envision that could happen to the ship to cause it to sink, or to sink so rapidly that the people on board wouldn't have ample time to be safely evacuated.

If the ship were to ram another ship, which was a fairly common occurrence in those days, the damage would be absorbed by the bow and the three watertight bulkheads and four watertight compartments located there.

If *Titanic* was rammed by another ship, it was possible that two of the watertight compartments would be ruptured, but there wasn't a ship large enough to rupture three compartments, including its sister ship *Olympic*.

If the ship ripped open its keel by grounding, the double bottom would prevent generalized flooding.

Finally, *Titanic* was equipped with the most powerful wireless station of any ship afloat. Ships for hundreds of miles around could be summoned immediately if there was a need for help. Ship traffic in the North Atlantic in the early 1900's was intense, and few ships traveling the normal traffic lanes ever went more than a few hours without coming into visual contact with another ship.

■   No White Star Line officer or any other official ever called *Titanic* "*unsinkable*," however newspapers in the United States and Britain were always trying to find new names for the ship.

It was called "*the Wonder Ship*", the "*Last Word in Luxury*" and Wall Street called it "*the Millionaires' Special*".

It was, however, the very prestigious journal *Shipbuilder Magazine* that called *Titanic* "*practically unsinkable*," and it was the title "*unsinkable*" that captured the imagination of the public.

A WALKING TOUR OF TITANIC

■ There were ten decks on *Titanic* and her sister ships. If you were to take a tour of the ship starting on the bottom deck and walking from the bow to the stern, this is what you would see:

Tank top

■ Not considered a deck, this was the top of the double bottom. There was no direct access to this deck by passengers. It served as the foundation for all the engines, generators, boilers, coal bunkers, fresh water storage and contained some cargo storage.

Also, this is the deck where the electrically operated watertight doors were located in the watertight bulkheads.

Orlop Deck

■ The first (and considered the lowest) deck; no direct passenger access and completely below the waterline. From bow to stern, significant areas based upon the compartments created by the watertight bulkheads were (compartments are numbered from bow-to-stern, numbers 1 through 16 on this deck, 1 through 15 on the remaining decks):

Compartment 1: Forepeak (chain locker for anchor chains)
Compartment 2: cargo
Compartment 3: cargo, including motor cars
Compartment 4: mail sorting room, First and Second Class
    baggage room
Compartment 5: boiler room #6 and coal bunkers
Compartment 6: boiler room #5 and coal bunkers
Compartment 7: boiler room #4 and coal bunkers
Compartment 8: boiler room #3 and coal bunkers
Compartment 9: boiler room #2 and coal bunkers
Compartment 10: boiler room #1 and coal bunkers
Compartment 11: two reciprocating engines
Compartment 12: turbine engine
Compartment 13: electrical switchboard; beer, wine, spirits,
    mineral water storage, tobacco and cigar storage; general
    groceries, beef storage and thawing room, bulk storage.
Compartment 14: refrigerated cargo
Compartment 15: general cargo
Compartment 16: peak tank (this deck only)

G Deck (or Lower Deck)

■ This is the lowest deck that had passenger and crew accommodations. Because of the slope of the deck the bow and the stern were above the waterline so there were portholes to allow air and light in. The amidships portion was below the water line. There were no doors in the watertight bulkheads between Second and Third Class accommodations, so the two classes were totally isolated on this deck. The only access passengers had were from the deck above.

Compartment 1: chain locker.
Compartment 2: crew accommodations for 45 firemen and greasers; foundation for the two-four deck high spiral staircases used for crew access between the decks.
Compartment 3: 26 third class cabins.
Compartment 4: First Class baggage, Post Office, registered mail, 10 Third Class cabins, Squash Racquet Court for First Class passengers, accessible from the deck above.
Compartment 5-10: continuation of boiler rooms and coal bunkers.
Compartment 11: continuation of engine room, paint storage, engineers storage and workshop.
Compartment 12: continuation of turbine engine.
Compartment 13: bulk storage for groceries; store rooms for flour, ice cream, ice, butter, fruit, fish, bacon, vegetables, mutton, milk, ice making machine, plus ready storage of all of the above for the restaurants.
Compartment 14: 40 Third Class cabins (or, if needed some could be used for Second Class).
Compartment 15: 20 Third Class cabins and blanket storage.

F Deck (or Middle Deck)

■ This was the first deck completely above water line, contained mixed passenger and crew accommodations and equipment to operate the ship. Along the hull on both sides of the ship were the coal shutes, where colliers (coal barges) could be used to load coal into the coal bunkers.

Compartment 1: chain locker.
Compartment 2: crew accommodations for 57 firemen and greasers with access via the spiral staircase.
Compartment 3: 26 Third Class cabins.
Compartment 4: mail clerks, linen storage, 22 Third Class cabins.
Compartment 5: boiler casing, fan shaft, 33 Third Class cabins.

Compartment 6: boiler casing and fan shaft, swimming bath for First Class passengers with two showers and 13 dressing rooms, linen storage, washing and drying.

Compartment 7: boiler casing and fan shaft, Turkish Bath, three dressing rooms and two shampoo rooms for First Class passengers, Turkish Bath attendants cabins, steam rooms and hot air tanks for hot water, dormitory for 11 cooks and 42 Third Class stewards.

Compartment 8: boiler casing and fan shaft, one half of the Third Class Dining Saloon.

Compartment 9: boiler casing and fan shaft, one half of Third Class Dining Saloon, pantry.

Compartment 10: boiler casing and fan shaft, dormitories for six butchers, six bakers and Third Class stewards; bakery; Third Class galley (kitchen), pots and pans storage and washing. The dog kennels were also located here.

Compartment 11: engine casing, accommodations for all of the ships' engineers.

Compartment 12: turbine engine casing, 13 Second Class cabins.

Compartment 13: 33 Second Class cabins, base of Second Class elevator.

Compartment 14: 18 Second Class cabins and one steward's cabin.

Compartment 15: 34 Third Class cabins.

E Deck (or Upper Deck)

■ All the decks from the tank top to E deck were divided up into watertight compartments. Most of the bulkheads except where crew or passengers were prevented from entering engineering spaces or where two classes of passengers were prevented from making contact, had watertight doors in them. As on all the other decks, these doors could only be closed manually.

E deck was the first deck that lacked watertight bulkheads: eight of them were missing in the middle of the ship. There were still bulkheads in the first two compartments and the last five, but the majority of the ship on E deck was wide open to an inrush of water.

All three classes and the crew had accommodations on E deck.

Over two thirds of the starboard side was occupied by First Class passenger cabins while most of the port side contained crew dormitories and cabins.

■ One of the most noticeable features of E deck was the 12 foot wide corridor on the port side that ran along all of the boiler casings and almost the entire length of the ship. This was the primary crew corridor and the only access that Third Class passengers had from the bow to the stern of the ship. This corridor was called "Scotland Road" by the crew in reference to the busy working class road in Liverpool. "Scotland Road" was always a hive of activity as the crewmembers traveled about their duties and the passengers visited friends and family that had accommodations at the opposite end of the ship.

A narrower corridor connecting all of the First Class cabins on the starboard side was called "Park Lane" after a more fashionable street in London.

■ First Class cabins were virtually isolated from the rest of the deck. There were only three doors that would allow passage by Second and Third Class passengers into the First Class areas. They were always closed and locked because they opened onto "Scotland Road."

The deck plan for E deck is a case study in throwing things together. It probably made sense to the designers, but with its maze of corridors, one can understand why the Third Class passengers would have a hard time finding their way out of that portion of the ship.

Compartment 1: storage and chain locker.
Compartment 2: dormitories for 72 trimmers.
Continuing aft from compartment 2 to about where compartment 3 would end if the watertight bulkhead extended up this high was a dormitory for 44 seamen and numerous washrooms and toilets for the crew. Following this was a wide corridor extending to both sides of the ship. At each end of this corridor was the Third Class gangway where passengers entered the ship while in port. Facing this passageway, in the middle of the ship, was the Master-at-Arms office.

■ Next came the First Class accommodations on the starboard side. These ran all the way from about where the Compartment 3-4 bulkhead would have been if there had been a watertight bulkhead here to where the Compartment 12-13 bulkhead was.

"Park Lane" ran the entire length of this section, broken only by two watertight bulkheads with watertight doors at compartments 10-11 and 11-12. These doors were always kept open and could only be closed by a crewman.

There were 91 First Class cabins in this area, about one-third of which did not have an outside view. These cabins did not have toilet facilities so there were a large number of toilets and washrooms in this area.

Also in this area was the base of the three First Class elevators and the five story First Class Grand Staircase.

On the opposite side of "Scotland Road", moving aft from the Third Class gangway were eight Third Class cabins; crew dormitories for quartermasters; carpenters; plate washers (20); Second Class stewards (62); library, smoking lounge and pantry stewards; saloon waiters (106); First and Second Class bedroom stewards; First Class cooks; barkeepers and storekeepers; engineers' mess; the restaurant staff; plus numerous storerooms, including some for potatoes and a room in which to wash potatoes.

Compartment 13: Seven Second Class and three Third Class cabins and various storerooms, separated by Scotland Road. There was also a wide corridor that ran the width of the ship with a gangway door on each side that served as the main Second Class entrance to the ship.

Compartment 14: 11 Second Class and 23 Third Class cabins, again separated by Scotland Road, plus the Second Class Purser's Office and cabin and a dormitory for the musicians in the orchestra and a separate room for their instruments.

Compartment 15: 30 Third Class cabins and various storerooms.

D Deck (or Saloon Deck)

■   This deck contained accommodations for all classes and crew. This was also the deck where most people ate their meals. It was the first deck that didn't contain any watertight bulkheads or doors.

In the bow were dormitories for 108 firemen and the top of the two spiral staircases for crew use. There was a solid wall running across the ship to prevent the crew from entering into the passenger sections of the ship.

Next was a large open room, extending across the width of the ship. This was the Third Class open space which was just a huge room for social gatherings. Access to this room was from E deck below and C deck above. There was a solid wall between it and the next space aft.

■   Next came 49 First Class cabins, along with several cabins for stewards and stewardesses and a large number of toilets and washrooms.

Next was the opulent First Class Reception Room extending across the width of the ship.

Beyond the Reception Room through huge double glass doors was the magnificent First Class Dining Saloon extending across the width of the ship. Large floor to ceiling windows provided light into the room.

Then came the First Class Pantry, followed by the First and Second Class Galley, then the Second Class Pantry and all the attendant storerooms and food preparation areas, including the bakery and butcher shops.

■ Also located on the starboard side, next to the Second Class Pantry, were the seven rooms of the ship's hospital, including two rooms reserved for infants.

The next room was the Second Class Dining Saloon, again stretching across the width of the ship, followed by 39 Second Class cabins.

Following another bulkhead with a single door were another 11 Third Class cabins including large cabins for families with several members.

C Deck (or Shelter Deck)

■ This was the lowest deck have access to the open air. Only crew and First Class accommodations were located on it, but this deck contained the common areas for both Second and Third Class passengers.

In the forward section were the seaman's and firemen's mess and galley, crew hospital, various shops and storerooms and the windless gear used to raise and lower the anchors. There were no access doors to the forward well deck.

Next came the forward well deck, an open air deck that served as an area for the Third Class passengers to congregate. Also located here were two electrically powered cargo cranes.

■ From the solid wall at the end of the well deck down to the First Class entrance were 54 First Class cabins, Purser's cabin and stewardess's cabins.

On either side of the First Class entrance, with its Grand Staircase and three elevators, were 12 more First Class cabins, the Purser's Office and the Enquiry Office. Passengers used the Enquiry Office to arrange the sending and receiving of wireless messages or to pay for access to the Turkish Baths.

Next on the port side was the large stateroom containing cabins C62, C64 and C66 while on the starboard side was another three-cabin stateroom C55, C57 and C59. Each of these large staterooms was equipped with its own bathroom facilities.

■ Along the next one-half length of the ship were 72 First Class suites, some with doors that made them into adjoining suites. About half of the suites contained their own toilet and bathroom.

Also in this area were the pantry and saloon for maids and valets, a separate one for the Marconi operators and another for the postal workers. Cabins for the medical staff and the surgery were located here, along with the stewardesses cabin, the First Class barber shop and the aft Grand Staircase that went up to the Boat deck.

■ Next behind the First Class area and accessible through locked doors was the Second Class enclosed promenade with large floor to ceiling windows surrounding the Second Class Entrance and Second Class Library.

Next came the aft well deck which was the Third Class Promenade and which was also open to the air. Two more of the electrically operated cargo cranes were located here.

Following this was the Third Class Smoking Room on the port side and the Third Class General Room on the starboard side.

Finally, the last section of C deck contained the steering engines, capstan gear and the top of the rudder.

B Deck (Containing the Forecastle, Bridge and Poop Decks)

First Class accommodations and common areas were located on this deck.

■ **Forecastle Deck**: From the bow to the well deck were located the anchor capstans, anchor chains, center anchor and other mechanical equipment. This was all open to the air, and it is where Rose Dewitt Bukater (Kate Winslet) and Jack Dawson (Leonardo DeCaprio) did their flying scene in James Cameron's film *Titanic*.

On B deck there was a gap between the forecastle and the main part of the superstructure (called the Bridge deck). This gap was left for the opening created by the well deck, one level below.

■ **Bridge Deck**: After this gap came the First Class open corridor that ran the width of the ship and looked down into the well deck. The front of this corridor was open to the weather.

■ Between the open corridor and the First Class entrance were another 49 First Class cabins plus toilets and washrooms.

Next came the huge First Class entrance. On either side of the ship were two First Class gangways that passengers used to enter the ship, and in the center was the Grand Staircase and elevators.

Next on the port side was one of the two Grand Promenade Suites, cabins B52, B54 and B56, with its own bathroom, servants quarters and a private thirty-foot enclosed promenade. On the starboard side was the other suite, B51, B53 and B55.

Following these were 24 First Class suites, each with its own bathroom and 22 other First Class cabins without bathrooms.

Next was the aft Grand Staircase, the à la carte restaurant, galley and pantry. Located on the starboard side was the Café Parisian.

■ The next section of C deck contained the Second Class promenade, entrance, gangway, bar and the Smoking Room which overlooked the aft well deck. There was another gap here for the aft well deck, one level down on C deck.

■ **Poop Deck:** Beyond the aft well deck was the Poop deck, the raised open area at the stern of the ship. This deck was open to Third Class passengers and contained many capstan's and other equipment required to operate the ship.

On top of the Poop deck, running across the width of ship, was the Docking Bridge which was used by the ships officers when docking the ship.

A Deck

This deck was reserved for First Class passengers and contained the covered First Class Promenade that was also enclosed on the forward half of the deck. This enclosure was unique to *Titanic* and it is the only visible difference between it and its sister ship *Olympic*. The enclosure was added shortly before *Titanic* was completed because passengers on *Olympic* had complained about spray from the bow blowing across the deck.

■ Next came 34 First Class cabins followed by the First Class entrance and Grand Staircase.

From the First Class entrance, a corridor with a revolving door extended to the First Class Lounge. This corridor was originally designed to allow passengers an enclosed passage between the entrance and the lounge, because when designed and built, the promenade deck wasn't enclosed.

Adjoining the Lounge on the port side were the Reading and Writing Room and Library.

After the First Class Lounge and its bar, another enclosed corridor and revolving door led to the aft First Class entrance and its Grand Staircase. Located along this corridor were various lounges and bars for the outside decks.

Next was the First Class Smoking Room followed by the Verandah and Palm Court. This court was divided into two parts, one on each side of enclosed Second Class Grand Staircase.

Finally, on the open deck at the aft end of A deck were two more electrically operated cranes.

Boat Deck

The Boat deck was the open top deck where much of the drama of *Titanic* would be played out. Most of the deck was either open promenade for the passengers or the deck house used by the crew. There were, however, two items that dominated the Boat deck: the four funnels and the 20 lifeboats.

■ The forward end of the Boat deck was occupied by the bridge which is where the ships' officer's operated and navigated *Titanic*. Glass enclosed the middle third of the bridge to keep the weather off the crew who worked there. Located in this area were the telemeters which telegraphed instructions to the engine and boiler rooms and docking bridge.

On either side of this enclosed area was the open bridge which extended all the way to the sides of the ship. Each of the port and starboard ends of this open area had a small room enclosed on three sides with windows. These rooms were called the bridge wings. It was from these little cubes that the ship's officers could look directly down to the water and along the entire side of the ship.

Behind the glassed-off middle section of the Bridge was the Wheel House. Located in here was the huge wheel that the quartermaster turned in order to steer the ship. The Wheel House was completely enclosed because it also contained the compass, the master control to close the watertight doors and other electrical equipment.

■ Behind the Wheel House on the starboard side was the Navigation Room where charts were kept to track the ship's voyage.

Next behind the Navigation Room was the Captain's Sitting Room, followed by his bedroom and then his bathroom.

The Fourth Officer's cabin was next, followed by the Officers Smoking Room, a pantry and finally some storerooms.

■ On the port side behind the Wheel House was located the Chief Officers' cabin, followed by the First, Second, Third, Fifth and Sixth Officer's cabins and several other rooms.

■ Located on a passageway connecting the cabins on the port and starboard sides, and directly behind the boiler casing for the first funnel, were the three Marconi Wireless rooms: an office in the center, a silent room where transmissions were made to one side, and a bedroom for the operators on the other side.

Located on both sides of the deck house was the Officer's Promenade, open deck space normally reserved for the ship's officers.

■ Behind all the ship's offices came the Grand First Class entrance with its magnificent Grand Staircase and, above it all, the huge glass and wrought iron dome to let the daylight in. This was also the top floor of the three elevators that carried passengers down to E deck.

Next came the boiler casing for the second funnel and on the port side was located the Gymnasium.

Then came a long, low and flat structure that was really the raised roof of the First Class Lounge. This roof covered the glass windows that extended around the ceiling of most of the lounge to provide light. There was also a raised skylight in the middle of this roof.

Next followed the boiler casing for the third funnel, on the port side of which was the Officer's Mess.

Located on both sides of the ship, from the closed off Officers' Promenade to the end of the third funnel was the First Class Promenade.

■ The next deckhouse was reserved for machinery and holding tanks for water, gravity being used to run drinking water throughout the ship. There was also an engineer's smoking room and the dome over the aft First Class Grand Staircase.

Following this was another low structure that was the roof over the First Class Smoking Room with windows that provided sunlight into that room.

On top of this was a deckhouse that housed the casing for the fourth funnel and storage rooms for deck equipment, games, and other miscellaneous items.

Surrounding this area was the Second Class Promenade, which was accessible from B deck via an enclosed room that contained the top of the Second Class grand staircase.

■ Just aft of the first and the third funnels were the expansion joints that ran all the way from the Boat deck down to the keel. These joints were placed there to allow for the expansion and contraction of the ship as the steel from which it was made heated and cooled due to fluctuations in the temperature.

■ **Funnels:** Topping off the boat deck were the four funnels, each 60 feet high and 22 feet wide. The first three vented the boiler rooms and the fourth was a dummy for appearance's sake, although it was used to vent steam and smoke from the galleys.

Each funnel was held in place by several huge cables attached near the top of the funnel and to the deck. Some of the cables for the forward funnel actually attached to the deck aft of the forward expansion joint.

The lower two thirds of the funnels were painted a buff color and the top third was painted black.

LIFEBOATS, PART I

■ The most prominent items on the Boat deck were the objects for which it was named: the 16 lifeboats (14 large and two small) and four Englehardt Collapsible lifeboats.

The 14 large wooden lifeboats were each 30 feet long, nine feet wide, four feet deep and had a capacity of 65 people.

The two smaller emergency boats had a capacity of 35 people each.

The sixteen regular wooden boats with a total capacity of 980 people were all the lifeboats required by the British Board of Trade regulations.

The builders of the *Titanic* also added four extra boats, the Englehardt Collapsibles, each 27 feet long, eight feet wide and three feet high. All had a capacity of 49 people, for a total of 196 additional people.

In all, there was lifeboat capacity for a total of 1,176 people. Unfortunately, *Titanic* was designed to carry 3,295 people and, on its maiden voyage, would carry 2,234 passengers and crew.

■ The lifeboats were numbered 1 through 16 and the collapsibles were lettered A through D.

The odd numbered boats 1, 3, 5, 7, 9, 11, 13 and 15 were on the starboard side of the ship. The even numbered boats 2, 4, 6, 8, 10, 12, 14 and 16 were on the port side, directly opposite the odd-numbered boats.

Boat number 1 on the starboard side and number 2 on the port side were the two small emergency boats. These were located closest to the bridge and were permanently swung out to be ready to lower in case of an emergency such as someone falling overboard.

All sixteen of the boats were already attached to falls and davits and were covered with canvas. All had oars, a pole and a sail, but none of them had any sort of supplies except for a gallon tin of water.

■ On the deck next to emergency boat number 1 was collapsible C, and next to emergency boat number 2 was collapsible D. Both of these boats already had their canvas sides made up.

Stored on the starboard side roof of the officers' cabins was collapsible A and on the port side was collapsible B. These boats were stored right side up but with their canvas sides down. They were securely tied down. Because of their weight, they would not be easy to maneuver off the roof. It is unknown why they were placed on the roof, but for all intents and purpose, they were useless in an emergency.

"They just builds 'er and shoves 'er in."

CHAPTER 3

FITTING OUT

The keel of the *Titanic* was laid down at Harland and Wolff's Belfast shipyard on March 31, 1909, three months after construction of its sister ship *Olympic* had begun. Construction of the two ships at the same time would severely tax the ability of Harland and Wolff to construct them. Because of their size, most of the existing engineering or mechanical equipment couldn't be used, so everything had to be built specifically for these ships.

■ Over 15,000 Belfast workers were be involved in the building of the two ships. It was a city-wide event as most of the residents of Belfast were involved to some extent in the construction. Everyone in town knew about the ships and they were the pride of the city.

The citizens were awed by the size of the 840 foot long, 240 foot wide and 214 foot high gantry that stood higher than any structure in town and dwarfed all other buildings in the shipyard.

■ There was a 200 ton floating crane that could lift 150 tons which made it ideal for lifting the engines and boilers.

Titanic was fully framed on April 6, 1910 and plating was completed on October 19, 1910.

Olympic and *Titanic* were built side-by-side and the hull of *Olympic* was painted white and *Titanic* black so that workers could tell the two apart.

While construction of the twin ships took place in Belfast, the port authorities in New York were using taxpayer money to dredge out part of the Hudson River and extend two of the White Star Line piers another 100 feet into the river to accommodate them.

■ On May 2, 1911 *Olympic* started her fitting-out trials in the basin of the River Lagan, and on May 29 she started two days of sea trials in the

Olympic (right) plated and *Titanic* framed but barely visible. *National Archives*

Titanic (left) now plated while *Olympic* is being prepared for launch. *National Archives*

Belfast Lough. When the trials were completed on May 31st, *Olympic* returned to Belfast and made preparations to steam to Southampton to prepare for its maiden voyage. But something else was happening in the Harland and Wolff shipyard in Belfast that day that was far more interesting to the 100,000 Belfast residents who turned out to witness it: the launch of the *Titanic*.

LAUNCH

■ The residents of Belfast and the surrounding areas started to gather early on the morning of May 31, 1911 to watch the launch of *Titanic*. People lined all the docks and stood on any vantage point they could find on both sides of the river.

The best views were reserved by the harbor commissioners who charged a small admission fee with the money going to several local hospitals.

A local ferry boat stopped in the middle of the river and served as a platform for those willing to pay even more for a clear view.

At 7:30 a.m. the chartered ship *Duke of Argyll* arrived at the Harland and Wolff yard with a load of reporters and special guests.

Three flags flew at the top of the gantry: the British Union Jack, the American Stars and Stripes and, in the center, the White Star Line flag, solid red with a white star in the center.

■ At 11:30 Lord Pirrie and his wife, both celebrating their birthdays, arrived from the yard office with, among others, J.P. Morgan and J. Bruce Ismay.

Pirrie made a final inspection of the launch area then returned to his guests while the red launch flag was hoisted on the stern of the *Titanic* and a red rocket was fired to warn away all ships.

■ Twenty-two tons of soap and tallow coated the 772 foot launching ramp to help the ship slide stern first into the water.

■ Several steps were taken to prevent the ship from grounding itself on the opposite bank:

Three sets of anchors were set in the river and attached to seven inch cables which in turn were attached to the ship.

Two piles of drag cables, each weighing over 80 tons, were attached to the bow.

As the ship slid into the water, the anchors and drag cables would slow, and then stop, the ship within a few feet of the launch ramp.

■   During the morning workers knocked out and removed most of the huge supports on the bottom and sides of the ship, leaving only enough to hold the ship upright with the aid of the hydraulic rams.

At 12:05 p.m. Lord Pirrie gave the order, whistles blew, workers knocked out the rest of the supports, another red rocket was fired and hydraulic rams, specially designed to give the ship a push, were released.

Then a support fell on top of a worker, but other workers came to his aid and pulled him out from under it. However, 43 year old James Dobbins died the following day from his injuries. He was the second confirmed fatality during the construction.

At thirteen minutes after noon on May 31, 1911, the bow of the *Titanic* started to slide backwards down the soap and tallow coated ramp as thousands of people started to cheer. Sixty-two seconds later the anchor chains and drag cables brought the hull to a stop, and *Titanic* floated for the first time.

Workers removed the anchor chains and drag cables and harbor tugs pushed the hull over to the Harland & Wolff dock where the *Titanic* would be fitted out.

Lord Pirrie and his guests went off to a lunch in Belfast while the thousands of spectators started for home. The day was an unpaid holiday for all of the Harland and Wolff workers.

■   There was no "christening", no breaking of a champagne bottle across the bow, no official speeches. A shipyard worker explained to a visitor that the White Star philosophy was *"They just builds 'er and shoves 'er in."*

■   After lunch, Lord Pirrie, Morgan, Ismay and a whole group of guests boarded *Olympic* in Belfast harbor. At 4:30 p.m. the ship departed, bound for Liverpool, White Star Line's headquarters and *Olympic's* home port. It arrived in Liverpool the following day and was opened to the public for tours.

FITTING OUT

Olympic began its maiden voyage with a full load of passengers on June 14, 1911 under the able command of White Star Line's senior captain, Edward J. Smith.

Titanic launched May 31, 1911. National Archives

The voyage was generally uneventful until *Olympic* arrived in New York when the tug *O.L. Hollenbeck* was almost sunk under the stern of the *Olympic* by the suction created by the huge ships' propellers.

■ When launched, *Titanic* was just a huge hull with absolutely nothing completed other than the shell. The fitting out process would turn the shell into the most beautiful ship afloat. That, however, was almost a year away.

■ During the next ten months, all of the thousands of finishing touches were added to the ship.

Hundreds of miles of electrical cable.
Thousands of tiles in the swimming bath and the Turkish bath.
Miles of carpeting and floor tile.
Hundreds of bathroom fixtures.
Tons of furniture.

■ Harland and Wolff created a book with over 300 pages that detailed the instructions White Star Line and Harland and Wolff had agreed upon for the completion of the ship. Every conceivable item had been included:

"The verandah to have three settees with small square tables in front...the servant's rooms to be finished in dark mahogany and fitted with bed having Pullman over, sofa wardrobe..."

"Bells, 1 - 23" dia. Brass ship's bell for F'csle on Foremast, 1 - 17" dia Brass ship's bell for look-out cage in foremast, 1 - 9" dia Brass ship's bell for Captain's bridge..."

"Twelve rooms to have furniture in oak (A design)...14 rooms to have furniture in oak with brass beds (B design) six rooms in Adams style, white; four rooms in Louis XVI style, in oak; two rooms in Louis XV style, in grey; two rooms in Empire style, in white..."

■ Sometime in July 1911, Ismay asked Lord Pirrie when he could expect *Titanic* to be completed and turned over to White Star.
White Star Line still had many preparations to make before *Titanic* could make its first voyage: coal ordered and delivered, crew hired, food ordered and prepared, announcements of the maiden voyage made and tickets sold.

After some consideration about what Harland and Wolff still had to do, Pirrie gave the date of March 20, 1912 as the date *Titanic* could depart on its maiden voyage.

■ On September 18, 1911 White Star Line announced the date for the maiden voyage of the *Titanic:* March 20, 1912.

Two days later, an event happened that would throw this schedule out the window: *Olympic* was involved in an accident.

THE COLLISION BETWEEN *OLYMPIC* AND *HAWKE*

■ On September 20, 1911 *Olympic* was leaving Southampton, beginning its fifth trip to New York.

Off the Isle of Wight and following a parallel course was the British cruiser HMS *Hawke*, doing routine engine tests.

Olympic, weighing over ten times more than *Hawke*, slowed and made a turn toward the open sea, but on a converging course with the *Hawke*. As *Olympic* increased speed, *Hawke* seemed to fall behind, but suddenly it changed course hard to port and headed straight for the *Olympic*.

While the crew of the *Hawke* vainly tried to change course, the current created by the massive hull of the *Olympic* sucked the cruiser into the side of the *Olympic*.

Hawke rammed the *Olympic* with a massive thud which crumpled the concrete filled bow of the *Hawke* and ripped open two of the watertight compartments near the stern of the *Olympic* and damaged its starboard propeller. (The bow of the *Hawke* was filled with concrete because, as a British warship, one of its duties was to ram an enemy ship in an attempt to sink it.)

Hawke limped home to Portsmouth, and the passengers on *Olympic* had to be off-loaded into tenders and taken back to Southampton.

Olympic itself was patched up in Southampton and then steamed back to Belfast where the only drydock in the country large enough to accommodate it was located. This drydock happened to be the drydock that *Titanic* was currently occupying as it completed its fitting out.

Enroute to Belfast, workers replaced the starboard propeller shaft with the one that was supposed to be installed on *Titanic*.

■ A false good came out of the collision: *Olympic* survived a major collision with a ship designed to sink another ship by ramming it. Only two of the major watertight compartments were breached and despite some serious flooding, *Olympic* did not sink. This seemed to convince some people of the myth that the two ships were unsinkable.

■ Initially *Hawke* was blamed for the collision because it had rammed the side of *Olympic;* however, further investigation revealed that *Hawke,* at 7,500 tons, was drawn into the side of the *Olympic* by forces beyond its control.

The experts were able to explain that when a ship is moving forward, large amounts of water is pushed away on either side, which then rushes back toward the stern of the ship, sucking in any smaller boat in the vicinity.

"...the collision was solely due to the faulty navigation of the Olympic." – Admiralty Report.

■ George Bowyer, the pilot who was guiding *Olympic* out of port, was the scapegoat for the accident, and not the Captain of the ship.

The White Star Line wouldn't blame the captain of *Olympic,* who had the ultimate authority to safely navigate his ship. He wouldn't be blamed because he was the senior captain and the Commodore of the White Star Line, Edward J. Smith. However, eventually White Star Line had to pay for the damage to both ships.

It was soon discovered that it would take six weeks to repair *Olympic,* that *Titanic* would have to vacate the graving dock it was occupying, and that repairs to *Olympic* assumed priority over *Titanic,* both in workers and material.

■ Because of this, it was soon decided that the maiden voyage for *Titanic* would have to be delayed. A new date was set: Wednesday, April 10, 1912.

LIFEBOATS, PART II

■ While *Olympic* occupied the graving dock, work continued on *Titanic* and the official steaming date grew ever closer.

In late November the repairs to *Olympic* were complete, and *Titanic* was returned to the graving dock to continue fitting out.

■ In January, the sixteen wooden lifeboats were installed on the Welin davits.

Although the original designer Alexander Carlisle had requested 32 boats and had ordered davits designed to accommodate them, only sixteen were installed at Bruce Ismay's request because he felt the extra row of boats would take up too much deck space. Carlisle had at one time proposed that 64 boats be installed, but that proposal was never seriously considered.

■ In 1894 the British Board of Trade created the Merchant Shipping Act of 1894 that dealt with lifeboat capacity, which was based entirely on the cubic footage of a ship and *not* how many people the ship would be carrying.

The largest ship considered by this act was 10,000 tons, meaning that once a ship had met this maximum tonnage, a number totally unrealistic by 1912 standards, no more lifeboats were required. For *Titanic*, regulations required 9,625 cubic feet of lifeboat space, or enough for about 960 people at 10 cubic feet per individual.

The sixteen lifeboats totaled 9,821.5 cubic feet, which is all that was required. However, White Star Line included the four Englehardt Collapsible boats which added another 1,506.4 cubic feet, giving *Titanic* a total of 11,327.9 cubic feet, enough lifeboat capacity for 1,132 people. This exceeded Board of Trade requirements by seventeen percent.

A few days prior to *Titanic's* departure from Southampton, Board of Trade inspectors noted that *Titanic's* lifeboats exceeded requirements and *Titanic* was certified to be capable of carrying a total of 3,547 individuals.

In reality, to accommodate all 3,547 individuals *Titanic* was certified to carry, would have required 63 lifeboats, or one less than Alexander Carlisle had originally proposed.

MARCONI WIRELESS SYSTEM

■ Wireless communications was still a fairly new innovation in the early 1900's. In 1909 its use had prevented major loss of life when the White Star liner *Republic* sank after colliding with the *Florida*, an Italian owned liner. Only two people had been lost because wireless was used to summon help from many other nearby ships.

By 1912 almost all commercial ships carried wireless provided by one of several competing companies. Many, including *Titanic*, used the Marconi wireless system and the Marconi system on *Titanic* was the most powerful available on any ship.

■ Marconi wireless operators were employed by the Marconi Company and *not* by the ship or its owners. The operators were contracted out and reported to their company offices *first* and to the ships officers *second*. The operators were only expected to pass information on to the crew of the ship if the information was related to an emergency or if it pertained to the navigation of the ship.

■ Stretching between the two masts on *Titanic* was the wireless antenna. Guaranteed working range for the Marconi wireless was 250 miles but communication could usually be maintained up to 400 miles. Sometimes, at night when atmospheric conditions were right, messages could be sent and received up to 2,000 miles away.

The wireless system on *Titanic* was powered by a five kilowatt generator that received power from the ships electrical system, with a backup generator on the roof of the deckhouse and another battery-powered backup system.

■   In January 1912 *Titanic* was assigned the call letters "MGY" which would identify the ship to anyone who was listening in on its transmissions.

CONSTRUCTION CONTINUES

■   From November 1911, when *Olympic* returned to service, until early March 1912, *Titanic* made several moves from the pier to the drydock in the Harland and Wolff shipyard as construction progressed.

In late February, *Olympic* lost a propeller blade on a trip from New York and had to return to Belfast for repairs. *Titanic* had to vacate the drydock once again to allow repairs to *Olympic*

Then on March 6, *Titanic* had to be placed into drydock to make room for *Olympic's* departure in the restricted waters of the River Lagan.

■   The constant delays and movement in and out of the drydock kept squeezing the time available prior to the April 10 voyage, so the decision was made to forego the planned stop in Liverpool that would allow citizens to board the ship to view it. Instead, *Titanic* would proceed directly to Southampton.

■   J. Bruce Ismay had traveled to New York on the maiden voyage of *Olympic* to see how well the ship performed. In conjunction with the Harland and Wolff design team, Ismay had decided to make some last minute design changes on the *Titanic*. During the last few weeks of March, 1912, and only weeks before its maiden voyage some noticeable and major modifications were made to *Titanic*.

■   Passengers on the *Olympic* had complained about spray from the bow blowing across the A deck promenade.

The open windows on the forward end and along the sides of the A deck promenade of the *Titanic* were removed and replaced with sliding windows. This change would create the only visible difference between *Olympic* and *Titanic*.

Fitting Out. Note crow's nest a quarter way up the mast and the private promenade (the dark window openings on B deck between number 2 and 3 funnels). *National Archives*

The windows could only be opened by a special crank, and they would supply their own drama for some of the passengers in a few short weeks.

■ Another of Ismay's changes was made shortly after the maiden voyage of *Olympic*. Ismay felt that there was too much open deck space on the ship, so, instead of allowing more lifeboats, he added more First Class cabins and created the two Promenade Suites. Each of these suites had its own private promenade that could be opened to the sea and each came with a room for a private maid.

■ Time was running out, and painters were falling over carpet layers who were challenging tile layers for room, who in turn were trying to stay out of the way of the plumbers and electricians.

Thousands upon thousands of details were being completed. Furniture arrived before the floors were ready or it arrived in the wrong sequence. Bedding arrived before it was needed. Kitchen equipment arrived by the train load. Thousands of workers crawled all over the ship adding last minute touches or touching up paint and woodwork.

The huge 21-light candelabra arrived for the Grand Staircase, to be placed under the huge glass dome.

Still, material continued to arrive: coat hooks, hangers, 3,560 lifebelts, more furniture, signal equipment, beds, basins, tools and ever more material.

■ In March the engineering crew began to arrive. Some had been with the ship during construction and many were now living on board.

Some of the ship's officers also arrived in March, including Charles Herbert Lightoller, the First Officer of the liner *Oceanic* which was out of service because of a lack of coal due to a nationwide coal strike.

Lightoller would later write, *"It is difficult to convey any idea of the size of a ship like Titanic, when you could actually walk miles along decks and passages, covering different ground all the time...it took me fourteen days before I could with confidence find my way from one part of that ship to another by the shortest route...there was a huge gangway door through which you could drive a horse and cart on the starboard side aft. Three other officers, joining later, tried for a whole day to find it..."*

■ On March 25, the huge center anchor was lowered and then raised, the watertight doors were tested, and all sixteen lifeboats were swung out and lowered, then raised back into position.

On March 26, four other White Star Line officers met at the company offices in Liverpool to meet transportation to Belfast, where they arrived around noon on March 27. They were the junior officers Boxhall, Lowe,

Moody and Pitman, and when they arrived on *Titanic*, they reported to Chief Officer William Murdoch.

■ While workers continued to add the final touches, a partial load of coal was loaded into the coal bins through the coal shutes located along the side of the ship. There was enough coal for *Titanic* to complete her sea trials and steam to Southampton, England. When coaling was completed, the entire ship had to be wiped down to clean up the coal dust which had settled everywhere. Then the painters returned and continued their work.

■ On March 29, firemen, stokers, greasers and support crew signed on as part of the crew: 79 of them, in preparation for the April 1st sea trials. Escort tugs from Liverpool arrived in Belfast along with builders, owners and Board of Trade representatives and food for them all.

■ Still the finishing touches were being added, but on April 1, 1912 the sea trials for *Titanic* were expected to take place. *Titanic* was only ten days away from the start of its maiden voyage.

Titanic preparing for sea trials. *National Archives*

CHAPTER 4

SEA TRIALS

Olympic had been put through two days of sea trials before its maiden voyage. Because *Titanic* was a copy of *Olympic*, it was felt that only one day of trials would be required. The trials were scheduled to begin at 10:00 a.m. on April 1 and would be held in the River Lagan and Belfast Lough. There would also be a steaming trial in the Irish Sea.

■ On the big day, all preparations had been made and the tugboats were along side to maneuver the ship away from the dock, but sometime before 10:00 the decision was made to postpone the trials because a heavy wind was blowing which churned up the river and made navigation hazardous. Because there was very little clearance in the river for a ship the size of the *Titanic*, it was decided to postpone the trials until the next day.

■ The weather was clear and calm on April 2 as about 200 people boarded *Titanic* to attend the sea trials. Included in the list of people on the ship that day were:

Engine room personnel consisting of 78 stokers, firemen and
    trimmers.
Other crewmen, including electricians, deck crew, stewards and
    cooks.
The officers and other senior crewmen.
Marconi operators Jack Phillips and Harold Bride who were setting up
    their wireless equipment.
Designer Thomas Andrews, representing Harland and Wolff.
Harland and Wolff's senior architect Edward Wilding.
Board of Trade ship surveyor Francis Carruthers who would sign off on the
    trials.

Harold A. Sanderson, IMM board member (representing IMM because
Bruce Ismay could not attend).
Finally, there were several other individuals representing various compa-
nies who had supplied equipment or machinery that would need ad-
justment during the trials.

■   By 6:00 a.m. five harbor tugs were ready to assist in getting *Titanic*
away from the dock and into the channel of the River Lagan.
The first tug to attach a line was Harland and Wolff's yard tug *Hercules*,
followed by harbor tugs *Huskisson, Herculaneum, Hornby* and *Herald. Herald* at-
tached to a line directly to the bow of *Titanic* and pulled the ship into the
river.
Once again, hundreds of spectators turned out to watch as the ship
was guided into mid-river and faced toward Belfast Lough.

■   As the stokers built up the fires in the boilers, huge plumes of
black smoke poured out of her funnels while the tugs pulled and nudged
Titanic down the river for more than three miles.
Once inside the wide and deep waters of Belfast Lough, the tugs cast
off and returned to Belfast. *Titanic* was now on her own.
Instructions were passed from the bridge to start the engines. Slowly
the engines started to turn over, the propellers began to turn and *Titanic*
was under way for the first time. On the bridge that day as the captain of
Titanic was the senior captain and Commodore of the White Star Line,
Edward J. Smith.

UNDER WAY

■   The first event was to work *Titanic* up to a speed of 20 knots then
stop the engines and let the ship coast to a dead stop.
Throughout the morning the ship repeated the pattern of being start-
ed and stopped. Numerous rudder tests, engine tests and turning tests
were conducted and the results discussed and recorded.
During one test, traveling a straight line at 20 knots, the ship was set
into a hard full circle and the distance measured. The diameter was mea-
sured at about 3,850 feet, 1,283 yards or about 4 lengths of the ship.

■   Next came the stopping test. A marker buoy was dropped into
the water and *Titanic* steamed away a couple of miles then turned around
to face the buoy. The ship then steamed toward it at 20 knots and, just
when the ship was along side the buoy, orders were given to put the en-
gines into full reverse to stop the ship.

At 20 knots, it took 2550 feet or 850 yards to come to a complete stop. That was just short of three times the length of the ship itself.

■ Next came the open water straight run out into the Irish Sea: two hours straight out averaging 18 knots, then two hours back to the entrance of Belfast Lough.

It was getting to be late afternoon and the sun was starting to set, but a series of huge "S" turns were made to test the handling of the ship.

It was almost dark when the final test was made to drop both anchors.

■ Board of Trade representative Carruthers was satisfied that *Titanic* had met or exceeded every one of the Board's requirements, and after dark he signed off the official paperwork with the notation *"good for one year from today, 2.4.12."*

Titanic was going to proceed directly to Southampton, so the individuals that weren't going there were placed on a tender and sent back to Belfast.

Sometime during the evening another set of papers were signed, these by Sanderson accepting ownership of *Titanic* and by Andrews, representing Harland and Wolff as the builders transferring ownership to White Star Line.

■ Around 8:00 p.m. *Titanic* steamed out of Belfast Lough and into the Irish Sea on a critical timeline: the ship had to be at Southampton in time for the midnight tide which was just 30 hours away.

During the entire trip, tests of various types were being conducted. Everything from the engines to the kitchen stoves and potato peelers was tested.

Wireless operators Phillips and Bride were awake and working most of the trip, testing their equipment, communicating with other ships and passing progress reports on to the White Star offices in Liverpool.

■ Around 10:30 a.m. on April 3rd, *Titanic* steamed into the English Channel, and around the coast of England, until she approached the entrance of Southampton harbor in late evening in time to meet the high tide.

A harbor pilot was brought aboard and, once in the harbor, five tugs (*Ajax, Hector, Hercules, Neptune* and *Vulcan*) secured their lines onto the great ship and guided her up the channel of the River Test.

Titanic would be departing Southampton at low tide and there would not be much room to maneuver. As the ship approached the White Star Line dock, it was turned 90 degrees and pushed stern first into the dock.

The trip from Belfast was over 570 miles, but around midnight *Titanic* was secured to its dock, and preparations were made for its brief stay in Southampton.

*"This is a magnificent ship, and I feel very disappointed
I am not to make the first voyage."*

CHAPTER 5

FINISHING TOUCHES

Southampton, England, located about 80 miles south-west of London, has been a major British seaport since the 15th Century.

■ The White Star Line was headquartered in Liverpool (which is why the name would appear under the *Titanic* name on the stern of the ship), but in 1907 passenger service from Southampton to New York was started.

Southampton is a short cruise across the English Channel from the French port of Cherbourg, giving White Star Line a port on the European continent.

From Cherbourg, it is another short cruise to Queenstown, Ireland where White Star ships made their third, and last, stop before steaming out into the North Atlantic Ocean enroute to their final destination.

By steaming two sides of a triangle, White Star ships were able to make a port call in three countries in a convenient steaming pattern.

Several White Star Line ships, including *Adriatic, Majestic, Oceanic* and *Teutonic,* served Southampton, but it was the trio of the *Olympic* class ships, *Olympic, Titanic* and *Gigantic,* that were being built to provide weekly service from Southampton to New York City.

■ In 1911 the White Star Line dock in Southampton was enlarged and the River Test dredged out in preparation for the arrival of the three huge ships.

The dock itself was enlarged so it contained six berths with over 3,800 feet of dock footage and it was 122 feet wide.

Berths 43 and 44 were almost 1,500 feet in length and were designed especially for two of the *Olympic* class liners to be tied up at the same time. It was into Berth 44 that *Titanic* was placed after its trip from Belfast.

■ In 1912 Southampton was home to over 120,000 people, most of whom were employed or influenced in some fashion by the shipping industry. It was from the small districts in and around Southampton that the vast majority of the crew for *Titanic* would come.

Because there had been a long national coal strike, few ships had left the port during the past months; in fact, dozens of ships were laid up all around England. Thus, when the time came to sign on a crew for *Titanic*, the enrolling officers could pick and choose from thousands of applicants, and for the most part they picked the best from the over 17,000 unemployed men and women in and around Southampton.

Titanic would be staffed by a premier crew for its maiden voyage.

■ Early on the morning of April 4, *Titanic* was tied up and ready for the next step in its journey. It was due to begin its maiden voyage in six days, and still there were thousands of details to be accomplished. Its stay in Southampton would be a busy one.

MAKING READY

■ Because of the coal strike which had been ongoing since early January, all the berths in Southampton were full of stranded ships that didn't have coal to operate.

Since there were several White Star Line ships stranded in port, their remaining coal plus coal left behind by *Olympic* which had just left for New York, was added to what *Titanic* had brought from Belfast.

■ Colliers pulled up next to the starboard side of the *Titanic*. Coal was loaded into buckets, hoisted up the side of the ship and dumped into the hinged coal shutes located all along the side of the ship on F deck. From there the coal fell into the coal bins along G deck and the Tank Top, and crewmen inside the ship distributed the coal throughout the width of the ship in carts and shoveled it into those bins that didn't have shutes.

Titanic had arrived from Belfast with 1,880 tons of coal on board, and during the coaling phase another 4,400 tons were added.

While in Southampton some of the boilers were kept lit to provide light, power and heat. During that time 415 tons of coal was consumed.

In all, *Titanic* had enough coal to make the trip to New York, but there wasn't much to spare. Because of this, it was decided in advance that instead of steaming at the proposed 23 knots to New York, *Titanic* would only maintain an average speed of approximately 20 knots (or 23 miles per hour) in order to conserve fuel.

■   Saturday, April 6: Most of the crew was hired and those not needed prior to departure were sent home so that they could enjoy Easter Sunday with their families, knowing that they would soon have a good paying job on the world's newest and largest steamship.

■   There was a shakeup in the officer assignments in Southampton.
Captain Smith, having just come from *Olympic*, decided he needed an experienced officer from that ship to act as his Chief Officer, so White Star Line ordered the Chief Officer of *Olympic*, Henry T. Wilde, to join *Titanic* for one trip.

Wilde's arrival just a few hours before the start of the voyage caused a domino effect among the officers, with the current Chief Officer William M. Murdoch being bumped to First Officer and first officer Charles H. Lightoller bumped down to Second Officer.

Second Officer David Blair was bumped by Lightoller, but instead of continuing the bumping process, Blair left the ship for another assignment. Although upset about losing his berth on *Titanic*, orders were orders. Later Blair would say that this was one of the best moves he had ever had to make, but for now he wanted to make the trip.

"This is a magnificent ship, and I feel very disappointed I am not to make the first voyage." – David Blair.

In his haste to depart, Blair pocketed the keys to a storage locker in his cabin and Lightoller never tried to open the locker. This was unfortunate because in the locker were the binoculars that were assigned to the lookouts in the crow's nest. The lookouts had used them on the trip from Belfast, but now they were safely stored away.

Seven of the eight officers on *Titanic* belonged to the Royal Naval Reserve, and all had served with White Star for various lengths of time. Overall, they were a very capable set of officers.

Final officer assignments for *Titanic's* maiden voyage were:

> Edward J. Smith, Captain
> Henry T. Wilde, Chief Officer
> William M. Murdoch, First Officer
> Charles H. Lightoller, Second Officer
> Herbert Pitman, Third Officer
> Joseph Boxhall, Fourth Officer
> Harold Lowe, Fifth Officer
> James Moody, Sixth Officer

Captain Edward J. Smith on the deck of the *Titanic*. *Illustrated London News, April 20, 1912*

CAPTAIN EDWARD J. SMITH

"When anyone asks me how I can best describe my experience in nearly forty years at sea, I merely say, uneventful...I have never been in any accident...or any sort worth speaking about. I have seen but one vessel in distress in all my years at sea. I never saw a wreck and never have been wrecked nor was I ever in any predicament that threatened to end in disaster of any sort."
—Edward J. Smith, 1907

■   A look at Smith's record indicates that although he was considered a safe captain, he wasn't exactly telling the truth in his 1907 comment. During his career he had some mishaps:

1889: Smith was captain when *Republic* ran aground off New York
       and was stranded for several hours.
1890: Smith grounded another ship off Rio de Janeiro.
1899: *Germanic*, tied up to a dock in New York, capsized due to ice
       accumulations during an ice storm.
1904: There was a serious fire on board the *Majestic*.
1906: There was a serious fire on board the *Baltic*.

After his 1907 statement, Smith also:

1909: Grounded *Adriatic* off New York.
1911: Commanded *Olympic* when it collided with the British
       cruiser *Hawke*.

In none of these instances was Smith found at fault, although White Star Line paid the penalty in every case, including losing the court case over the collision with the *Hawke* and having to pay for damage to both ships.

■   Known as "E.J." by his friends, Smith was 62 and planning to retire. The maiden voyage was supposed to be his last trip, although there is indication that he actually planned to work for a few more years, at least until the third ship of the *Olympic* class trio, *Gigantic*, was put into service.

Smith had been with White Star Line for 26 years. Since 1886, he had served aboard most of White Star's major ships.

Since he was the senior captain for White Star, Smith carried the title of Commodore of White Star Line.

For many years Smith was given the honor of being the captain of each of White Star's new ships, and he was on *Olympic* and now *Titanic*.

Smith was an honorary commander of the Royal Naval Reserve and had made two transport runs to South Africa during the Boar War, earning the right to fly the coveted Blue Ensign on any ship he commanded.

One crewman once said of Smith *"this crew knew him to be a good, kind hearted man, and we looked upon him as a sort of father."*

Many passengers traveled on ships commanded by captains they most liked, and Smith had a huge following. Many of *Titanic's* passengers gave up accommodations on ships that departed earlier in order to travel with Smith.

■   North Atlantic ocean travel was extremely safe, there being only four fatalities among passengers in over 30 years, and Smith had never been involved in a collision of any sort until the incident with the *Hawke.* This may have meant he wasn't equipped to deal with a serious accident if he was involved in one.

Finishing Touches

■   Three major events were taking place in Southampton prior to the arrival of the passengers and crew on April 10: workers were still finishing the final touches on the ship; arrival of most of the furniture, food and china; and the loading of cargo.

■   Due to the short time available and the delays caused by the two unplanned dockings of *Olympic* in Belfast, many of the finishing touches to *Titanic* were done enroute to and while docked at Southampton.

Painters, plumbers, electricians, carpet layers, tile layers, drapery hangers: all got into each other's way as everyone struggled to get the ship ready for the Wednesday departure.

Some of the finishing work wasn't completed in time, and plans were made to complete it when the ship returned to Southampton after its first trip to New York. With so much work going on, White Star had to cancel plans in Southampton to allow visitors to board the ship for a tour, the "open house" that most new ships allowed.

■ However, the day before *Titanic* left Southampton and before being displaced by Charles Lightoller, Second Officer David Blair did manage to take his sister on a tour: *"... this took several hours and the ship was still a hive of activity with carpets still being laid and decorators busy until the last moment..."* – Miss Nancy Blair.

■   Among the people on board for the maiden voyage, not counted as passengers or crew, were nine senior employees of Harland and Wolff, including Thomas Andrews. They were known as the Guarantee Group and were making the trip to continue doing testing of equipment and systems.

■ While workers continued to add the finishing touches, the dishes, linen and food arrived.

Dishes, Glass and Silver

All of the following were loaded at Southampton:

BASIN		GLASSES		SHAKER	
Sugar	400	Celery	300	Pepper	2,000
BOTTLE		Champagne	1,500	Salt	2,000
Water	2,500	Cocktail	1,500	SPOONS	
BOWLS		Liqueur	1,200	Dessert	3,000
Finger	1,000	Wine	2,000	Dinner	5,000
Salad	500	JUGS		Egg	2,000
CUPS:		Claret	300	Mustard	1,500
Breakfast	4,500	Cream	1,000	Salt	1,500
Bouillon	3,000	KNIVES		Tea	6,000
Coffee	1,500	Butter	400	TUMBLER	
Tea	3,000	Dessert	4,000	Cut Glass	8,000
DISHES		Fish	1,500	VASE	
Bouillon	3,000	Fruit	1,500	Flower	500
Butter	400	Table	4,000		
Crystal	1,500	PLATES		MISCELLANEOUS	
Entrée	400	Breakfast	2,500	Asparagus Tongs	400
Fruit	400	Dessert	2,000	Grape Scissors	100
Meat	400	Dinner	12,000	Nut Crackers	300
Pie	1,200	Ice Cream	5,500	Sugar Tongs	400
Pudding	1,200	Soup	4,500	Toast Racks	400
Soufflé	1,500	POTS		Vegetable	400
Coffee	1,200				
FORKS		Tea	1,200		
Dinner	8,000	SAUCERS			
Fruit	1,500	Breakfast	4,500		
Fish	1,500	Coffee	1,500		
Oyster	1,000	Tea	3,000		

TOTAL ITEMS   127,000

Linens

CLOTHS		TOWELS		Aprons	4,000
Cooks	3,500	Bath	7,500	Bed Covers	3,600
Glass	2,000	Fine	25,000	Blankets	7,500
Table	6,000	Lavatory	8,000	Counterpanes	3,000
SHEETS		Roller	3,500	Napkins	45,000
Single	15,000	Pantry	6,500	Pillow Slips	15,000
Double	3,000			Quilts	800
				Miscellaneous	40,000
TOTAL ITEMS					199,900

■ White Star Line maintained a huge laundry facility in Southampton that employed 50 people to process almost 200,000 items a week.

Victuals (Food)

DAIRY		VEGETABLES	
Condensed Milk	600 gallons	Asparagus, Fresh	800 bundles
Fresh Butter	6,000 pounds	Green Peas, Fresh	2,250 pounds
Fresh Cream	1,200 quarts	Lettuce heads	7,000
Fresh Milk	1,500 gallons	Onions	3,500 pounds
Ice Cream	1,750 quarts	Potatoes	40 tons
FISH		Tomatoes	2 tons
Fresh	11,000 pounds	MISCELLANEOUS	
Salt & Dried	4,000 pounds	Cereals	10,000 pounds
FRUIT		Coffee	2,200 pounds
Grapes	1,000 pounds	Eggs, Fresh	40,000
Grapefruit	50 boxes	Flour	200 barrels
Lemons	16,000	Jams	1,120 pounds
Oranges	36,000	Sugar	10,000 pounds
MEAT		Rice & beans	10,000 pounds
Bacon & Ham	7,500 pounds	Tea	800 pounds
Fresh Meat	75,000 pounds	DRINKS	
Poultry & Game	7,500 pounds	Beer & Stout	20,000 bottles
Sausage	2,500 pounds	Mineral water	15,000 bottles
Sweetbreads	1,000	Spirits	850 bottles
		Wines	1,500 bottles

■ With over 200,000 pounds of food on board, passengers on *Titanic* were certainly going to eat well on this trip.

Smokers would fare well too, because also taken aboard were 8,000 cigars.

Cargo

■ While the stewards and cooks managed the loading of the food and eating utensils, other members of the crew were overseeing the loading of the cargo destined for New York. The cargo ranged from common items to those which were unique.

Although this isn't a complete list, the cargo manifest included the following:

Wine	300+ cases	Cork	6 bundles
	3 barrels	Mussels	225 cases
	26 hogsheads	Wood	35 bags
Whisky	1 case	Opium	4 cases
Liquor	192 cases	Skins	100+ bundles
Brandy	110 cases	Horsehair	2 cases
Cognac	17 cases	Feathers	7 cases
Anchovies	75 cases	Calabashes	16 cases
Walnuts, shelled	300+ cases	Argols	33 bales
Cheese	480+ bundles	Dragon's blood*	76 cases
Leather		Earth	1 barrel
Books	hundreds of boxes	Rabbit hair	15 cases
Printed matter	hundreds of cases	Tulle	65 cases

*Dragon's blood is a natural substance. It comes from a tree in Asia and was used to manufacture stains and varnishes.

■ Also listed on the general cargo manifest were boots, soap, tennis balls, golf balls, auto parts, tissue, rubber, a load of solid oak beams, five grand pianos, a jeweled copy of *The Rubáiyát by Omar Khayyám* with the binding inlaid with 1,500 precious stones, and passenger William E. Carter's 25 horsepower Renault automobile.

■ Shippers paid a premium to ship cargo on *Titanic,* but they saved most of the additional cost in their insurance premiums. Insurance companies gave excellent rates because *Titanic* was considered the safest ship in the world.

Olympic (left) entering a drydock while *Titanic* (right) is being fitted out. March 1912.
National Archives

"Six hundred and ninety-nine called Southampton their home."

CHAPTER 6

THE CREW

In the early 1900's the crew of a liner, except for the officers, were only hired or "signed on" for one round trip, and had to re-sign for every voyage. They were not guaranteed a job on the next trip.

"When a ship docked in those days the men. . . were paid off. Well, if that ship was in for 2 or 3 weeks they were put ashore and there was no unemployment benefit. . . so they couldn't afford to stay, so they usually jumped on some other ship."–Seaman Alan Fanstone

Occasionally crew members would manage to sign on for many trips, often for several years on the same ship, which gave some sort of continuity and permanence. Some passengers would alter their travel plans to make sure they could travel with a favorite steward or waiter.

■ There were over a hundred different jobs on a ship like *Titanic*, divided into the Deck Crew, Engineering Department, Stewards Department and Victualling Department.

DECK DEPARTMENT

■ The Deck Department consisted of one master and seven mates (Captain Smith was the master and the officers were the mates); two Surgeons, seven Pursers and clerks, two Carpenters, one Boatswain, eight Boatswains' Mates, 39 Seamen, two window washers, two Mess Room Stewards and two Masters-at-Arms.

The Officers

■ Henry T. Wilde was born in 1872 and went to sea when he was 15. Joining the White Star Line in 1905, Wilde worked his way up from second officer of several White Star ships to Chief Officer of the *Olympic*, a job he held when *Olympic* collided with the *Hawke*. He was on the docking bridge when it happened, so he had one of the best views of the collision.

When Captain Smith assumed command of *Titanic*, he asked for Wilde to join him as Chief Officer because of his experience handling such a large ship.

Wilde joined *Titanic's* crew on April 8 and assumed the Chief Officer's position on April 10, the day *Titanic* left Southampton.

■ William M. Murdoch was born in 1873 and was apprenticed to the sea in 1887.

In 1899 Murdoch served on a ship with Stanley Lord, who was an apprentice officer and who would command the *Californian* the night *Titanic* sank.

In 1900 Murdoch joined the White Star Line as a Second Officer. Between 1900 and 1910 a total of six of his family members were lost at sea in various accidents.

In 1905 Murdoch prevented a collision with another ship by countermanding the orders of a senior officer who had ordered an incorrect change of course. Overruling a senior officer did not endear him to that officer, but it marked Murdoch as a capable officer willing to make difficult decisions.

■ Charles H. Lightoller was 38 years old and had been at sea since he was 13. Lightoller joined White Star Line in 1900 and served on several of the company's ships before being assigned to *Titanic* as First Officer two weeks before the start of its maiden voyage. He served in that position during the trials and the trip to Southampton.

■ Third Officer Herbert J. Pitman was 35 years old and had been with White Star Line for nine years. He was one of three officers who did not come over from *Olympic.*

■ Although only 28 years old, Joseph G. Boxhall had already spent 13 years at sea. He joined White Star Line in 1905, served on *Olympic* and on March 26, 1912 he received orders to report to *Titanic* as Fourth Officer.

■   Harold G. Lowe was another officer who did not come over from *Olympic*. Lowe was 29 years old when he joined *Titanic* as Fifth Officer.

■   James P. Moody was 24 years old and had just recently graduated from nautical school and passed his Masters Examination. Moody was the third non-ex-*Olympic* officer, and he signed on as Sixth Officer of *Titanic*.

The Deck Department Crew

■   Surgeon William F.N. O'Loughlin had spent 40 years at sea and transferred over from *Olympic*.

"Whether he had any premonitions about the Titanic...I cannot say, but I do know that during a talk with him...he did tell me that he was tired at this time of life to be changing from one ship to another..." — J.C.H. Beaumont

One of O'Laughlin's jobs was to review the entire crew muster sheet on the day the ship sailed to ensure that a healthy crew was on board. O'Laughlin would not survive the voyage, and would be last seen partaking in some of the spirits from his medicine cabinet.

■   John H. Hutchinson from Southampton, transferred from the *Olympic* as a Joiner. He would die on the voyage.

■   Alfred Nichols of Clouds Hill signed on as a Boatswain after transferring from *Olympic*, and he would also die on the voyage.

■   Another transfer from *Olympic* was Boatswain's Mate Albert M. Haines from Southampton. Haines would survive the voyage.

■   Signing on as quartermaster's were Robert Hichens, George T. Rowe and five others, all of whom would survive.

■   Able Seaman Edward J. Buley, Thomas Jones, George A. Moore, Joseph Scarrott and Frank Osman signed on, along with Able Bodied Seaman Walter T. Brice, William H. Lyons and Robert J. Hopkins. All except Lyons would survive the voyage.

■   Able Bodied Seaman Frank O. Evans had spent over 9 years in the Royal Navy before moving onto merchant ships. On April 10, Evans was one of about 18 sailors who took part in the lifeboat drill on *Titanic*, and he would command one of the lifeboats after the ship sank.

■ John T. Poingdestre was an Able Bodied Seaman, one of twelve children, and he had five of his own before he signed up for the maiden voyage of *Titanic*. Only a month earlier Poingdestre had been on another ship, *Oceana*, when it sank. Poingdestre would survive the *Titanic* disaster, and later during World War I he would also survive the sinking of another ship that was torpedoed out from under him.

■ Boarding in Belfast and in Southampton were the six crow's-nest lookouts who were all residents of Southampton: Reginald Lee, Alfred F. Evans, George K. Hogg, George T.M. Symans, Archibald Jewell and Frederick Fleet. All six would be drafted as lifeboat commanders and survive the sinking. Jewell and Fleet transferred from *Oceanic*, and Fleet had been at sea since the age of thirteen.

ENGINEERING DEPARTMENT

■ The engineering department consisted of 24 engineers, six electricians, two boilermakers, 177 firemen and stokers, 73 trimmers, 24 greasers, six mess stewards and four storekeepers.

■ Fifty-one year old Joseph Bell was the Chief Engineer and had been with White Star for 26 years and transferred from *Olympic*. Bell would not survive.

■ Chief Engineer Peter Sloan was thirty-one years old and had worked for White Star all of his life and he, too, transferred from *Olympic*. Sloan and the entire electrical department would stay by their equipment to keep the lights working, and all would go down with the ship.

■ Firemen William Nutbean, John Podesta, the three Slade brothers Alfred, Bertram and Thomas and trimmer V. Penney signed on and appeared for muster the morning the ship left Southampton. Then the six of them headed off to a nearby pub.

■ Fireman Walter Hurst and his father-in-law William Mintram signed on. As *Titanic* was sinking, Mintram would give his son-in-law his own life vest. Hurst would survive, Mintram would not.

STEWARDS AND VICTUALLING DEPARTMENT

■ The Stewards and Victualling Department was divided into the Purser's Staff (which also included the two Marconi operators), First Class,

Second Class and Third Class Stewards (and stewardesses) and the Kitchen and Galley Staff.

■ Hugh W. McElroy was signed on as Purser whose duty, among other things, was to safeguard the passengers valuables and oversee the Enquiry Office. After the collision, McElroy would remain in the Purser's Office until he had handed out all of the passengers valuables. McElroy would last be seen on the Boat deck helping the passengers board lifeboats.

■ John G. "Jack" Phillips and Harold S. Bride were the two Marconi operators and they boarded *Titanic* in Belfast. They were not employed by the White Star Line, but were employees of the Marconi Company and were contracted to White Star to operate the wireless equipment. The night *Titanic* sank, they would remain at their stations until the very end. Bride would survive but Phillips would not.

■ There were 217 men and women assigned to the First Class Stewards department, including saloon stewards and waiters, bedroom, pantry, plate, lift, deck and boots stewards, Turkish Bath, Swimming Bath, Reception Room and Smoke Room stewards and a host of miscellaneous bell boys, printers, baggage masters, telephone operator, the bugler, gymnasium instructor and the squash racquet court attendant.

■ There were also 75 Second Class and 53 Third Class stewards and 65 galley workers, cooks and bakers.

■ Twenty-four year old First Class Stewardess Violet Jessop supported her mother and five younger siblings. The seventeen hour days and meager salary paid by White Star was offset by the tips she could expect on each voyage.
Jessop had a unique story to tell in later life: she had already survived one White Star disaster, having been on the *Olympic* when it collided with the *Hawke*. She next would survive the sinking of *Titanic*. Then, just a few years later during World War I, Jessop would be a nurse on the last ship of the *Olympic* class, *Britannic*, (ex-*Gigantic*) when it was sunk after hitting a mine in the Aegean Sea. She would survive that sinking, too.

■ P.W. Fletcher was the ship's bugler whose primary function was to call passengers to meals, which he would do by wandering around the ship in all class areas blowing his bugle. Fletcher would not survive the sinking.

Stewardess Violet Jessop as
a nurse on *Britannic.*

National Archives

■ Frederick Wright was a professional squash player whose job was
to provide lessons to the First Class passengers in the squash-racquet
court. He didn't survive the voyage.

■ Gym instructor T.W. McCawley was hired to help the First Class
passengers make use of the gymnasium on the Boat deck. McCawley
would not survive.

■ Twenty-two people on the ship were not classified as part of the
crew although they were gainfully employed (this is in addition to the two
Marconi operators): five postal employees, eight members of the orchestra
and the nine members of the Harland and Wolff Guarantee Staff.

■ There were three American (William L. Gwinn, Oscar S. Woody
and John S. March) and two British (John R.J. Smith and James B.
Williamson) postal clerks whose job was to sort all of the letters and
parcels carried on the ship. They were employed by their respective postal
departments. None would survive.
Postal clerk Gwinn was supposed to make the trip on another ship,
but he requested a transfer to *Titanic* when he received word that his wife
in New York was seriously ill.
A British postal inspector recommended changes to the cabins occu-
pied by the postal clerks because *"the cabins are situated among a block of third*

class cabins, and it is stated that the occupants of these...who are mostly low class conti-
nentals, keep up a noisy conversation...and music."

■ The eight orchestra members were employed by the Liverpool
firm of C.W. and F.N. Black, and were contracted out to the White Star
Line. Most had been on voyages on other ships, and all of the musicians
were carried as Second Class passengers.

■ Bandmaster Wallace H. Hartley was 33 years old and was highly
respected by the rest of the orchestra and by the First Class passengers
who had seen him on other ships. Hartley was engaged to be married after
the completion of *Titanic's* maiden voyage.

■ There were also 68 employees of the À la carte Restaurant which
was a private concession managed by Mr. Luigi Gatti and staffed with em-
ployees from his two London restaurants. A number of his employees
were family members. These individuals were paid by Gatti, although
they had signed on as employees and received a token wage from White
Star Line. Most of them were asleep down on E deck when *Titanic* struck
the iceberg. They were mostly from France and Italy and considered low-
life continentals by the British crew who were afraid that they would try to
storm the lifeboats. So they were locked into their cabins. All but one, in-
cluding Gatti (who wasn't locked up) went down with the ship.

The Marconi Wireless Operation

■ Most ships only had one operator and generally the wireless sys-
tem was shut down around midnight so the operator could get some sleep.
It was not required by law for the wireless to be manned continuously.
Because of the size of *Titanic* and the number of First Class passengers on
board, however, two operators were assigned.
With its nominal range of 250 miles and a night range of up to 2,000
miles, *Titanic* had one of the strongest wireless sets of any ship at sea.

■ The wireless was provided mainly as a service for the passengers.
Passengers paid for the sending or receipt of messages and tipped the op-
erators for their services. Operators normally took care of passengers' busi-
ness needs before handling official business of the ship unless the ship or
another nearby ship was in distress.
Another duty of the wireless operators was to relay messages from
one ship to another or to shore because few other ships had a wireless set
with enough power to transmit more than a few hundred miles.

One problem with the wireless service was that ships carried service from competing companies, and if an operator was asked to relay a message from a ship with a competing service, he might or might not do so, but it normally had low priority. Occasionally, operators from competing companies would turn up the power to drown out the weaker signal of a competitor or actually refuse to respond to signals from them.

SOUTHAMPTON

■ The crew was amazed by the size of the ship and most never learned their way around it. In fact, once *Titanic* left Southampton, most of the engine and fire room crews spent their entire voyage in the mechanical spaces and never saw daylight again.

Not counting those few who transferred from the *Olympic,* most of the crew, officers included, were totally unfamiliar with the ship and their duties.

■ In all, there were 892 (871 male and 21 female) crew members (including the two Marconi operators, but not counting the orchestra, postal workers, the à la carte restaurant staff and the Harland and Wolff Guarantee group) on *Titanic* at noon on April 10, 1912, when it steamed out of Southampton harbor. One crewman jumped ship in Queenstown, so there were actually 891 on board when *Titanic* sank.

■ Of this number, 699 crewmen called Southampton their home.

CHAPTER 7

DEPARTURE, APRIL 10, 1912

Shortly after 5:00 a.m. on Wednesday, April 10, 1912 the sun rose over Southampton for what would be a cool but clear and windy morning. Hundreds of the members of the crew began to arrive to spend their first day aboard *Titanic*.

The ship dwarfed all of the surrounding buildings and on this day was visible for miles around the White Star Line dock on the River Test.

As the crew began to arrive and assemble on the decks of the *Titanic*, some of the major players in the events of the day also boarded and headed directly to the bridge. Also, during the next few hours as the crew was making its preparations, the passengers began to arrive. Berths 43 and 44 would soon be a hive of activity as final preparations for sailing were made and hundreds of passengers and visitors were gathering on the dock and on the ship.

■ At 7:30 a.m. Captain Edward J. Smith arrived and headed for his cabin to wait for Chief Officer Wilde to report. Smith said good-bye that morning to his wife and twelve-year-old daughter, possibly with the happy thought that this might be his final voyage prior to his retirement, then he could spend more time with them.

Also at 7:30 a.m. the Board of Trade's emigration officer, Captain Maurice H. Clarke, arrived to oversee the crew muster with the aide of the ship's officers.

■ By 8:00 a.m. all of the crew had reported aboard and most had stowed their gear in time to report to their mustering stations on the various decks.

Also at 8:00 a.m. the Blue Ensign was raised at the stern. This was a flag the Royal Naval Reserve authorized Captain Smith and certain other RNR officers to fly on commercial ships.

■   As the crew assembled on the various decks, they were read and then signed the ship's articles while roll was called. Each crew member had to pass before a medical officer and Clarke, who then signed the crew list as each department was completed.

More headcounts were made and each of the ship's departments was checked to make sure there were enough crew members signed on, and the master list was given to Captain Clarke who then signed it.

■   While the crew was being mustered and counted, Clarke ordered the manning and lowering of two of the lifeboats. The lowering of lifeboats 11 and 15 on the starboard side was supervised by Fifth Officer Lowe and Sixth Officer Moody. Each boat with a crew of eight was lowered into the water, rowed around the ship to the dock, rowed back around the ship and hoisted back up into the davits.

■   By 9:30 the crew muster and boat lowering was complete and the crew released for breakfast. Crew members on the 8-to-12 watch were sent to their work areas, the 12-to-4 watch was ordered on standby and the 4-to-8 watch was released to do as they wished. Many of these crew members went ashore, most of them to their favorite drinking establishment for a final ale before leaving port.

■   Many of the crew members who had signed on earlier in the week did not show up for the morning muster. This was a common occurrence. Consequently, it had been arranged in advance that several additional men for each department would show up at muster to fill in as a substitute for anyone who didn't show. Several substitutes were mustered in at this time while the rest of those who were potential substitutes were asked to remain on board until the ship actually departed in order to replace any other shortages. This ensured that a full complement would be available for the voyage.

■   It took a good portion of the morning for the paperwork to be completed by Captain Smith and Captain Clarke.

In the end, Clarke signed off that he had observed a boat drill and that *Titanic* had enough coal, 5,892 tons, to allow it to steam to New York, its final destination.

There was also a "Report of Survey of an Immigrant Ship" which was prepared as required by the Board of Trade and signed by Smith and Clarke.

■ Finally, there was the "Master's Report to the Company:"

"I herewith report this ship loaded and ready for sea. The engines and boilers are in good order for the voyage, and all charts and sailing directions up-to-date. - Your obedient servant, Edward J. Smith."

About the time the official paperwork was completed, Bruce Ismay and Thomas Andrews arrived on the bridge to greet Captain Smith and wish him a safe voyage.

■ Originally, Lord Pirrie had planned to make the trip but he became ill so Andrews was sent in his place. Andrews had a First Class cabin on A deck (A36), which had been one of the late additions after Ismay's decision to add more cabins was made after the maiden voyage of *Olympic.*

Andrews' responsibility during the trip was to make sure everything that Harland and Wolff had done was completed satisfactorily and to see what changes should be made to the third ship of the trio.

Andrews was also responsible for the nine-man "Guarantee Group" of Harland and Wolff engineers.

■ Ismay had come aboard about 9:30 with his wife and three children and took them on a tour of the ship. Ismay was making the trip, his family wasn't. Once the tour was completed, his family departed and Ismay settled into his suite of rooms B52, 54 and 56 with its private prom-

Thomas Andrews, Managing Director of Harland and Wolff. Andrews did not survive the sinking.

Author's Collection

enade. His manservant Richard Fry had already unpacked Ismay's clothes and had prepared the suite for him.

Ismay was going to New York for the International Mercantile Marine Directors' meeting, so accompanying him was his secretary, W.H. Harrison. Both Fry and Harrison would die on this voyage.

■ One item not mentioned in any of the reports or to the Board of Trade representative was the fire that had been burning for almost a week in a coal bunker in boiler room 6 next to the bulkhead adjoining boiler room 5. This fire somehow got started during the coaling process in Belfast and had smoldered ever since.

Smith, Andrews and the "Guarantee Group" were aware of the fire, but until it could be put out, little could be done to check for any potential damage to the hull or the bulkhead.

Stokers in boiler room 6 had been working for a week trying to move enough coal to get to the bottom of the pile to put out the fire. However, it wasn't until a full complement of crew was on board that serious headway could be made toward reaching the bottom.

Chief engineer Bell felt, without being able to examine the bulkhead, that there was little cause for worry and that the fire hadn't damaged either the hull or the bulkhead. With this assurance, Smith never said anything to the Board of Trade inspector.

The fire was still smoldering at noon when *Titanic* left Southampton.

THIRD AND SECOND CLASS PASSENGERS

At 7:30 a.m. the boat-train carrying the Second and Third Class passengers left London's Waterloo Station for the two hour trip to Southampton.

Upon arrival, Second Class passengers immediately began to board through the Second Class entrance, aft on C deck, while Third Class passengers entered near the bow on the well deck or further aft on C deck.

Third Class Passengers

■ There were 497 Third Class passengers boarding in Southampton, many (150 adults and 30 children) of them emigrants from various Scandinavian countries. Most of these emigrants had purchased passage on *"the first available ship"* and, for these lucky people, the first available ship was the *Titanic*.

There were 183 Third Class passengers from Britain including two families, the Goodwins (eight members) and the Sages (11 members), with a total of 19 people between them. All 19 would die during the voyage.

Loading the Third Class passengers was extremely chaotic. Many did not speak English and in conjunction with the crew who mostly had been on the ship only for a few hours, it was difficult to get the passengers sorted out and to their proper cabins.

No one attempted to show the Third Class passengers where the public rooms were or where the corridors and stairs led to or where the exits were. They were allowed to wander aimlessly, up and down stairs, down blind corridors, careening off walls and each other, looking for lost children and, more often then not, running into locked gates with signs that said "First Class" or "Second Class" passengers only.

Third Class passengers were checked by a health inspector who also reviewed their identification cards. For the most part, British or American subjects were quickly approved, but foreigners were closely checked. White Star didn't want to carry anyone to New York only to have them denied entry into the United States. If this happened, White Star would then have to carry them back to Britain at no cost.

■ Third Class passengers were often referred to as "steerage" because in the past that is exactly where they were quartered: in the holds of the ship and most often at the stern where the steering mechanism was located. There was a time when human passengers traveled in one direction and cattle on the return trip, all occupying the same area. Up until the late 1800's there were often signs posted asking First and Second Class passengers not to throw food or money to steerage passengers because it could cause a disturbance.

Although there had been dramatic improvements in the quality of accommodations for Third Class passengers, American immigration laws required that gates be placed between Third Class and other passengers. The gates were to be locked at all times to prevent the spread of infectious disease. American law also required that Third Class passengers be given 20% more space per passenger than what the British Board of Trade mandated. American law did not, however, require more lifeboats than what the Board of Trade required.

■ Third Class single men were sent to their accommodations in the bow of the ship, the single women and families were sent to their cabins on D, E, F and G decks toward the stern.

■ Traveling from Sweden to Worcester, Massachusetts, was forty-year-old Carl and thirty-eight-year old Selma Asplund and their five children, ages 13, 9, 5, 4 and 3. Mr. Asplund and three of the children would not survive this trip and their bodies were never recovered.

■ Twenty-three year old Miss Wendla Heininen was traveling alone from Finland to New York. She would not survive either, but her body was recovered and is buried in Halifax.

■ Mr. Karl Backström, 32, was returning to the United States from Finland with his wife Maria, 33, along her two brothers Johan and Anders Gustafsson. Of the four, only Maria would complete the trip and none of the bodies of the men were recovered.

■ Mrs. Belia Moor, 27, and her son were from Russia and had purchased passage on *Adriatic*, but because of the coal strike, they were transferred to *Titanic*. Both of these passengers would survive the trip.

■ Mr. Ernst Danbom, 34, was born in the United States and worked as an emigrant recruiter in Iowa. He had traveled to Sweden with his bride and son for a vacation, and the family was now returning to the United States, along with three family friends, Alfrida and Anders Andersson and Anna Nysten. Only Anna Nysten would survive and none of the bodies were recovered.

■ Mrs. Stanton (Rosa) Abbott, 35, was from Rhode Island and was the wife of former middleweight champion Stanton Abbott. Rosa and her two sons Rossmore, 16, and Eugene, 13, traveled to England on *Olympic* in August 1911 and were now heading back to Rhode Island. Rosa would survive the trip but her sons would not.

■ Eighteen year old Leah Rosen Acks was from Russia and was enroute to Norfolk, Virginia, with her infant son to meet her husband Sam Acks. Leah and her son would survive the trip, but it would be a very trying experience for Leah.

■ Mrs. Maria Panula, 41, was married to John Panula and lived in Michigan, but returned to Finland in 1910 to sell the family farm and convince the rest of their family to emigrate. John Panula was in the United States, but Maria, her five children and Sanni Riihivuori, the daughter of a neighbor, all boarded in Southampton. All seven would perish on the voyage.

■ Jules Van Der Planke, 31, and his wife Emilie, 31, were from Ohio, had gone to Belgium before Christmas. For the trip back to the United

States two other family members Augusta, 18, and Leon Van Der Planke, 16, would accompany them. They all would die on the trip.

■ Ernst Persson, 25, was emigrating to the United States from Sweden along with his sister Elna Ström and niece Telma Ström. Ernst Persson would complete the trip but the two women would not.

■ Mr. Olaus Abelseth, 26, emigrated from Norway in 1902 and lived in North Dakota. He left New York in late 1911 to visit his family in Norway, and he was now returning home with five friends and family members: Peter Soholt, a cousin, Sigurd Moen, his brother-in-law, Adolf Humblen and Anna Salkjelsvik, friends and sixteen-year-old Karen Abelseth, not related but the daughter of a close friend. Peter, Sigurd and Adolf drowned but the rest made it to North Dakota.

■ Twenty-two year old Hilda Hellström was traveling to Evanston, Illinois to help her widowed aunt. Hilda would survive the voyage.

■ Miss Berta Nilsson, 18, was traveling from Sweden to Montana with her fiancé Edvard Larsson-Ronsberg. Berta would survive, Edvard would not.

■ Miss Carla Jensen, 19, was traveling to Portland, Oregon with her uncle Niels Jensen, 48, her brother Svend Jensen, 17, and her fiancé Hans Jensen, 20. Carla alone would survive.

■ Brothers Alfred, 24, John, 21, and seventeen-year-old Joseph Davies and their uncle James Lester were traveling together to Pontiac, Michigan. None of them would survive the trip.

■ Miss Elizabeth Dowdell, 30, was traveling as a nurse, escorting five-year-old Virginia Emmanuel to her grandparents in New York City. They shared a cabin with twenty-four year old Amy Stanley who was traveling to New Haven, Connecticut, to become a children's maid. All three of them would survive.

■ Another twenty-four year old passenger was Mrs. Elisabeth Johnson, who was traveling back to St. Charles, Illinois with her two children after a visit to Sweden. All of them would make it back to St. Charles.

■ Nils Johansson, 29, had traveled to Sweden after having spent eight years in Chicago. He was returning with his fiancé Olga Lundin and three friends Paul Andreasson, Albert Augustsson and Carl Jonsson. Olga and Carl would survive but the rest of the men would not.

■ Traveling to Los Angeles, California was thirty-two-year old Thure Lundström and his fiancé Elina Olsson, 31. Lundström was the de-facto leader for a group of ten people all traveling to California. Thure would tell many versions of how he survived, but witnesses would claim that Thure saved himself and left Elina behind to die.

■ Twenty-two year old Helga Hirvonen and her daughter were traveling to Monessen, Pennsylvania to meet her husband. Traveling with them were her brother Eino Lindqvist and friend August Abrahamsson. All but Eino would survive the voyage.

■ Frederick Goodwin, his wife and six children were traveling to Niagara Falls, New York so Frederick could begin a new job at a power station there. All eight members of the family perished.

■ Oscar Hedman was leading a group of 17 Swedish emigrants, most of whom could not speak English, to Sioux Falls, South Dakota. Oscar would survive but most of the rest would not.

■ Mrs. Agnes Sandström, 24, and her two daughters were traveling home to San Francisco after visiting friends in Sweden. All would survive to make it home to San Francisco.

■ Thirty-two year old Oscar Olsson was a sailor on a Swedish ship who was returning to New York with friends Karl Johansson and Samuel Niklasson to sign on with another ship. Oscar would survive but the other two would not.

■ Twenty-seven year old journalist August Andersson from Sweden was traveling to New York under the name "Wennerström" with two friends Carl Jansson and Gunnar Tenglin. All would survive the trip.

■ Adolf Dyker, 23, and his wife Elisabeth were returning home to New Haven after having traveled to Sweden to arrange the final effects of his father who had just passed away. Shortly, Elisabeth would be attending another funeral for her husband.

■ Miss Aina Jussila, 21, and her sister Katriina, 20, were enroute to New York to obtain work with their uncle who owned an employment agency. Both sisters would perish.

■ Anton Kink, his wife and four year old daughter were traveling from Zurich, Switzerland, to Milwaukee, Wisconsin. The entire family would be saved.

■ And so the Third Class passengers continued to board: August Abrahamson from Finland traveling to Hoboken, New Jersey; Mrs. Johanna Ahlin and her brother Johan Petterson from Sweden, traveling to Minnesota; Josef Arnold, his wife Josephine and friend Aloisia Haas traveling from Switzerland; Mrs. William Coutts and her two children traveling to Brooklyn, New York. Only Mrs. Coutts and her children would complete the voyage.

Second Class Passengers

■ While the Third Class passengers were boarding the ship and sorting themselves out, 234 Second Class passengers began to board. There was somewhat less chaos and better organization for these passengers befitting their more expensive accommodations and the smaller number of them.

■ Percy A. Bailey was eighteen years old, traveling to New York to visit his uncle. Bailey was traveling with two friends Harry Cotterill, 20, and George Hocking, 23. None of them would survive.

■ Reverend Ernest C. Carter, 54, and his wife Lilian, 44, were enroute to New York City. Mrs. Carter befriended Marion Wright and Kate Buss during the trip. On Sunday night Carter led the hymn service in the Second Class dining saloon. Marion Wright sang a solo. Neither of the Carters would survive.

■ Marion Wright was traveling to Cottage Grove, Oregon to join her fiancé. She reported the collision with the iceberg as a "huge crash of glass." She is also one of the survivors who reported that the orchestra last played *"Nearer, My God, To Thee."*

■ Kate Buss, 37, was traveling to San Diego to meet up with her fiancé. Kate didn't want to watch as the boats were being loaded, and she decided she didn't have a chance to get on one. At some point, though, she managed to get on a boat. She lived to be 96 but she was never able to discuss the sinking without becoming very emotional about it.

■ The only Japanese passenger on the voyage was Masabumi Hosono, a civil servant from Tokyo. He was found almost frozen to death laying on top of a piece of wreckage and was picked up by a passing lifeboat. He survived, but was ostracized in his own country for doing so when so many others had died. He lost his job, Japanese newspapers called him a coward, schoolbooks cited his shameful behavior and he was called immoral. Although he died in 1939, he was still being cited as a coward even in 1954 when another ship sank and newspaper articles referred to him.

■ Mrs. Arthur H. Wells, 29, was enroute to Akron, Ohio with her two children to meet up with her husband whom they hadn't seen for two years. All would survive, but the boat they were on was so overcrowd they had to stand the entire time until rescued.

■ Thirty-four year old Lawrence Beesley was a science teacher in London and was making a lengthy tour around the United States. He had specifically chosen *Titanic* because it was the maiden voyage. Beesley wanted to *"stand some distance away to take in a full view of her beautiful proportions, which the narrow approach to the dock made impossible."* He decided that he would have to wait until arrival in New York to get his view.

■ Mrs. Allen (Nellie) Becker, 36, was traveling to Benton Harbor, Michigan from India with her three children Ruth, 12, Richard, 1, and Marion, 4. Mr. Becker was still in India, and Mrs. Becker and the children were traveling to the United States for treatment of a disease Richard had contracted. All would survive and Ruth would live to be 90 years old.

■ Father Thomas R.D. Byles was a highly respected member of the clergy who was traveling to New York to officiate his brother's wedding.
By many accounts, Father Byles was a hero to the end, hearing confessions and praying with those who couldn't escape. His body wasn't recovered.
His brother had his wedding as planned, then the couple went home, changed into their mourning clothes and returned to the church for a memorial mass.

■ Mrs. Elizabeth Nye, 29, had already suffered through appendicitis, the loss of her first fiancé and the loss of two children and a husband. Mrs. Nye was returning to New York after a visit in Britain. She was supposed to travel on *Philadelphia* but because of the coal strike was transferred to *Titanic*. She was loaded into a lifeboat and while waiting for the boat to be lowered, she caught baby Frank Acks as he was tossed like a football into the boat. She wrapped him in a steamer blanket to keep him warm and

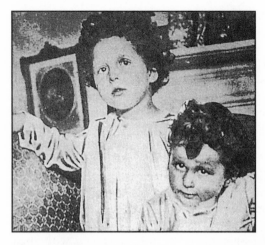

Left: The Navratil children kidnapped by their father. *Harper's*

Below: Father Thomas Byles. *National Archives*

didn't know who his mother was until Leah Acks was found on the rescue ship *Carpathia.*

■   William H. Harbeck, 44, was a successful cinematographer who had taken the earliest movies of the San Francisco earthquake in 1906. He had been in Europe making films to show American audiences and was hired by the White Star Line to film the maiden voyage. Harbeck was carrying over 100,000 feet of exposed motion picture film with him on *Titanic.* Harbeck died and he and his film went down with the ship.

■   John, 28, and Elizabeth Chapman, 28, were just married and were celebrating a belated honeymoon on *Titanic* as were several other couples. Both died on the trip, his body being recovered and buried in Halifax.

■   Benjamin, 43, and Esther Hart, 45, were traveling with their daughter Eva, 7, to Winnipeg, Canada. Benjamin would not survive.

■   "Louis Hoffman" from Nice, France boarded with his two children, two year old Edmond and three year old Michel. The Hoffman's were enroute to an unknown destination in the United States and were traveling under fictitious names. Hoffman was really Michel Navratil who was kidnapping his two children from his estranged wife in France, who had no idea where he or the children were. The children survived but "Louis Hoffman" did not.

■   Thirty-one year old Harvey Collyer, his wife Charlotte and daughter Marjorie had sold their home in Britain and were traveling to Payette, Idaho with everything they owned. Harvey would die on this voyage.

■   Six year old Nina Harper was traveling home to Chicago with her widowed father, Reverend John Harper and her aunt, Miss Jessie Leitch. One of the more memorable photographs that survive of the voyage show Reverend Harper and his daughter walking on the Boat deck of the *Titanic.* Jessie and Nina would survive but John would not.

■   Mrs. Elizabeth Hocking was moving to Akron, Ohio with her son George, 23, daughters Nellie and Emily and grandsons George and William, plus two of her son George's good friends, Percy Bailey and Harry Cotterill. Everyone except George survived the voyage.

■   Henry Morley told his friends he was traveling to Los Angeles when, in fact, he was eloping with Kate Phillips. They were traveling un-

Reverend John Harper and daughter, Nina, on the Boat deck in Queenstown. Nina would survive, her father would not. *Cork Examiner*

der the names of Mr. and Mrs. Marshall. Henry would perish but Kate would survive. It would take a long time before family and friends sorted out the issues caused by the couple traveling under assumed names.

■　Three single women ended up sharing the same cabin: Miss Edwina "Winnie" Troutt, Susan Webber and Nora Kean. Their cabin adjoined that of the orchestra. The musicians were willing to perform special musical requests for the ladies and all of the other nearby passengers during their off-duty hours. All three women survived, and Winnie lived to be 100 years old.

FIRST CLASS PASSENGERS

The train carrying most of the 193 First Class passengers left Waterloo Station at 9:45 a.m. and arrived at the White Star Line dock at 11:30, thirty minutes before scheduled departure. They boarded the ship via the main entrance on B deck where they were met by the chief steward and his staff and escorted immediately to their cabins. This was First Class: there wouldn't be any aimless wandering of the corridors for these passengers.

■ Confronting them as they entered the B deck entrance was the huge 16-foot wide, 60-foot (six deck) tall Grand Staircase with a massive glass and iron dome and a huge 32-light chandelier overhead.

■ Because of its size, luxury and the tremendous amount of publicity concerning *Titanic*, sailing on the maiden voyage was to the rich-and-famous of 1912 what the Academy Awards would be to their counterparts in the latter part of the century. Many of the biggest names in politics, business or entertainment had booked passage, some even adjusting the length of their stay in Europe in order to do so.

In 1998 dollars, a "cheap" First Class cabin cost about $2500 and the two First Class parlor suites with the private promenade cost $73,000, one way.

After the final port call in Queenstown, there would be 337 First Class passengers. Most of the First Class male passengers were captains of industry or politics, and just 12 of them alone were worth $3.2 billion 1998 dollars. The lot of them were estimated to be worth almost $8.5 billion.

■ Major Archibald W. Butt was a close personal friend of President William H. Taft. He was a journalist who had served in the Spanish-American war in Cuba and the Philippines. He became military aide to President Theodore Roosevelt and later to President Taft. He tried, unsuccessfully, to remain neutral during the personal quarrels between Roosevelt and Taft and finally, needing rest, took a leave and traveled to Europe with a close friend Francis D. Millet. They were returning to Washington DC. Neither would complete the voyage.

■ Twenty-nine year old Thomas Pears was a very successful businessman who owned manufacturing sites all across Europe. He was an avid sportsman and had participated in automobile and motorcycle races. Pears was traveling to the United States to scout new business locations with this wife of two years, Edith. Thomas Pears would not survive, however his wife did. Within five years, three of Edith's four brothers would become casualties of the First World War.

■ Colonel John Weir was president and owner of several mines in the western United States and had served during the Spanish-American War. He was well respected and gave generously to various charities. Weir had sent a letter to friends on April 6 stating he was going to be coming home on the *Philadelphia*. Because of the coal strike, he was transferred to the *Titanic*, but his friends didn't know this until he was listed as lost in local newspapers.

■   Mr. Charles M. Hays, 55, was the former president of the Southern Pacific Railway and was the current president of the Grand Trunk Railway. The Hays party included Hays' wife Clara, his assistant Vivian Payne, Clara's maid, their daughter Orian and her husband Thornton Davidson. Hays was returning the United States after having wrapped up a business deal with the White Star Line to transport European emigrants from White Star ships to their final destination in America. Charles Hays, Vivian Payne and Thornton Davidson would all die when the ship sank.

■   Mr. Hudson J.C. Allison, 31, was a successful Canadian business-man and breeder of horses. Allison's wife Bess, their two children Helen, 3, and Hudson Trevor, 1, were traveling back to Canada with Mrs. Allison's maid, young Hudson's nurse Alice Cleaver and two servants Mildred Brown and George Swane. Young Trevor, Alice and Mildred would sur-vive. One of the most tragic stories in a long night of tragedy would affect the Allison family.

■   George Bradley was traveling under the alias George A. Brayton. He was a professional gambler who made a livelihood by making the cir-cuit of First Class passengers on various steamships. His luck would hold out and Bradley would survive.

■   Miss Elisabeth Allen, 29, was returning to her home in St. Louis with her aunt, Mrs. Edward Robert and her fifteen-year old cousin Georgette Madill and a maid. Miss Allen was engaged to a British physi-cian and was returning home to gather her belongings. All three would survive the sinking.

■   Isador and Ida Straus usually traveled on German liners whenever possible, but for their return to New York City this trip they decided to travel on *Titanic* and occupied parlor suite C55. Isidor, 67, was involved in blockade running for the Confederate States during the Civil War, had been a Congressman from New York and currently was the owner of Macy's Department Store. Traveling with the Strauses were Mr. Straus' manservant and Ms. Ellen Bird, Mrs. Straus' maid. After having spent a life-time together, the Straus's preferred to go down with the ship, together, rather than be separated.

■   Traveling home to Scituate, Massachusetts, was a famous fiction writer, Jacques Futrelle and his wife May. Mrs. Futrelle would make it home, her husband would not.

Isador Straus (left) and Ida Straus (right). They decided to remain together and went down with the ship. *National Archives*

■ Major Arthur Peuchen, 52, was president of Standard Chemical Company, had a military career in the Queen's Own Rifles and was Vice-Commodore of the Royal Canadian Yacht Club in Toronto. Major Peuchen would survive but $300,000 in securities he was carrying with him would not.

■ Another of the several professional gamblers on this trip was Charles H. Romaine who was planning to make some money off the affluent First Class passengers. His luck would hold out—he would survive this voyage.

■ Lucy Noel Martha Dyer-Edwards, the Countess of Rothes, 33, whose home was at Kensington Palace in London was traveling with her cousin Gladys Cherry and her maid to Vancouver, British Columbia. The Countess would survive, spending her night on the lifeboat manning the tiller while Gladys helped with the rowing.

■ Miss Kornelia Andrews, 63, was vice-president of the Hudson City Hospital in Hudson, New York and was returning to New York with her sister Anna Hogeboom and niece Gretchen Longley. All three of them would survive the ordeal.

Above: Lucy Noel Martha Dyer-Edwards, the Countess of Rothes.

New York News

Left: Fiction writer Jacques Futrelle on the Boat deck. Futrelle would not survive.

National Archives

■ Mrs. Edward Appleton and her sisters Mrs. John M. Brown and Mrs. Robert C. Cornell had gone to England to attend the funeral of another sister, and they were now returning home to New York. During the voyage they met up with old friends Archibald Gracie and Miss Edith Evans. All but Miss Evans would survive the trip. Gracie escorted Mrs. Brown and Miss Evans to one of the last lifeboats and because there was only time for one of them to get in, Edith Evans stepped back and told her friend, *"You go first, you have children waiting at home."*

■ Mr. Mauritz Björnström–Steffansson, 28, was the son of the owner of a major Swedish paper company and was living in Washington DC while completing his studies. During the voyage back to the United States, he befriended passenger Hugh Woolner and the two of them took it upon themselves to be the personal escort of Mrs. Edward Candee, a young and beautiful widow. All of them survived.

■ Mrs. Lucien P. Smith was only eighteen, but she was traveling to Huntington, West Virginia with her husband. Although Mrs. Smith would survive, her husband would not. Later, Mrs. Smith would marry fellow survivor Robert Daniel.

■ Forty-six year old Herbert Chaffee was a multi-millionaire busi-
nessman from North Dakota. The Chaffee holdings included 42,000 acres
of farmland, dozens of grain elevators and several company towns.
Chaffee and his wife Carrie were returning home from a European vaca-
tion. Mrs. Chaffee would complete the trip home but Mr. Chaffee would
not.

■ William Thomas Stead, 62, was a world famous and controversial
journalist and author. In the 1880's he was editor of a liberal publication,
the "Pall Mall Gazette," and in 1883 he was elected to parliament. In 1885
Stead published a controversial book exposing child prostitution.

Starting in the 1890's Stead devoted himself to pacifism and became
interested in spiritualism. He was enroute to New York City to speak at a
peace congress at the request of President Taft.

In 1886 Stead wrote an article entitled "How the Mail Steamer Went
Down in Mid-Atlantic, by a Survivor", in which a steamer collides with
another ship and there is large loss of life because of a shortage of
lifeboats.

In 1892 he wrote a fictional story entitled "From the Old World to the
New" about an accident involving a ship that collided with an iceberg and
a White Star Line ship, the *Majestic*, that arrived to rescue the survivors.

On this trip, Stead would have the opportunity to witness first hand
what he had written about. However, he didn't survive to write about it
later.

■ Henry B. Harris and his wife Rene were world famous Broadway
theater owners and producers. Mrs. Harris would survive the trip.

■ Dr. and Mrs. Washington Dodge were traveling to New York with
their four year old son, and they would all survive.

■ Mr. Washington A. Roebling III, 31, was the president of the
Roebling Steel Company, grandson of John A. Roebling, designer of the
Brooklyn Bridge and nephew of Washington A. Roebling who actually
built the bridge. He was returning to New York after a business trip to
Britain. Roebling would not survive the trip.

■ Counted among First Class passengers was J. Bruce Ismay.

Ismay occupied Promenade Suite B52 which was one of two such
suites, and the one designed especially for J.P. Morgan. Pittsburgh steel
magnate Henry C. Frick had reserved the suite, but had to cancel his trip
when his wife sprained her ankle. Morgan then planned to use the suite,

but had to cancel because of business. The suite was then reserved by Mr. and Mrs. J. Horace Harding, but they too canceled and transferred to *Mauretania*. So it ended up that Ismay would occupy the suite.

DEPARTURE

■ By noon just about everyone who was going to depart Southampton on *Titanic* was aboard the ship.

■ At 11:15 harbor pilot George Bowyer boarded and his red-and-white stripped pilot flag was raised while Bowyer made his way to the bridge.

Bowyer had been a harbor pilot for over 30 years and was the White Star pilot of choice for ship movements in Southampton. Bowyer had been the pilot commanding the *Olympic* the day it collided with the *Hawke*, but he wasn't held responsible for that collision.

J. Bruce Ismay, Chairman of the White Star Line.

National Archives

After reaching the bridge, Bowyer conferred with Captain Smith and the ship's officers prior to their returning to their various stations and duties associated with the departure.

■ Chief Officer Wilde was assigned to the forecastle, far forward, to oversee the mooring lines and tugboat hawsers.

First Officer Murdoch was on the Poop Deck at the stern, in charge of the mooring lines and tugboat hawsers there.

Second Officer Lightoller was at the aft end of the forecastle to assist Wilde as needed.

Third Officer Pittman was on the docking bridge above the Poop Deck, assisting Murdoch and passing orders along to him that were telegraphed from the bridge.

Fourth Officer Boxhall was on the navigating bridge, passing orders via the engine room and docking bridge telegraphs and logging every order, command or maneuver into the scrap log (a temporary place to write orders before they are written into the official log) and taking his orders directly from Smith and Bowyer.

Also on the bridge with Boxhall was Fifth Officer Lowe who worked the ships telephones and communicated directly with all departments.

At the gangway was Sixth Officer Moody who was overseeing late arrivals. The gangway also remained open until the last minute to allow anyone aboard who might have gone onto shore.

■ With less then one minute until noon, Smith gave the order and the two huge whistles blasted the surrounding waters, thrilling the estimated 50,000 people who were perched on every piece of available space to watch the departure of the world's largest ship from their port.

■ Two more times the whistle blew and Sixth Officer Moody began to lower the gangway. As he did so, two stokers, John Podesta and William Nutbean, came running up and jumped the few inches between the end of the gangway and the hatch.

Podesta, Nutbean, the three Bertram brothers, Tom and Alfred Slade, and three other crewmen had been at one of the local pubs and were returning to the ship when they were held up on the dock by a passing train. Podesta and Nutbean managed to cross the tracks but everyone else waited.

Podesta and Nutbean crossed the gangway and jumped aboard *Titanic.* Their six drinking buddies came running up behind them, but Moody made the decision to continue to lower the gangway, thus preventing them from boarding. Moody immediately passed the word and six substitutes waiting at the aft entrance, which was still open, were signed onto the ship. The remaining substitutes were allowed to go ashore.

The three Slade brothers and their friends were obviously upset over this action, but within three days their disappointment would change to relief. Both Podesta and Nutbean would survive the voyage but none of the substitutes would.

■ Three other brothers scrambled onto the ship at the very last minute. Alfred and Percy Pugh actually made it, but a third brother literally missed the boat. Alfred would be saved but Percy would be drowned.

■ As Sixth Officer Moody was lowering the gangway, five tugs (*Ajax, Hector, Hercules, Neptune* and *Vulcan*) began to pull the ship sideways away from the dock just as all of the mooring lines were dropped into the water and then hauled onto the dock by the dock workers.

The tugs pulled the ship away from the dock then out into the newly-dredged turning circle in the middle of the River Test. After *Titanic* was towed into the turning circle, the tugs pushed and pulled it 90 degrees to port so it was facing down the channel.

It was just a few minutes after low tide and *Titanic* drew 35 feet of water, so extreme caution had to be used to prevent damaging the hull. It was for this reason that *Titanic* had been backed into the berth at Southampton.

Once the turn was completed, orders were telegraphed to the engine room to move "Ahead slow" and the two huge wing propellers began to turn.

The lines to the tugs were dropped and they pulled away, the *Vulcan* actually moving around the stern to the open door on E deck to pick up the last of the standby crew who weren't needed but were waiting to be taken to shore.

A CLOSE ENCOUNTER

■ As *Titanic* picked up speed and the tugboats began to drop behind, the forward motion of the ship combined with low water and the incoming tide caused a surge of water in the channel.

On the starboard side this surge flowed into the River Test, but on the port side the wave rolled toward the docks and had nowhere to go.

Because of the coal strike, two idle passenger ships, *Oceanic* and *New York*, were tied up in tandem at Berth 38, facing downstream with *New York* on the outside.

■ The surge of water lifted *New York* up and its mooring ropes slackened. Then, as *Titanic* passed by, the volume of water decreased and *New York* dropped back to its old level, then bobbed up and down like a cork. These movements caused too much of a strain on the mooring ropes, and every one of them started to snap. The stern ropes broke first with a loud bang, and the ropes flailed across the decks of the two ships and the bystanders on the dock. Fortunately no one was hit by the ropes.

Now the stern of *New York* was loose, and the increasing speed of *Titanic* was drawing water and the stern of *New York* toward it. *New York* came within four feet of colliding with the *Titanic.*

■ Quick action by the captain of the tug *Vulcan* prevented a collision. *Vulcan* was able to get some ropes on the stern of *New York* to try to hold it in check. At about the same time, Captain Smith ordered *"Full astern"* which stopped the forward motion of *Titanic* and actually caused the ship to begin backing up. The flow of water now forced *New York* back toward its former position.

In the meantime, *Titanic* backed past Berth 38 and the stern of *New York* and, as a precaution, Captain Smith had the starboard anchor lowered part way so it could be dropped immediately if required.

■ Meanwhile, *New York* drifted down river, controlled by the tugs which had managed to get more ropes on it, and forward progress was finally halted after *New York* had drifted past the end of the docks. The ship was then moored to an open dock while additional ropes were attached to *Oceanic* to prevent the same thing from happening to it.

Later it was found that a large, sunken barge in the river had been dragged nearly half a mile down river by the suction created by *Titanic.*

■ Finally, an hour late, *Titanic* was given permission to continue its twenty-four mile journey down the River Test to the English Channel, this time, though, a little slower and with much more caution. Half way down the river, *Titanic* passed the spot where *Olympic* and *Hawke* had collided in a situation vary similar to what *Titanic* had just encountered.

Captain Smith gave four blasts on the whistle as *Titanic* passed the Royal Yacht Squadron to acknowledge all of the people lined up to see the ship, in particular one photographer named Frank Beken who waited out in a boat with his camera. As *Titanic* passed Beken, he took some of the most remarkable photographs of the ship ever made.

■ While Beken was taking his photographs, another amateur photographer, Father Francis M. Browne, was taking pictures on the ship. Father Browne spent most of the daylight hours searching for good camera angles, and he took several pictures of the near collision with *New York*

Titanic leaving Southampton April 10, 1912. Note passengers lining the decks and the now partially enclosed A Deck Promenade. *Author's Collection*

and of life on the ship. Browne was a transit passenger. He was only going as far as Queenstown, Ireland, *Titanic's* last port call before heading to open water and New York. Browne's photographs are some of the most famous ones that exist of the ship.

■ As *Titanic* approached the English Channel, it slowed long enough to drop Bowyer off onto a waiting pilot boat, then picked up speed for a routine crossing of the Channel to Cherbourg France, 67 miles away and its next port stop.

■ The April sun was beginning to set at 3:00 p.m. when the passengers were called for dinner (or, more correctly, the ships bugler P.W. Fletcher went from deck to deck announcing meal call with his bugle) and the passengers began to settle in for their first meal on the great ship *Titanic*.

Probably much of the dinner conversation centered around the near collision that most of the passengers had seen. Mrs. Henry Harris remembered speaking to a stranger who asked her, *"Do you love life?" "Yes, I love it"* she replied. The stranger then said, *"That was a bad omen. Get off this ship at Cherbourg, if we get that far. That's what I'm going to do."*

Mrs. Harris laughed about the episode, thinking as many others did that the ship was unsinkable, however she never saw the stranger again after Cherbourg.

The American flag fluttered from the mast of ship, announcing its final destination of New York. Cherbourg was just a couple of hours away.

"...each porthole gleaming like a star..."

CHAPTER 8

CHERBOURG, FRANCE

White Star Line had been using Cherbourg as a port for ready access to the continent ever since White Star began using Southampton as a port in 1907. Cherbourg had a great deep water harbor and was a prime location, being only 75 miles from Southampton. What Cherbourg didn't have was docking facilities for large passenger ships.

■ To overcome this problem, White Star used tenders to ferry passengers out to the ships from the passenger terminal on shore.

Built at the same time as *Olympic* in Harland and Wolff's Belfast shipyard and actually steaming along with *Olympic* on its sea trials, were White Star Line's two newest passenger tenders, *Nomadic* and *Traffic* which had been built specifically for use in Cherbourg.

Nomadic was designed to carry 1,000 First and Second Class passengers and their luggage while *Traffic* was built to carry 500 Third Class passengers and luggage. It was also equipped with conveyers to load mail onto the liners.

■ About the same time that the First Class train was leaving Waterloo Station in London for Southampton, another train was leaving Paris bound for Cherbourg with 274 First, Second and Third class passengers destined for an afternoon rendezvous with *Titanic*.

At 3:30 p.m., about six hours after leaving Paris, the train pulled into the Gare Maritime station in Cherbourg. There the passengers were notified that because of the near collision that *Titanic* had with *New York* in Southampton, the ship would not depart at 4:30 but would be at least an hour late.

Most of the 102 third class passengers were emigrants from Middle Eastern countries like Syria and Croatia, and few could read or understand English or French. Normally they would have been routed through a Mediterranean port, but for some unknown reason they had instead been routed through Cherbourg onto the first available ship...*Titanic.*

■ At 5:30 the passengers were gathered up and escorted onto the two tenders where they could await the arrival of *Titanic* inside and out of the cold air.

■ At 6:30 p.m. the passengers watched as *Titanic* slowly entered the harbor. Everyone commented on what a beautiful sight it made with all of its lights on as the last glow of sunset appeared behind it.
As one observer wrote:

> *"Perhaps then, more than at any other time, she was the lovely ship that people thought her to be. Her outline was etched clearly in light, with each porthole gleaming like a star..."*

The trip across the English Channel took over four hours while steaming at 15 knots. There had not been any attempt to make up for lost time.

■ At 6:35 p.m. *Titanic* came to a stop about one mile from shore and dropped anchor with its starboard side facing the dock. The passenger shuffle at Cherbourg was about to begin.
Before passengers were allowed to board, there were fifteen First and nine Second Class passengers traveling only to Cherbourg that were allowed to board *Nomadic* with their baggage and some cargo.

SECOND AND THIRD CLASS PASSENGERS

■ Among the 102 Third Class passengers was thirteen-year old Miss Ayout Banoura who was traveling from Syria to Detroit with her cousin Shawneene Whabee, 38, and three male cousins. Ayout and Shawneene would survive the trip. The three men would not survive.

■ Mr. Said Nackid, 20, was enroute to Waterbury, Connecticut, with his wife Mary, 19, and 18 month old daughter Mary. All three would be rescued, but young Mary would die of meningitis three months later...the first survivor to die.

■ Mrs. Solomon Baclini, her three daughters and the daughter of a friend were enroute from Syria to New York. They had already missed another ship because of illness so they took the next available one. All five would survive the sinking and Mrs. Baclini's husband did-n't even know they had been on *Titanic* until they arrived home. Tragedy struck though when their three-year-old daughter died four months later...the second *Titanic* survivor to die.

■ Another Syrian traveling to Ottawa, Canada to meet up with his wife was Joseph Elias and his two sons. Three other children remained in Syria. Joseph and his sons died, and their bodies were not recovered. It would take months before the three remaining children would be reunited with their mother and then only with the assistance of the American Red Cross.

■ There were only 30 Second Class passengers boarding in Cherbourg, including twenty-eight year old Joseph LaRoche from Haiti, his French born wife and their two children. Mrs. LaRoche was pregnant. Since Joseph was black he had sustained much racial discrimination in France, so the family was moving back to Haiti so he could find a high paying engineering job. Joseph LaRoche would die on this trip but the rest of his family would survive. It also appears that Joseph was the only black on the ship. His body was not recovered.

■ An interesting individual boarding in Cherbourg was a German named Alfred Nourney, 20. Nourney traveled under the name "Baron von Drachstedt." Upon boarding he decided he didn't like his accommodation, so he demanded First Class accommodations and was upgraded to First Class. He survived, but nobody seems to know why he was traveling under that name.

■ Samuel Ward Stanton was a well-known American marine artist who was returning home from Spain after making sketches for murals he would paint back in New York. Stanton would not survive the trip.

FIRST CLASS PASSENGERS

April was the end of the high-travel season in Europe and some of the most interesting individuals to board *Titanic* did so in Cherbourg. In addition to many regular business travelers, there were many who were socially prominent among the 142 First Class passengers.

■ By far the wealthiest passenger on board was Colonel John Jacob Astor IV, 48, of New York City and Rhinebeck, New York. Estimated to be worth $100 million (1912 dollars), Astor managed the

John Jacob and Madeleine Astor. John   Margaret (Molly) Brown.   *Daily Mirror*
Jacob Astor would perish at sea. *National*
Archives

Above left: Benjamin Guggenheim. **Above right:** James Clinch Smith. Neither
Guggenheim or Smith would survive the disaster. *National Archives*

family fortune while writing novels and inventing mechanical devices like bicycle brakes.

In 1897 Astor built the Astoria Hotel in New York, which was later joined with its neighbor, the Waldorf Hotel, and was renamed the Waldorf-Astoria. Astor also owned the St. Regis and Knickerbocker Hotels. During the Spanish-American War he was appointed a colonel in the US Volunteers. Astor was married and had two children when in 1909 he did something that was so socially unacceptable that he would spend the rest of his life dodging the gossip it created: Astor divorced his wife.

In the late Victorian era, socially prominent men did not divorce their wives. They had mistresses—sometimes many of them and often very public ones. Having a mistress was fine, but divorce was not. However, Astor did divorce his wife Ava and two years later in 1911, Astor married an eighteen-year-old girl named Madeleine Force who just happened to be one year younger than his son.

The gossip and rumormongers had a field day with this and in order to create some stability in their lives, the Astors decided to spend the winter in Egypt and Paris and to travel home to the United States on board *Titanic*, occupying the suite C62-C64 on the port side. Traveling with the Astors were Victor Robbins, Astor's manservant; Miss Rosalie Bidois, Mrs. Astor's maid; and Miss Caroline Endres, a private nurse hired because young Mrs. Astor was pregnant. Rounding out the Astor clan was Colonel Astor's pet Airedale dog Kitty. Madeleine Force Astor and the two women survived, John Jacob, his servant and Kitty did not.

■ A friend of the Astor's boarding at Cherbourg was Mrs. James J. (Molly) Brown, wife of a rich gold miner who had made and lost several fortunes in the midwest. Molly had to change her reservations from another ship in order to travel with the Astors. Molly would have an interesting evening on a lifeboat, but she would survive.

■ At least millionaire Benjamin Guggenheim had his social priorities in order. He was enroute home to his wife in New York with his mistress Madame Leontine Aubert from Paris. Mr. Guggenheim was also accompanied by his valet Victor Giglio and his chauffeur Rene Pernot, while Madame Aubert was accompanied by her maid. Miss Aubert would survive but the rest of the group would not.

One of the more memorable last acts was played out as the ship sank by Guggenheim and his valet Victor Giglio, who returned to their rooms and dressed in their most formal attire. They then camped out in the First Class Smoking Lounge awaiting the end. When asked why he wasn't trying to get onto a lifeboat, Guggenheim replied *"we are dressed up in our best and are prepared to go down like gentlemen."*

■ Mrs. James W.M. Cardeza, 58, from Germantown, Pennsylvania, was traveling with her son Thomas D.M. Cardeza, 36, her maid Anna Ward, his manservant and fourteen trunks, four suitcases and three crates of baggage. They occupied the other Promenade Suite B51-53-55 on the starboard side. All four would survive the trip, but the luggage is still at the bottom of the North Atlantic Ocean. Mrs. Cardeza would later file a claim for $177,352 (in 1912 dollars) for the lost luggage and clothing.

■ Colonel Archibald Gracie IV, 54, was the son of a Confederate general killed during the Civil War. He lived in New York and Washington, DC and had four daughters who all died very young. One of Gracie's ancestors built Gracie Mansion which is the official residence of the mayor of New York City.

A graduate of the United States Military Academy, Gracie was colonel of the US Army's Seventh Regiment and a amateur historian. He spent several years researching and writing a book titled *"The Truth About Chickamauga"* about the famous Civil War battle his father had fought in. After the book was published, Gracie decided it was time to relax, so he took a trip to Europe, traveling on *Oceanic* and making friends with one of that ship's officers, Herbert Pitman. During his trip he had taken notes and did considerable research for a new book he was going to write about the War of 1812. Although Gracie would survive the trip, his notes did not.

Once aboard *Titanic*, Gracie formally offered his service to several "unprotected ladies" (women traveling alone). It was a custom for gentlemen at this time to do so. Accepting his offer were three sisters returning from a funeral in England: Mrs. E.D. Appleton, Mrs. R.C. Cornell and Mrs. John M. Brown and their friend, Miss Edith Evans. Of this group, only Miss Evans, who stood back to let her friend and a mother of small children, Mrs. Brown, enter a boat ahead of her, did not survive.

■ George D. Widener, 50, was from Elkins Park, Pennsylvania, and very wealthy. He was also the son of P.A.B. Widener, a board member of the Fidelity Trust Company in Philadelphia, which in turn controlled the International Mercantile Marine, who owned the White Star Line. George Widener was heir to the largest fortune in Philadelphia. He was now traveling home from vacation with his wife Eleanor, son Harry E. Widener and two servants.

Sir Cosmo Duff Gordon. *National Archives*   Lady Lucille Duff Gordon. *National Archives*

Photograph of survivors of lifeboat 1 taken on board *Carpathia*. Lady Duff Gordon is standing in the center, Sir Cosmo is to the right. *Daily Mirror*

George Widener, son Harry and the manservant would die. George and Harry helped Mrs. Widener and the maid into a lifeboat then stepped back to await their fate.

■ Enroute home to Cooperstown, Pennsylvania, was Mr. Arthur L. Ryerson, 61, his wife Emily, three children Emily, John and Suzette and their maid. Unknown to them, also on board was a distant cousin William Ryerson, a steward in the dining saloon. Arthur L. Ryerson would not survive the trip, but William and the rest of the family did.

■ Sir Cosmo and Lady Lucille Duff Gordon were an interesting couple. Sir Cosmo basically lived off the family wealth after having graduated from Eton (England's premier men's academy) and then married Lucille, who was a famous fashion designer in London, Paris and New York. Sir Cosmo represented Britain in the 1908 Olympics as a fencer, and beyond that Sir Cosmo did little else. He and Lucille were now enroute to New York and they occupied staterooms A16 and A20 which were not only not connected but were across the hall from each other. For some never explained reason, they had booked their trip under the names of Mr. and Mrs. Morgan. Their actions the night of the sinking would cause them a lifetime of grief.

■ James Clinch Smith, 56, was the brother of Bessie Smith White and the brother-in-law of the late architect Stanford White (another person who did not have his social house in order). In 1906 Harry Thaw, until recently married to White's mistress, murdered White while Clinch Smith was watching.
Clinch Smith and Archibald Gracie were good friends. Smith would die and his body wasn't recovered.

■ Mr. Dickinson H. Bishop, 25, was already a widower from Dowagiac, Michigan, who had recently re-married a lady from Sturgis, Michigan, named Helen Walton. The Bishops were returning from a four-month honeymoon in Europe and had delayed their return so they could travel on *Titanic*. Helen was also pregnant. The Bishops were unique: most of the honeymooning couples on *Titanic* lost one or both of their partners, but both of the Bishops survived. Their tragedy would come later.
The child Mrs. Bishop carried would die two days after birth. In 1916 the Bishop's divorced and Helen died on March 16, two days after Dickinson had remarried. The announcement of her death would appear on the same page as his marriage in the local newspaper.

■ William E. Carter, 36, from Byrn Mawr, Pennsylvania was traveling home from vacation with his wife Lucile, their two children, a maid, a chauffeur, their two dogs and Mr. Carter's 25 horsepower Renault automobile. This was another rare case of an entire family and the maid surviving the trip. However, the chauffeur, the automobile and the two dogs weren't as fortunate.

■ Miss Margaret B. Hays, 24, of New York City was touring Europe with two friends Lily Potter and Olive Earnshaw and Margaret's Pomeranian dog. They, too, had a self-appointed "escort" named Gilbert Tucker who had met the three ladies while traveling in Europe with his parents. Tucker decided to return home with them because he had fallen madly in love with Miss Hays.

After the collision with the iceberg, Tucker helped get the three women up to the boat deck where he helped them into their life jackets. Margaret was holding onto her dog which was wrapped up in a blanket. At some point James Clinch Smith walked by an commented, jokingly, *"Oh, I suppose we ought to put a life preserver on the little doggie, too."*

Margaret, Lily and Olive and survived as did Gilbert Tucker. However, although they remained friends for years, Margaret Hays later married someone else.

■ Mr. Arthur W. Newell, 58, from Lexington, Massachusetts had been on a trip to the Middle East with his two daughters Madeleine, 32, and Marjorie, 23.

After the collision, Mr. Newell went to the girls room and told them to get dressed in their warmest clothes and to follow him to the boat deck. Once there, he helped them get into lifeboat number 6, commenting to them that, *"It does seem more dangerous for you to get into that boat than to remain here with me but we must obey orders."*

Newell continued to help load passengers into other boats, and he died when the ship went down. His body was later recovered and identified and he was later buried in Cambridge, Massachusetts. His wife never remarried and lived until 1957, passing away at the age of 103. She spent the rest of her life in mourning, usually wearing black and sleeping with his watch under her pillow and never allowing mention of *Titanic* in her presence.

■ Englehart Ostby, 65, was very successful in the jewelry business in Providence, Rhode Island. He was returning home from vacation in Europe with his daughter Helene and a bag full of gems and jewels he had bought in Paris.

After the collision, Ostby managed to get to the boat deck with his daughter, but went back to his room to get some warmer clothes. In the meantime Helene was placed into lifeboat number 5, and she never saw Ostby again. His body was recovered and he is buried in Providence.

■ The Spedden family, Frederick, wife Daisy and son Douglas plus two servants were another success story: all were saved. Frederick had actually placed his wife and child into a lifeboat and stepped back after saying good-bye, but before the boat was lowered about 20 men were allowed to enter because there weren't any more women or children around. One of the more endearing *Titanic* photographs that survive is of young Douglas spinning a top on the Promenade Deck as his father looks on.

Douglas Spedden, spinning a top on the Promenade Deck as his father watches.

■ Mr. Ramon Artagaveytia, 72, was returning to Argentina by way of New York. In 1871 he survived the sinking of the ship *America* in Uruguay, where only 65 of the 205 passengers survived, most of the dead dying of burns. He had nightmares throughout his life, even writing a relative two months before he sailed on *Titanic* that he kept hearing the words "Fire! Fire! Fire!" and said he often wore his lifebelt when he was on a ship.

Artagaveytia also thought that wireless communication would prevent the type of disaster of a sinking ship because help could now be called. He died when *Titanic* went down, and his body was recovered. He was eventually buried in Uruguay.

■ Mrs. Walter Stephenson, 52, from Haverford, Pennsylvania, had already survived the 1906 San Francisco earthquake. She was now returning home from a vacation in Europe with her sister Elizabeth Eustis. Both women would survive this disaster too.

It was completely dark at 8:00 p.m. when the loading process was completed. In just ninety minutes the 274 embarking and 24 departing passengers had been taken care of. At 8:10 p.m. *Titanic* got underway, turning around and heading out of Cherbourg harbor. The ship and all aboard were now heading west into the night, to cross the English Channel once more to make the next and last port call at Queenstown, Ireland the next afternoon.

Titanic at the Southampton dock. *Author's Collection*

CHAPTER 9

QUEENSTOWN, IRELAND

Even before *Titanic* left Cherbourg, Mr. P.W. Fletcher made his second round of the ship, blowing his bugle to announce the evening meal. Most, if not all, of the passengers took advantage of the opportunity to make their way to the various dining saloons.

Once the ship departed Cherbourg and everyone finished eating, it was time for people to begin what was called by some as the grand escapade or the big search: now was the time when many of the passengers began exploring their floating hotel. The sea that evening was somewhat rough, and several passengers remarked at how smoothly *Titanic* handled the waves. There was little notice of any rocking or motion, and people commented that the only real sense of motion came from the distant, hollow sound of the thumping of the engines.

■ While the passengers were settling into the routine that would last until they arrived in New York, the crew also settled into their own routine: the stokers, firemen, trimmers, greasers and other members of the Engineering Department stood their four hour shifts. Meanwhile in the Victualling and Stewards Department, the stewards and stewardesses, cooks, bakers and anyone else that was responsible for running the hotel portion of the ship were preparing for their twelve and eighteen-hour days. Some stewards were on call twenty-four hours and would only get to rest early in the morning when their passengers no longer needed their services.

All of the ship's officers except Captain Smith stood normal four-hour deck watches, but they had other duties as well. All had various rounds to keep and duties to attend to. Each had his own cabin and would retire there whenever possible to catch up on his rest, but the normal routine was eight-to-ten hours on and two-to-four hours off.

A typical First Class stateroom. *National Archives*

Café Parisien. *National Archives*

■ Marconi operators Phillips and Bride had settled on their own watch schedule prior to leaving Southampton: Phillips took the 8:00 p.m. to 2:00 a.m. watch and Bride the 2:00 a.m. to 8:00 a.m. watch. During the rest of the time usually both were on duty although they did manage to take time off to rest when the workload allowed it.

■ The Harland and Wolff guarantee group was up and about offering their services to the various departments, but for most of the voyage there was little for them to do.

■ Down on F deck near the Third Class Dining Saloon and close by where the butchers prepared the meals were the dog kennels and on this night the animals, too, were settling in for a long trip. These four legged passengers would be as well treated as their masters up in First and Second Class.

■ What the roaming passengers discovered in their travels around the ship was almost beyond belief for all but a very few of them: for while many of the First Class passengers were used to the very finest accommodations, most of the rest had never seen anything like the luxury offered on the *Titanic*.

AMENITIES FOR THE FIRST CLASS PASSENGERS

■ First Class passengers boarded the ship through the main entrance on B deck, and the first thing they saw was the magnificent Grand Staircase that towered two stories above them, topped off by a huge glass and wrought-iron dome that allowed light to flood into the enclosed First Class entrance on the boat deck. This staircase had a landing and a right-angle turn between the decks on each level, so that passengers descending the stairs would have a view of the entire room they were descending into. Also, there were two wells, or light shafts, that went all the way from the Boat deck down to the bottom of the stairwell on D deck so that light from the dome could enter those decks as well.

The staircase and the landings were fully carpeted in light beige, the banisters were of carved wood and iron, and the walls were done in light oak.

"Carpet...you sank in it up to your knees...furniture so heavy you could hardly lift it...she was a beautiful, wonderful ship" wrote one crewman.

First Class staircase between the Boat deck and A deck with glass dome above. Note the right angle turn. The wood carving of "Honour and Glory Crowning Time" surrounds the clock on the wall. This photo is from *Titanic's* sister ship *Olympic. National Archives*

There was a second, smaller Grand Staircase aft of the third funnel that also had a dome and a light shaft, and this staircase also extended all the way down to D deck.

Most of B deck was occupied by First Class suites including the two Promenade Suites with their own private promenade decks.

Further aft on B deck were the reception room for the à la carte restaurant at the base of the aft Grand Staircase, and further aft was the restaurant itself. The Café Parisian was on the starboard side, and many of the younger adult passengers would gather here during the trip.

■ From B deck, the Grand Staircase led up to A deck where the partially enclosed and fully covered promenade ran almost two-thirds the length of the ship on both sides. This promenade surrounded several rooms: the First Class Lounge which was finished in green velvet and dull polished oak; the reading and writing room with its huge fireplace, finished with plush carpeting done in old rose; the smoking room done in dark Georgian style, surrounded by the finest mahogany, mother of pearl inlay work and stained glass windows; and the Verandah and Palm Court rooms with their floor-to-ceiling windows that opened to let the air in, carpeted with thick heavy carpeting and surrounded with live plants. The corridors were oak paneled and there were revolving doors to keep the cold air out. Mirrors and cut glass were everywhere.

■ Going up the Grand Staircase toward the boat deck, passengers saw the beautiful wood carving of Honour and Glory Crowning Time on the wall of the landing.

■ Once on the Boat deck, people could look up through the huge dome and then go outside to the deck which contained both the First and Second Class promenade. Noticeable on this deck were the abundance of chairs and benches for the passengers to sit on as well as the four funnels and the 20 lifeboats.

The enclosed entrance had a linoleum floor, but the walls were all covered in dark oak, and there were several electric heaters to keep the room warm.

■ A First Class passenger who entered the ship on B deck and went down the main Grand Staircase to C deck would find the majority of the First Class cabins (as opposed to multi-room suites on B deck).

■ Continuing down one more level to D deck, a First Class passenger would find more First Class cabins and the huge First Class Reception room that extended the width of the ship and had large floor-to-ceiling windows. Thick Axminster carpet covered the floor. Wicker chairs and Chesterfields were placed for the passengers comfort. A huge grand piano was placed in this room.

■ Passing from the reception room through two large iron and wooden doors brought passengers into the First Class Dining Saloon, the largest single room on the ship, so large that the room could seat every First Class passenger.

After a meal if someone wished to return to the boat deck for some air or exercise but didn't want to climb back up five levels, he or she could always take one of the three elevators located behind the staircase, each manned by an attendant.

■ Down one more level of the Grand Staircase were the First Class accommodations on the starboard side of E deck. Running the length of E deck on the port side was the corridor called "Scotland Road" by the crew, used by them and Third Class passengers to move from one end of the ship to the other.

■ The First Class accommodations were designed to emulate the best hotels of the world, and they were fabulous. All were decorated in various styles popular at that time: Louis XIV, Louis XVI, Italian Renaissance, Queen Anne, Modern Dutch, Old Dutch, Georgian. The finest brass, wood, cloth and carpeting was used in these rooms. Many of the fixtures cost hundreds of dollars each and all were fully authentic to the period.

■ Over 400 live plants in five-inch or larger pots were loaded in Southampton for placement in the First and Second Class portions of the ship. Also, climbing ivy was used in the Palm Court and the Café Parisian.
Also, thousands of fresh flowers and roses were loaded for use in the cabins and on the dining tables in the First and Second Class areas.

■ In an age when some of the best hotels did not have private rest room facilities, most of the suites on *Titanic* had private facilities including full size bathtubs. The suites also had storage areas for trunks and closets for clothes, and all rooms had call buttons to summon attendants.
Many of the suites also came with separate rooms for servants and maids, and all came with electric heaters, four-foot wide brass bedsteads, wicker armchairs, ceiling fans, marble fixtures in the bathrooms, thick carpeting and heavy drapes to block the outside light.
All the cabins were connected by long corridors, all painted white and carpeted, and all corridors led to one of the two huge Grand Staircases. Cabins came with one, two, three or four beds.
There was a barber shop, a dark room for amateur photographers, a library, a separate dining room for personal maids and valets and a hospital equipped with a modern operating room.

■ To keep the idle rich occupied, *Titanic* was equipped with a heated 30-foot long, 14-foot wide indoor saltwater swimming bath, a Turkish and electric bath with adjoining cooling room, a squash racquet court (30 feet long, 20 feet wide) with spectators areas. On the Boat deck was the gymnasium measuring 44 feet long, 18 feet wide and containing several pieces of exercise equipment including cycling, rowing and horse-riding equipment.
The Turkish and electric baths were forward on F deck, and they were open to ladies between 10 a.m. and 1 p.m. and to gentlemen from 2 p.m. to 6 p.m. The cost to use the baths was $1.00.
The swimming bath was across the corridor from the Turkish bath, and it was open the same hours in addition to being open for gentlemen

from 6 a.m. to 9 a.m. Cost was twenty-five cents if you didn't buy a ticket for the Turkish bath. The pool wasn't filled with water until after *Titanic* left Queenstown because it was filled directly from the sea and the water too close to shore was dirty and polluted.

Located on the Boat deck next to the First Class entrance was the gymnasium, open the same hours as the swimming pool except between 1 p.m. and 3 p.m. when children only were allowed.

Also located forward on G deck was the squash racquet court. Open by appointment only during the day, this cost $1.00 per hour and included the service of Frederick Wright the racquet professional.

In addition to Frederick Wright, there was an instructor for the gymnasium and assorted attendants for the swimming and Turkish baths.

SECOND AND THIRD CLASS PASSENGERS

■   Passengers who didn't have the funds or the social stature to travel in First Class were forced to travel in Second Class. Those who were emigrants or who wanted to travel cheaply Third Class.

Passenger Lawrence Beesley and instructor T.W. McCawley in the gymnasium prior to departure from Southampton. *National Archives*

Second Class accommodations on *Titanic* were said to be better than First Class on any other ship, and even Third Class was supposed to be better than First Class on a lot of the liners of the day.

Second Class passengers had their own grand staircase leading down six decks from the boat deck. *Titanic* and *Olympic* were the first ships to have an elevator for Second Class passengers. There was a separate library, smoking room, enclosed promenade and a huge dining saloon. The Boat deck had a separate, open promenade area.

■ Third class passengers didn't get all of the amenities and trappings the other classes did, but they were well taken care of. Instead of the usual dormitories that other ships had, *Titanic* provided individual rooms with anywhere from two to six beds. All rest room facilities were common, but then many of the Third Class passengers had never seen indoor plumbing. The food was great and there was a lot of it. Most Third Class passengers had more to eat on this ship than they had ever had.

In an era when Third Class passengers knew their status, they weren't at all upset by the locked gates or the segregation, and few ever took it upon themselves to take charge of a situation because they were used to being told what to do. This, in large part, is why so many of them didn't survive the sinking. There wasn't anyone to tell them what to do or where to go, and they perished while waiting for instructions.

■ While First Class accommodations were in the center of the ship (the most stable portion), Second Class cabins were mainly aft of the First Class areas, and the Third Class passengers were in the bow or stern areas. Third Class families and single women were placed in the stern while single men were placed in the bow, and their only route of communication was down "Scotland Road", the wide corridor down on E deck.

■ The crew quarters were jammed into just about every available nook-and-cranny available. Separate cabins or dormitories were provided for complete departments: postal clerks, the band, the bakers, the cooks, the quartermasters each had their own cabin while the larger crews such as the stokers, firemen, trimmers all had a bunk in a dormitory, some of which held over 50 men. Most of the different departments had their own mess (meal) areas. The only crew members who had their own rooms were the officers and some of the stewards and stewardesses who were on call for the First Class passengers.

QUEENSTOWN

Throughout the night and into the morning, *Titanic* steamed toward its final port call at Queenstown, Ireland. In the morning breakfast was served and afterwards the passengers started to congregate on the decks watching for landfall that would be the coast of Ireland.

■ Around 6:45 a.m. Father Francis Browne went up on the Boat deck and started taking pictures, including the one of six-year-old Robert Spadden spinning a top while his father Frederick looked on.

Browne took a lot of pictures that morning: pictures of passengers and of the crew. One shows that *Titanic* wasn't steering in a straight line because the officers were making course changes to test the compass.

■ Near the Cobh Harbor light vessel, *Titanic* slowed to a stop and picked up the pilot who would guide the ship into the harbor and at 11:30 a.m. *Titanic* stopped in the harbor, about two miles from land because once again, the harbor didn't have facilities for a ship the size of *Titanic*.

■ Ferried out on a half-hour run from the dock in Queenstown on the tenders *Ireland* and *America* were 7 second class and 113 third class passengers and 1,385 sacks of mail. Seven First Class passengers disembarked, including Father Browne who was clutching his photographic plates. While waiting on the tender, Father Browne took more pictures, including one of Captain Smith looking over the side from the starboard bridge wing.

■ While the loading and unloading process was going on, a flotilla of merchants in small boats, called bumboats, pulled up next to the tenders. The merchants started showing off their wares by hanging them all over the sides of the boats. Many of the owners of these boats (the respectable looking ones at least) were allowed to board *Titanic* with their goods by crossing over the decks of the tenders. One enterprising bumboatman got really lucky when John Jacob Astor approached him and bought a lace jacket for Madeleine on the spot for $800. At today's rate, that jacket would cost over $13,000.

■ One unauthorized departure in Queenstown was stoker John Coffey. His home was in Queenstown and he probably signed on to get a free trip home. In any event, he managed to get off the ship and onto one of the tenders and hide behind some of the cargo coming off the ship.

Since leaving Southampton the day before, many of the passengers and crew had taken the time to write letters or address some of the many

Captain Edward J. Smith looking over the side from the starboard bridge wing (top of photo). Lifeboat 1 hangs on its davits. *National Archives*

Titanic postcards provided them, and there was a lot of outbound mail to take to shore.

Little is known or said about Chief Officer Wilde, but he did mail a letter to his sister from Queenstown, and he made the comment *"I still don't like this ship...I have a queer feeling about it."*

■ Loading the Third Class passengers was less hectic here. The stewards and the crew knew their way around now, and *"At least this lot spoke English,"* one steward said.

■ Sometime during the boarding process occurred one of the highlights of the stop in Queenstown. An unnamed stoker, totally covered in black soot, climbed up the 165-foot ladder inside the aft funnel to get a look out and some fresh air. The appearance of his black head popping out of the funnel scared a number of people and was thought to be an ill-omen by some.

■ Two hours after *Titanic's* arrival, the huge whistle blew again and the propellers started to turn. As preparations were being made to close the gangway door, a local photographer took a photo of Fourth Officer Boxhall and Second Officer Lightoller standing in the door opening for the last time.

The anchor was brought up and Father Browne, now standing on the tender, took one last photo of the stern of the *Titanic* as the tender moved away.

■ On the stern of the ship, newly arrived Third Class passenger Eugene Daly propped himself up on a bench and began playing the dirge "Erin's Lament" on his Irish pipes as the green hills of Ireland began to fall away from the ship. There was another brief stop to drop off the pilot, then *Titanic* picked up speed. As the sun was beginning to drop into the horizon, a French fishing boat came so close to *Titanic* that it was splashed with water, but nothing serious happened and as the fishing boat fell astern, so to did the Irish coast. The next stop would be New York City in five days. *Titanic* was now steaming west into the sunset and into history.

The last photograph of First Officer Murdoch and Second Officer Lightoller looking out the gangway door prior to closing it. Photographed from the tender in Queenstown. *Cork Examiner*

"God himself could not sink this ship."

CHAPTER 10

DESTINY

There were 2,234 people on *Titanic* as it steamed west into the afternoon sun on April 11, 1912. One of the many questions that has not been and never will be answered to everyone's satisfaction is exactly how many people were really on board.

Researchers use their own methods of tracking and counting people, and the numbers range from a low of 2,212 up to 2,240, but 2,234 seems to be the most accurate. In any case, this is the number used here, but no number diminishes the fact that over two-thirds of the people on *Titanic* that afternoon would never see land again.

■ There were accommodations for 1,024 third class passengers and there were 721 of them on board, or 70% of capacity.

■ In second class there was room for 674 passengers and there were a total of 285 on board, or 42% of capacity.

■ First class accommodations for 735 passengers existed yet only 337 were on board, or 46% of capacity.

■ In addition to the 1,343 passengers (there were actually accommodations for 2,433, so *Titanic* was steaming at 55% of capacity) there were 891 crew members.

FIFTY-FIVE VERY LUCKY PEOPLE

■ For various reasons, fifty-five ticketed passengers did not make the trip on *Titanic*.

Several canceled because they didn't like their accommodations. Most had booked First Class passage on another ship but were transferred to *Titanic* because of the coal strike and given Second Class accommodations for the same price they had paid earlier for First Class.

Several more canceled because they had premonitions of disaster or didn't like to travel on maiden voyages.

■ Mr. and Mrs. E.W. Bill were planning on making the trip but a few nights before they were supposed to leave Southampton, Mrs. Bill had a nightmare about a sinking ship, and the Bills canceled their trip.

■ Millionaire George W. Vanderbilt and his wife also canceled the day before their departure because his mother talked them out of the trip as she did not like maiden voyages. Since their huge collection of luggage (even more than the Cardeza's haul) was already aboard the ship, their servant Frederick Wheeler was sent on with it as a Second Class passenger to collect the luggage in New York. Neither the luggage or Mr. Wheeler survived the trip.

■ Robert Bacon, United States Ambassador to France, had to cancel because his replacement was late arriving in Paris.

■ Finally there were the Fricks, the Morgans and the Hardings that had all booked a Promenade Suite and had to cancel for various reasons, giving Bruce Ismay his opportunity to occupy it.

■ In addition to the fifty-five passengers, there were about 20 crewmen who missed the boat, as the saying goes, for various reasons.

■ Lucky also were the over 1,100 people who could have booked passage on *Titanic*...it was designed to carry that many more...and didn't.

LIFE AT SEA, PART I

■ Other than meals and Sunday church services, there weren't any organized activities for the passengers. They were expected to provide their own entertainment.

■ Meals were scheduled for:

> 8:30 a.m. to 10:30 a.m. for breakfast
> 1 p.m. to 2:30 p.m. for lunch
> 6 p.m. to 8 p.m. for dinner

The á la carte restaurant was open to First Class passengers from 8 a.m. to 11 p.m. daily for anyone wanting a snack or not wanting to partake in the regular daily meals.

■ The First Class library on A deck was open from 8 a.m to 11 p.m. There was also a library for Second Class passengers. Third Class passengers could spend some of their time in the great general room on C deck that had a piano and was used for dances which seemed to take place most hours.

A large selection of card and board games were available to all classes, and each class had its own outside promenade where chairs and tables were available.

It seems that most people read or wrote letters, played card games or visited with friends. In the days before radio, television or slot machines, there was little else to do.

There were several high stakes card games going on the First Class areas, and there were also several professional gamblers who were doing their best to part the rich from their money. White Star Line had given all of the passengers a written warning about the possibility of the gambler's presence.

■ One thing that occupied the minds of many of the First Class men was the board in the Smoking Lounge that listed the number of miles in the previous day's run, posted from noon one day until noon the next:

Thursday to Friday, 386 miles
Friday to Saturday, 519 miles
Saturday to Sunday, 546 miles

It looked like *Titanic* was on time for a morning arrival in New York City on Wednesday, but several of the passengers were taking bets on the next day's run and at what time the ship would arrive in New York.

■ Several passengers had overheard conversations or rumors that an attempt was going to be made to try to set a record on the run, but that was neither possible or practical.

Titanic wasn't designed to beat *Mauretania's* current 26-knot record on the transatlantic run and, because of the coal strike, there wasn't a full load of coal. Steaming at high speed for too long could have consumed so much coal that there was a chance *Titanic* would have run out before making port. The fastest the ship ever steamed was a short run of 23 knots.

Titanic probably could have beat its sister ship *Olympic's* maiden voyage record, however to do so would have put *Titanic* outside New York harbor in the middle of the night. Given the problems of getting the ship out of

Southampton in the middle of the day, docking *Titanic* in New York in the dark probably would have been out of the question. Also, many of the passengers didn't have any arrangements to get picked up on Tuesday night, so they wouldn't have been overly excited about an early arrival. About all that could have been done is to have the ship wait outside the harbor until morning which wouldn't have set any records and would not have made much sense to the passengers.

MEALS

■ Meals were the only organized activity of the voyage and, for the First Class passengers anyway, the evening meal was a signature event.

The First Class Dining Saloon could seat 532 people in one setting, so all 337 of the First Class passengers on this trip could eat at the same time.

All 285 of the Second Class passengers could also be seated in one sitting in the Second Class Dining Saloon which could hold 394 at one time.

The two Third Class Dining Saloons could hold 473 in one setting, so the 721 passengers on this voyage had to be accommodated in two meal settings.

Before *Titanic* left Southampton, over 200,000 pounds of fresh food was loaded on board along with 35,000 bottles of beer, wine and spirits and 9,000 cigars. Nobody on this trip would go hungry or thirsty.

■ Lunch served to the First Class passengers on April 14 included the following: Consommé Fermier, Cockie Leekie, Fillets of Brill, Egg À L'Argenteuil; Chicken À La Maryland, Corned Beef, Vegetables, Dumplings, Grilled Mutton Chops, Custard Pudding, Apple Meringue, Salmon Mayonnaise, Potted Shrimps, Norwegian Anchovies, Souses Herrings, Plain and Smoked Sardines, Roast Beef, Veal and Ham Pie, Bologna Sausage, Corned Ox Tongue and eight types of cheese.

■ First Class dinner on April 14 was a seven course meal. There was a whole selection of hors d'oeuveres; two soups; sauté of chicken Lyonnaise or stuffed marrow; lamb, duckling or sirloin of beef; salmon; filet mignon; various vegetables, several special dishes including asparagus vinaigrette and pâté de foie gras and four deserts including Waldorf pudding and French ice cream.

Captain Smith usually didn't eat his meals at the head of a large table. He had his small personal table in the Dining Saloon. More often then not, he ate his meals in his own room.

Meals in the First Class Dining Saloon was strictly a formal affair. In an era when gentlemen always wore a coat, tie and a hat, mealtime didn't provide an opportunity to dress down.

■ While First Class passengers were being pampered with a limitless meal selection, Second Class passengers weren't treated badly either.

The Second Class dinner meal on April 14 included Consommé, Tapioca, Baked Haddock, Sharp Sauce, Curried Chicken and Rice, Spring Lamb and Mint Sauce, Roast Turkey, Cranberry Sauce, various vegetables and assorted desserts.

■ It's been said that some of the Third Class passengers ate better on this voyage than they had ever eaten before. If the selection wasn't all that great, the amount of food was more than they were accustomed. No one complained about the quantity.

Third Class breakfast included oatmeal porridge with milk, smoked herring and potatoes, ling fish with egg sauce, fried tripe and onions, boiled eggs, fresh bread and butter, marmalade, tea and coffee.

Dinner was served at mid-day, and a typical Third Class dinner might include soup, beefsteak and kidney pie; boiled mutton and caper sauce; various vegetables and desserts.

The evening meal for the Third Class passengers was called "tea," and might include cod fish cakes; cheese and pickles; fresh bread and butter and plum and apple jam.

While much of the menu might seem rather unappetizing to the late 20th century American palate, it was perfectly acceptable to the passengers of *Titanic*.

■ In addition to the dining saloon and the Café Parisien, First Class passengers could take their meals at the à la carte restaurant up on B deck, adorned with French walnut paneling and two-tone Dubarry rose carpeting. Mr. Luigi Gatti was the operator of the restaurant and had recruited most of his staff from his employees at the two London restaurants he owned, Gatti's Adelphi and Gatti's Strand.

Gatti brought his own staff of chefs, waiters and a manager. All of them were French or Italian, and ten of them were Gatti's cousins. Although not counted as part of the crew, all 68 of Gatti's employees did sign the ship's articles indicating that they would take orders from the ship's officers.

Gatti had been on *Olympic* when it collided with the *Hawke,* and now Gatti's wife didn't want him to go on this voyage, but he told her not to worry because he was an excellent swimmer.

THE ORCHESTRA

While the First Class passengers were enjoying their meals or lounging around the First Class Lounge and Smoking Room, they were entertained by the ship's orchestra which played for both First and Second Class passengers.

The leader of the orchestra was Wallace Hartley, a 33-year-old violinist who had been recruited from the *Mauretania*. There were a total of eight members of the orchestra which was divided into two sections, one with three members who performed in the Second Class Lounge and Dining Saloon. The remaining five, led by Hartley, played in the First Class Dining Saloon during meals and at after dinner concerts.

Their cabins were down on E deck, and when they weren't playing for the First and Second Class passengers, they would often take musical requests from the passengers who had cabins near theirs.

They played from a published list of 352 musical selections. Each member was expected to know all of the selections and its assigned number so that Hartley could call for the next selection by number only.

The members of *Titanic's* orchestra weren't employed by White Star Line, but were contracted out by the Liverpool company of C.W. and F.N. Black. Consequently, they held Second Class tickets and they also had to sign the ship's articles.

Bandmaster Wallace H. Hartley did not survive. *National Archives*

First Class passenger, Archibald Gracie. *National Archives*

WIRELESS

Next door to the First Class Purser's Office on C deck was the Enquiry Office where passengers could pay for tickets to the Turkish Bath or the squash racquet court. However, most passengers would use the Enquiry Office to arrange for the transmission of wireless messages to friends, family or business partners.

■ For a small fee based upon a flat rate for ten words and each extra word being additional, passengers could give a handwritten message to the clerk who would send it by pneumatic tube to the wireless office up on the Boat deck. There the wireless operator would arrange to transmit the message in the order it was received.

Incoming messages were handled in reverse, being sent down another pneumatic tube to the Enquiry Office where it was given to a courier for delivery to the recipient.

■ Incoming messages for the ship were given directly to the officer on duty on the bridge which was just down the corridor.

Messages concerning navigation were supposed to be handled immediately, but because the wireless operators didn't work for the ship but for the Marconi Company and the majority of their pay came from tips, there were times when navigation messages would pile up if one of the operators wasn't available to take them to the bridge. With two operators on the *Titanic*, the wireless office was never allowed to be unoccupied.

■ Wireless operator John (Jack) Phillips was the senior wireless operator and had spent several years on various ships. The junior operator was Harold Bride who was fully competent at his job. Between them *Titanic* had two excellent wireless operators who managed a large volume of messages. It seems that most of the First Class passengers delighted in sending dozens of messages to tell their friends and family about their trip on the *Titanic*.

■ On Friday night, the wireless blew a circuit and shut down. Both Phillips and Bride worked on it all night and had it running again on Saturday morning, but now they had over ten hours of incoming and outgoing messages to catch up on, something they hadn't completed by Sunday night.

Shortly before dark on Sunday, the wireless land station at Cape Race, Newfoundland came into Marconi range. Bride, and later Phillips, knew they would have to spend the entire night catching up on both the message backlog and the influx of outgoing messages that had come in during the day after the passengers found out that Cape Race would be in range during the night.

Messages received at Cape Race would be forwarded via wireless or phone line to Montreal for distribution to the rest of North America.

Marconi wireless operator John (Jack) Phillips. *National Archives*

Harold S. Bride. Bride, junior wireless operator, survived the ordeal. *National Archives*

LIFE AT SEA, PART II

■ During the trip, there weren't any lifeboat drills nor were there any instructions about which lifeboat to report to if there was an emergency. Furthermore, there weren't any instructions posted about how to use the life belts.

■ Captain Smith and his officers made a complete inspection of the ship every day at 10:00 to check on the safety and operation of the ship, the crew and the passengers.

■ Second class passengers Benjamin and Esther Hart were traveling with their seven-year-old daughter Eva. Eva and her father seldom parted company and spent a good portion of the trip touring the ship and meeting with all of the other passengers. Before leaving home, Eva's mother had a premonition about the ship sinking and she seldom left her cabin except for meals. In addition, she slept during the day and sat up at night so she would be awake if something happened at night while her family slept. On Sunday night, Benjamin and Eva were sleeping while Mrs. Hart performed her nightly vigil. Before it was over, Esther and Eva would be on a lifeboat and Mr. Hart would be dead.

■ Some Second Class passengers complained that the heat didn't work in their cabins and only part of the fixtures in some of the washrooms were installed. Due to the haste in preparing the ship for departure, some of the finishing work wasn't completed.

■ Down on G deck the five postal inspectors, three American and two British, worked more than fourteen-hour days sorting and bagging 3,430 bags of mail and hundreds of packages.

■ Second Class passenger Nellie Hocking of Cornwall told several friends that she heard a rooster crowing late one night. According to Cornish folklore this was a sign of pending disaster. Her friends didn't believe her.

After the ship sank, passenger Mrs. J.S. White filed a claim for lost property including roosters and hens. So it's entirely possible that Nellie Hocking did hear a rooster on *Titanic*.

■ Mrs. Ruth Becker was assured by the Second Class purser's clerk that, *"You don't have to be afraid at all. If anything should happen to this ship the watertight compartments would keep it afloat until we get help."*

■ Second Class passenger Mrs. Albert Caldwell asked a deck hand, *"Is this ship really non-sinkable?"* His reply was, *"Yes, lady. God himself could not sink this ship."*

■ On Saturday morning it was reported to Captain Smith that the coal fire in boiler room 6 had finally been put out. All the coal in the bunker had been moved out and watered down. The fire had burned for almost two weeks.

■ Religious services for all classes were held in the First Class Dining Saloon at 10:30 Sunday morning. This was the only opportunity Third Class passengers would have to see the First Class sections of the ship.

■   First Class passenger William T. Stead had written about a ship that collided with an iceberg and sank. Stead believed in mysticism and spiritualism and had been advised by mediums to avoid ocean travel.

During dinner one evening, Stead told a story about an Egyptian mummy that carried a curse that caused death and destruction to all that viewed it. The mummy itself was on display in a London museum.

Passenger Fred Seward was so impressed by the mummy story that he told it to a reporter of the *New York World* after his rescue. The story was written that the mummy was actually being transported on *Titanic* and its spell had caused the disaster.

■   Sometime Sunday, Mrs. Henry Harris tripped and fell down one of the stairwells and broke a bone in her arm. The ship's surgeon set her arm in a plaster cast.

■   In the First Class section, many of the unaccompanied male passengers engaged in the tradition of formally offering their services to "protect" the "unprotected" ladies: single, widowed or otherwise traveling alone. Usually the services provided didn't involve any more strain than to call a steward to bring something for the lady, and it often provided the gentleman with a dinner companion. There wasn't any pretext for romance in offering one's services.

One of the busiest passengers involved in protecting the ladies was Colonel Archibald Gracie who offered his services to at least six women, including three sisters and the widow Mrs. Helen Churchill Candee. Mrs. Candee was an independent, strong willed woman and a successful author.

Mrs. Candee was so popular, in fact, that no less then six gentlemen offered to "protect" her during her voyage to the United States. She was traveling to meet up with her son who had been injured in an airplane accident, a rather rare event in 1912.

Colonel Gracie called Mrs. Candee and the six gentlemen "our coterie," and they all go along so well that several of the passengers later commented on the closeness of the group.

On Sunday, Mrs. Candee and one of her "protectors" Mr. Hugh Woolner spent an hour in the gymnasium up on the Boat deck where the instructor T.W. McCawley let them use all the new equipment, including the stationary bicycles and mechanical horse. Afterwards they had tea in the First Class Lounge.

■   Reverend Ernest Carter, traveling Second Class, spent much of Sunday preparing for Sunday night's hymn singing down in the Second Class Dining Saloon.

■ Third Class passenger Eugene Daly spent a good portion of Friday, Saturday and Sunday out on the aft well deck playing his bagpipes.

■ Meanwhile, Benjamin Hart and his daughter Eva spent much of Sunday exploring the ship while Eva's mother slept in the cabin. She had been up all night waiting for some catastrophe to happen to them and the *Titanic*.

■ Down in the Third Class common areas there was some sort of dance every night with music provided by the many musically inclined passengers.

■ Pretty much the same routine was followed every day by the passengers. When the weather permitted it, many spent a large portion of the daylight hours out on the open decks and whatever event occupied their time would give way to meal call when Mr. P.W. Fletcher made his appearance with his bugle.

ICE WARNINGS

■ The winter of 1912 was one of the mildest in over thirty years and this warm weather allowed huge chunks of ice to break off Greenland's ice fields and drift south into the North Atlantic shipping lanes. These shipping lanes were routinely moved further south at this time of year because of the potential for icebergs, but in 1912, even ships steaming in these southern lanes reported an increasing amount of ice.

Some of the ice resembled huge buildings or mountains and icebergs 100 feet tall weren't uncommon. There were also miles of sheet ice (also called field ice), ice that was ten or twenty or thirty feet thick and which no ship could penetrate without much low speed maneuvering. Most ships had to steer many miles out of their way to get around the ice and then only in the daylight.

There were also the growlers, smaller icebergs that broke off from the larger ones. All-in-all, the huge ice pack that was floating down from Greenland that April extended over 70 miles north-to-south, and it was sitting right in the middle of the main shipping lanes. The ice pack was so extensive that ships either had to stop for it or steam even further south. Neither option was considered good by Captain Smith.

■ Ice warnings were received by the wireless operators even before *Titanic* left Southampton. Between Thursday and Saturday over twenty ships reported ice in the area *Titanic* would be steaming. Many ships were forced to stop once they entered the ice field, and most of them had to stop at night to prevent a collision with an iceberg. This was pretty much standard practice for ships of the time.

On Friday morning the ship *Empress of Britain*, eastbound from Halifax to Liverpool reported ice. (This and all future ice warnings listed here were picked up by *Titanic's* wireless operators, either directly or passed on from another ship. The wireless operators would then pass the massages onto the ship's officers.)

That afternoon, *La Touraine*, eastbound from New York to Le Havre reported ice.

In all, there were ten warnings on Friday alone about ice in the area of 41° 41' N latitude. Ships all along the shipping lane reported ice, most of it right in the area *Titanic* was scheduled to cross on Sunday night.

■ On Saturday there were over a dozen ice warnings received by wireless operators Phillips and Bride, who were now fully occupied in trying to work through the backlog of messages created when the wireless broke down the night before.

■ Sunday, April 14 was a beautiful day to be steaming across the North Atlantic. The weather was perfectly clear and the seas calm. The outside temperature was such that many passengers spent most of the day on the promenade decks to enjoy the sun. The air temperature wasn't overly warm, raising only to the mid-50's during the day, but for the passengers coming from the winter months in the colder climates, the temperature was perfectly fine.

There was a White Star Line requirement that all liners conduct a lifeboat drill on Sunday morning after Services, but for some reason Captain Smith did not hold one this day.

■ 9:00 a.m.: The day's first ice warning was received from *Caronia*, eastbound from New York to Liverpool. This message was directed to *Titanic* instead of being the usual general warnings directed to all ships: *"Captain, Titanic—West-bound steamers report bergs, growlers and field ice in 42° N, from 49° to 51° W, April 12, Compliments, Barr."* This warning was passed onto Captain Smith, who posted it for his officers to read and take note of.

■ 10:30 a.m.: Religious services were held in the First Class Dining Saloon.

■ 11:40 a.m.: *Noordam* signaled to *Titanic*, "Much ice."

■ **12:00 noon:** The ships officers gathered to "shoot the sun" and take the noon position bearings. They also calculate the previous 24 hour distance of 546 miles. This information was posted in the First Class Lounge for all those taking bets on the previous day's progress.

■ **1:42 p.m.:** *Baltic*, eastbound from New York to Liverpool, relayed a message: *"...Greek steamer Athinai reports passing icebergs and large quantities of field ice today in latitude 41° 51' N, longitude 49° 52' W...wish you and Titanic all success. Commander."*
This message was handed to Captain Smith, who in turn handed it to Bruce Ismay with whom he was speaking at the time. Ismay put the message in his own pocket instead of passing it onto the bridge officers. A look at the map would have shown that *Titanic* was headed right into the mass of this ice field.

■ **1:45 p.m.:** A private message was relayed from *Amerika* through *Titanic's* wireless to the US Hydrographic Office that *Amerika* had passed several large icebergs in the same area reported by the *Athinai*. This message was not passed onto the bridge.
During the afternoon the temperature had steadily declined to 43 degrees at 5:30 p.m., but between then and 7:30 p.m. it dropped another 10 degrees to 33 degrees. Because of the rapid drop in temperature, most of the passengers moved inside for the remainder of the afternoon.

■ **5:20 p.m.:** There was a planned change of course that was to be made at this time to bring the ship to a more westerly direction from its current generally southwesterly direction. Captain Smith held off making this change for a few minutes in order to bring *Titanic* even further south, apparently in order to avoid the ice that was reported to be in the area of *Titanic's* original course.

■ **5:50 p.m.:** Captain Smith ordered the delayed course change which the officers thought would put *Titanic* south and west of any of the reported ice.

■ **6:00 p.m.:** Lightoller relieved Wilde on the bridge. Sixth Officer Moody shared the watch with him.

■ **7:15 p.m.:** During dinner, Ismay showed the *Baltic* ice warning message to several passengers and by now Captain Smith had retrieved it and posted it in the chart room.

■ **7:15 p.m.**: It was dark outside and very cold, just a couple degrees above freezing. First Officer Murdoch ordered lamp trimmer Samuel Hemming to secure the forward forecastle hatch and the skylight over the crew's galley to prevent light from reflecting up into the eyes of the lookouts in the crow's nest who were now on special alert to spot any ice.

■ **7:30 p.m.**: A message was intercepted from *Californian* to *Antillian*: *"To Captain, Antillian: Six-thirty p.m....latitude 42° 3' N, longitude 49° 9' W, Three large bergs, 5 miles to the southward of us. Regards. Lord."* This message was delivered by Marconi operator Bride to one of the officers on the bridge, but he later couldn't remember which officer.

The message wasn't passed on to Captain Smith either. He was down in the à la carte restaurant having dinner with the Wideners and several other First Class passengers. *Titanic* was steaming directly into this ice field, and it was only 50 miles away.

■ **7:30 p.m.**: Lightoller "shot the stars" and gave the information to Boxhall who updated the plot. If anyone had remembered to mark *Californian's* warning on the chart, it would have been obvious that *Titanic* was entering dangerous waters.

■ **8:00 p.m.**: Lightoller decided to check Moody's navigational skills by having him plot the estimated time *Titanic* would enter the area of the icefield. Moody estimated around 11:00 p.m., but Lightoller wasn't happy with that answer. He had already figured the time to be around 9:30 p.m.

■ **8:40 p.m.**: While Reverend Carter was conducting his evening hymn singing down in the Second Class Dining Saloon, the temperature was continuing to fall. Lightoller ordered the ship's carpenter to check the fresh water supply because there was a very good chance that it might freeze.

■ **8:55 p.m.**: Captain Smith returned to the bridge after his dinner with the Wideners and engaged Lightoller in a conversation, speaking about the weather. Lightoller later reported:

"There is not much wind" said Captain Smith.
"No, it is a flat calm, as a matter of fact" I replied.
"A flat calm. Yes, quite flat" replied Smith.

I said that it was a pity the wind had not kept up with us whilst we were going through the ice region. Of course he knew I meant the water ripples breaking on the base of the berg...I remember saying, 'Of course there will be a certain amount of reflected light from the bergs,' with which the Captain agreed. Even with the blue side toward us, we both agreed that there would still be the white outline.

■ **9:00 p.m.**: Captain Smith updated the chart to reflect the 7:30 position fix Lightoller had taken. This should have allowed Smith to see the location of the ice field that *Titanic* was rapidly approaching.

■ **9:30 p.m.**: Captain Smith retired to his cabin, telling Lightoller "If it becomes at all doubtful let me know at once. I shall be just inside."

■ **9:30 p.m.**: Lightoller sent a message to the crow's nest to keep a sharp lookout for ice. It was now about the time that Lightoller figured they would be entering the area of the icefield.

■ **9:40 p.m.**: Message received by Jack Phillips in the wireless room: *"From Mesaba to Titanic. In latitude 42° N to 41° 25', longitude 49° W to longitude 50° 30' W, saw much heavy pack ice and great number large icebergs, also field ice, weather good, clear."*

This message did not get delivered to the bridge. Phillips was working alone because Bride had gone to bed to rest for awhile before he relieved Phillips at midnight. *Titanic* had just recently come within range of the Cape Race land station and Phillips was extremely busy with all of the commercial traffic to be sent them. The message was laid on a desk by the door of the wireless office and a weight was placed on top of it to keep it from going astray.

Unfortunately, *Titanic* was already inside the area described in *Mesaba's* message, and Captain Smith knew nothing about it.

■ **10:00 p.m.**: Murdoch replaced Lightoller on the bridge for the next four-hour watch. Before returning to his cabin to sleep, Lightoller made his rounds through the ship. He observed that the temperature was continuing to drop and it was now 31 degrees. Down in the First Class Lounge, he found many of the passengers listening to Wallace Hartley and the orchestra while others were engrossed in one of the several card games.

■ **10:00 p.m.**: High up in the crow's nest on the fore mast, lookouts Frederick Fleet and Reginald Lee replaced George Symons and Archie Jewell. Word was passed to Fleet and Lee to watch for icebergs.

The crow's nest was an open platform, exposed to the wind and cold. The air temperature by this time had dropped to 31 degrees and, combined with the 22.5 knot speed of the ship, the lookouts had a real problem keeping their eyes open as the cold air stung and burned them. Fleet and Lee were probably spending as much time trying to keep warm as they were looking for icebergs.

The binoculars the lookouts should have had with them were those unknowingly locked up in Lightoller's cabin by David Blair. In his haste to depart the ship before leaving Southampton, Blair had taken the keys to the cabinet with him.

There was no moon, no haze and the sky was completely full of stars. The water was absolutely flat. Any item, iceberg or whatever, ahead of the ship would be difficult to see because there would be no wave action against the object to provide a warning.

Furthermore, the worst place to try to detect an iceberg ahead of the ship would be from the crow's nest. Located over 100 feet above the water, the lookouts would have the disadvantage of looking down at the sea, and any object would be even harder to see because it would tend to blend into the dark background of the water.

■ 10:15 p.m.: Somewhere north-west of *Titanic*, at a position logged as 42° 5' N, 50° 7' W, Captain Stanley Lord of *Californian* noticed a glow along the western horizon and concluded this was caused by an unseen icefield. Lord ordered full speed astern and turned his ship hard-a-port. Within minutes *Californian* slowed to a stop with its bow facing East-North-East. Lord ordered steam kept up all night just in case they had to move to keep from bumping into the ice.

■ 10:30 p.m.: A visual message by signal lamp was received from *Rappahannock* that it had just passed through a huge icefield. *Rappahannock* didn't report, though, that it had collided with an iceberg and damaged its rudder.

■ 10:30 p.m.: Before leaving the bridge of the *Californian*, Captain Lord thought he saw the light of an approaching steamer from the south and east, but Third Officer Charles V. Groves thought the light was from a star.

■ 10:35 p.m.: *Parisian* warned *Titanic* of ice, then its wireless operator shut down his system for the night.

■ 10:55 p.m.: Captain Lord on the *Californian*, still thinking he had seen the lights of a steamer to the south-east, asked his wireless operator Cyril Evans if there were any other vessels in the vicinity. *"Only the Titanic,"* replied Evans. *"That's not the Titanic,"* replied Lord, *"she's a vessel close to us in size. You'd better contact Titanic, however, and let her know we're stopped in ice."*

■ **10:55 p.m.**: Cyril Evans of *Californian* sent a message to *Titanic*: *"We are stopped and surrounded by ice."*

■ **10:55 p.m.**: Before the message was completed, Jack Phillips on *Titanic* broke in with *"Keep out! Shut up! You're jamming my signal. I'm working Cape Race."*

■ **11:30 p.m.**: On *Titanic*, the evening hours passed by. Most of the passengers were now in their cabins if not already asleep. Up in the First Class Lounge and Smoking Room, a whole group of passengers were involved in card games, reading or conversation. It was now 30 degrees outside and the water temperature had dropped to 28 degrees. Except for a few diehard passengers who were walking the decks and the two lookouts up in the crow's nest, everyone else was inside keeping warm.

■ **11:35 p.m.**: Evans listened to the some of Phillip's messages to Cape Race. Then, extremely tired after another eighteen-hour day as *Californian's* only wireless operator, Evans shut down his wireless for the night and didn't bother to rewind the detector system, figuring he would do that in the morning. Without the detector being rewound, there would be no way to detect incoming messages.

■ **11:35 p.m.**: High up in the crow's nest, lookouts Fleet and Lee were bitterly cold and they were looking forward to being relieved in thirty minutes.
Off in the distance and directly ahead they detected a slight haze on the horizon. Both men strained to see what was behind the haze.

■ **11:40 p.m.**: Staring into the haze, Fleet sees something. His reflexes taking over, Fleet grabs the cord for the crow's nest 16-inch warning bell. He gives it three sharp tugs, then grabs the phone connecting the crow's nest to the phone on the starboard side of the bridge. He urgently rings its bell.

"Are you there!" shouts Fleet.
"Yes. What do you see?" replies Sixth Officer Moody.
"Iceberg right ahead!" shouts Fleet.
"Thank you," is Moody's polite reply.

■ Disaster will strike in less than thirty seconds.

CHAPTER 11

ENCOUNTER

Four-fifths of an iceberg's mass is under water. As this mass melts the iceberg will turn over, exposing that portion which had been underwater. When this happens, the water still in the newly exposed portion turns the iceberg very dark. This is called blue ice. In the dark, blue ice is almost impossible to see.

It only takes a few hours for the water in the newly exposed portion to either drain out or freeze, at which time the exposed portion will turn white again. However, the various spurs that protrude from the iceberg below the water now turn rock hard, harder than the side of any ship which might brush against it.

The iceberg that Fleet and Lee saw directly ahead of *Titanic* was apparently one of those which had turned over less than two hours before they saw it looming out of the haze.

■ As Fleet and Lee looked at the iceberg, growing ever larger as *Titanic* approached it at 21 knots, it looked like a black mass surrounded by a white mist. Its height appeared to be slightly less than the crow's nest.

In almost the same instant that Moody said *"Thank You"* to Fleet, he turned to Murdoch who had just come in from the bridge wing. Moody repeated Fleet's message, *"Iceberg right ahead!"*

Murdoch, now fully aware of pending disaster, rushed to the engine room telegraph and ordered the engines stopped and then reversed while at the same time ordering quartermaster Robert Hichens to turn the rudder, *"Hard-a-starboard!"* Prompt action by Murdoch prevented a head-on collision with the iceberg.

Hichens turned the wheel until it stopped turning and waited for the bow of the ship to start its swing to the port.

■ Up until 1928 when the rules were changed, turning directions were based upon the direction a rudder tiller would have to be placed to make a vessel go in a given direction. Turning the tiller to starboard would make the rudder go to port which in turn would make the vessel turn to port. Thus, the command "Hard-a-starboard" meant to turn the tiller to the starboard in order to make the ship turn to port. To further confuse matters, to make *Titanic* turn to port, the command "Hard-a-starboard" was given but Hichens actually had to turn the wheel to port. After 1928, this process was reversed so in a similar situation today the order would have been "hard-a-port."

■ While Hichens was turning the wheel, Murdoch went over to the aft wheelhouse bulkhead to the switches that closed the watertight doors. He briefly pushed the warning bell to provide an alarm for anyone who might be near the doors, switched on the power to the doors, and then he turned the lever which activated the doors.

Just above the tank top far down inside the ship the 14 electrically operated watertight doors began to close.

■ With the rudder hard over and the engines slowing first to a stop and then into full reverse, *Titanic* started to make a great turn to port. The ship turned 2 points of the compass or 22.5 degrees and it seemed that *Titanic* would miss the iceberg. Fleet and Lee thought so as the iceberg kept growing in size but the bow was pointed away from it. The huge mass of ice passed by the bow and then past the crow's nest platform where the top of the berg rose 25 feet above it and then disappeared down the starboard side. There was absolute silence as the berg went by until the sound of falling ice as several large chunks of it fell onto the forecastle and forward well deck and broke into pieces.

■ From the time Fleet saw the iceberg until it passed even with the crow's nest, about 37 seconds had elapsed, enough time for *Titanic* to travel about 446 yards or 1,338 feet. Had Fleet seen the iceberg just five seconds earlier or had *Titanic* been steaming just two knots slower, the encounter with the iceberg might have been just a near miss, and maybe Captain Smith would have ordered the ship to stop for the night.

The iceberg bumped and scraped along 300 feet of the forward portion of the starboard side of the ship, a rock hard protrusion below the water punching small random holes into the one-inch thick steel plating. The ship was still moving forward at about 21 knots, the reversing of the engines as yet having little affect on the forward motion of the ship. At this speed, *Titanic* would have traveled the 300 feet in about 10 seconds.

As the iceberg passed the bridge, Murdoch ordered the wheel turned hard to port in order to try to get the ship to port-around the iceberg, a movement similar to trying to fishtail an automobile around an object.

The iceberg passed the bridge and disappeared into the darkness off the stern. As it went by the crow's nest, Fleet and Lee finally saw a tip of white at the very top of the berg, high above their heads. Forty seven seconds had elapsed since the iceberg was spotted. Murdoch had the time logged. It was 11:40 p.m., April 14, 1912. *Titanic* would only live for another two hours and forty minutes. Fifteen hundred people were about to die.

■ The iceberg made a 300 foot gash, probably no more than one quarter inch wide and about twelve feet above the keel. The total area opened up to the sea was probably less then twelve square feet.

The gash opened up the forepeak, number one, two and three holds, number 6 boiler room and extended for about six feet into number 5 boiler room. *Titanic* was designed to sustain flooding in four forward compartments and not sink or five forward compartments and still float long enough for a reasonable chance to evacuate the passengers and crew. However, six compartments were flooding, although the six foot gash in boiler room number 5 was small enough that the engineers could try to pump the water out as fast at it came in. In any case, five compartments were more than *Titanic's* design allowed for.

A Thousand Marbles

Depending on where they were at the time, survivors would tell some interesting stories about what the collision felt like.

■ Down in the first class dining saloon on D deck, several stewards were sitting around a table talking when a faint grinding jar came from somewhere deep within the ship. Not much of a jar, but enough to rattle the silverware that was being set for breakfast the next morning.

■ First Class passenger James B. McGough had his porthole open as the iceberg passed by, and chunks of ice fell into his room.

■ Mauritz Björnström-Steffansson, a First Class passenger having a drink in the First Class Smoking Room, felt a slight jar but not enough that he got up to investigate.

■ Colonel Archibald Gracie was asleep in his cabin, C51, which was six decks directly above boiler room 6. He was awakened by a jolt, so he opened his cabin door and looked out. He saw no one and heard no machinery running; he heard only the sounds of escaping steam.

■   Mrs. Walter Stephenson and her sister Miss Elizabeth Eustis were awakened by a *"ripping sound."* They heard a lot of noise in the corridor, so they decided to get fully dressed and go up to the Boat deck.

■   Third Class passenger Miss Jamila Nicola-Yarred was asleep and felt a slight bump. Her brother Elias was still asleep, but she woke him up and had him investigate. Soon they left their room and followed several other people up to the Boat deck.

■   Miss Margaret Hays was in bed and felt nothing until the engines stopped running.

■   Third Class passenger Victor Sunderland felt a slight jar and heard a noise *"similar to that of a basket of coal would make if dropped on an iron plate."* Victor and some of this cabin mates went up onto the forward well deck where they could see ice on the deck. They then went back to their cabin several decks down near the bow because they didn't think anything serious was wrong.

■   Quartermaster George Rowe was on duty high on the docking bridge at the stern of the ship, trying his best to stay warm. He felt a change in the motion of the engines then thought he saw the sails of a windjammer passing along the starboard side. Another glance showed it to be an iceberg, over 100 feet tall and passing by, then it quickly disappeared into the dark night.

■   Third Class passenger Miss Carla Jensen was sharing a cabin with three other single women. They all felt a bump but, after some discussion about it, they all went back to sleep. Carla's uncle would later awaken her and have her dress and follow him up to the boat deck. The other three ladies decided to stay in bed. They were never seen again.

■   Marjorie Newell felt the collision but before she and her sister could get dressed to investigate, their father knocked on their door and told them *"Get up, girls and get dressed. Put on your warmest clothes and follow me."*

■   Mrs. Louis Hippach heard someone say they had hit an iceberg, so she decided to go out on deck to take a look. One of the officers saw her and told her to, *"Go back to bed. You'll catch cold."*

■   One seaman on duty outside the seaman's mess said it felt like a heavy vibration, a rumbling noise that continued for about ten seconds.

■   Several crewmen thought that an anchor had been dropped and the chain was dragging along the hull. Others thought that the ship had thrown a propeller.

■   Passenger Lawrence Beesley down in cabin D56 reported that *"...no sound of a crash or of anything else; no sense of shock, no jar that felt like one heavy body meeting another...nothing more than what seems to be an extra heave of the ship's engines and a slight dancing movement of my bunk mattress."*

■   Mrs. J. Stuart White in cabin C32 said, *"It was as though we went over about a thousand marbles."*

■   First Class passenger Henry Blank was also in the First Class Smoking Room when he felt *"a slight jar."* Someone called out to the men in the room, *"Hey boys, we've just grazed an iceberg!"* The men went out on deck to see the berg but it had disappeared into the darkness, so they went back to their card game.

■   Miss Sarah Daniels, maid to Mrs. Hudson Allison, felt a bump and got up and dressed to see what was happening. She never went back to her cabin, but went straight to the Boat deck.

■   Miss Caroline Bonnell and relative Natalie Wick felt the collision and went up on deck. Caroline said to Natalie, *"Well, thank goodness, Natalie, we are going to see our iceberg at last!"*

■   Third Class passenger Edward Dorking was playing cards down in the public room, only a few decks away from the site of the collision. *"We were thrown from the bench on which we were sitting. The shock was accompanied by a grinding noise..."*

■   Third Class passenger Gunnar Tenglin felt a thud and, having just removed his shoes, went out on deck to check out the source. He never went back to his room to get his shoes and got into a lifeboat without them.

■   Third Class passenger Carl Jansson also went out on deck without his shoes. He went back to this cabin to get them, but by then the cabin was filling with water. He, too, did without his shoes that night and suffered severe frostbite.

■ Mrs. Arthur Wells were asleep and she awoke to a tremendous jolt. She heard someone yell, *"Dress quickly: there's some trouble I believe, but I don't know what it is."* She did dress, then went up to the Boat deck

■ Miss Marion Wright said the collision sounded like a *"huge crash of glass."*

■ Crewman Albert M. Haines heard air escaping from the forepeak tank and reported to Chief Officer Wilde that the tank was filling with water.

■ Steward Alfred Theissinger was on C deck when the collision occurred. He saw a fireman running past, shouting, *"There is water forward!"* and someone else shouted *"All watertight doors shut!"* Theissinger went to his station near the mailroom and he could look down into it and see water pouring in while the mail clerks were struggling to move the mail out of the way.

■ Steward James Johnson thought they had dropped a propeller blade, and told his friends that this would certainly mean *"Another Belfast trip!"* in reference to *Olympic's* two trips back to the shipyard. Second Class steward Walter Williams later reported that, *"The joker [Johnson] went down with the ship."*

■ Night baker Walter Belford noticed the collision mainly because several pans of freshly baked rolls were jarred off the top of a cabinet.

■ Second Officer Lightoller and Third Officer Pitman were just going to sleep when they felt the collision. Both went out on deck, but seeing no alarm on the bridge, went back to their rooms where they could be found if needed.

■ Harland and Wolff manager Thomas Andrews barely felt the collision and didn't know there was a problem until he was summoned to the bridge by Captain Smith.

■ Bruce Ismay felt the jolt, and decided to head up to the bridge to see what caused it.

■ Fireman George Beauchamp was on duty in boiler room 6 when he was told to shut the dampers to the boilers in order to cut off the air supply. He was still doing so when the icy water reached his waist.

Someone told him to leave the room, and he was able to go through the watertight door before it closed.

■ Leading fireman Frederick Barrett was also in boiler room 6 when the side of the ship was opened up and a flood of ice water poured in. Within moments there was eight feet of water in the compartment, six feet of which was below the iron grating he was standing on. The watertight doors started to close and two crewmen (including George Beauchamp) got through the door, but Barrett had to climb the emergency escape ladder up to E deck and then down a similar ladder into boiler room number 5. Enroute, Barrett ran into chief engineer Bell and told him what happened. There were no other survivors from boiler room 6.

■ Esther Hart felt a bump, as did Mr. Hart. He dressed and went out on to the deck. Shortly, he returned and told Mrs. Hart to dress herself and little Eva.

■ Moments after the ship struck the iceberg, Boxhall arrived on the bridge in time to see Captain Smith arrive.

"What have we struck" Smith asked Murdoch.
"An iceberg, Sir. I hard-a-starboarded and reversed the engines and I was going to hard-a-port around it, but she was too close. I could not do any more. I have closed the watertight doors."
"The watertight doors are closed? And you have rung the warning bell?" asked Smith.
"Yes, Sir!" was the reply.

Damage Assessment

■ Smith and Murdoch first walked to the starboard bridge wing and looked aft to see the iceberg, but it had disappeared into the darkness.

Smith next sent Boxhall down into the engineering spaces to check to see if there was any damage. Boxhall was back shortly, stating that he had gone down a few decks and saw no water. This was the last time in his life Smith would hear good news as things went from bad to worse from this time on.

While Boxhall was away, Smith ordered that the engines be reversed again and the ship to move forward at "Half Ahead," and a short time later he ordered the engines stopped. (Murdoch had ordered "Full Speed Astern" but in the few moments that had elapsed up to this time, the propellers had just started to turn in reverse; the ship still hadn't started moving in reverse.)

Cavitation, the effect of air bubbles caused when a propeller is stopped and then reversed, had set in. The reversing of the propellers and forward motion of the ship had caused a dead space in the water creating millions of bubbles, and this prevented the propellers from actually doing any good. Reversing the engines as Murdoch did in order to try to miss the iceberg had actually done more harm than good. The bubbles created did not allow the reversing of the propellers to slow the ship down and they prevented the rudder from performing its function. If Murdoch had simply ordered "Hard-a-starboard" and NOT reversed the engines, *Titanic* might have missed the iceberg because the rudder would have been more effective.

■ Chief engineer Bell next reported to the bridge, and Smith ordered him to sound the ship (check for damage.)

■ Smith then went into the Marconi office and told Phillips and Bride, *"We've struck an iceberg and I'm having an inspection made to tell what has been done to us. You had better get ready to send out a call for assistance, but don't send it until I tell you."* Bride later reported.

■ Next to arrive was carpenter J. Hutchinson with the news that the ship was taking water fast, followed by postal clerk Smith who reported that the mail room was flooding.

■ Smith then sent Boxhall on another tour, and as he was leaving, both Ismay and Andrews showed up on the bridge.

Ismay asked, *"Do you think the ship is seriously damaged,"* and Smith replied, *"I'm afraid she is."*

■ Smith decided to do his own tour with Andrews, so they set off, using the crew passageways so they wouldn't alarm the passengers. They were back in about ten minutes with enough information to predict the worst.

■ Fifteen minutes after he left, Boxhall returned to the bridge with more information about the damage he had seen. Smith then ordered Boxhall to work out the ship's exact position.

■ Smith, Ismay and Andrews then huddled in the chart room behind the bridge and discussed the situation. Six compartments were flooding and in less then ten minutes there was fourteen feet of water in the first five compartments. There was nothing that could be done to save the ship. The pumps could probably keep the water out of the sixth compartment, boiler room 5, but eventually the bow of the ship would sink so low that the water would lap over the top of the watertight bulkhead between boiler rooms 6 and 5 which would then flood boiler room 5. This process would be repeated from compartment to compartment until the ship sank. *Titanic* was doomed.

In the company of Ismay, Smith asked Andrews, *"How long have we?"* and Andrews replied, *"An hour and a half. Possibly two. Not much longer."*

■ Boxhall worked out the ships' current position. Using the 7:30 p.m. stellar position, his own guess of the ships' speed at 22 knots and the course *Titanic* had been on since 5:50 p.m., Boxhall figured the position to be 41° 46' N, 50° 14' W.

There were some errors in Boxhall's calculations. First, *Titanic's* speed had been 21.5 knots. Second, it is unknown if Boxhall had allowed for the one knot speed of the current that *Titanic* had been passing through since the last star sighting. These and other errors could place the ship as much as four miles south and six miles east of the reported position. This error would cause many problems in the future when the issue of the position of the *Californian* relative to the *Titanic* was debated.

■ Boxhall handed Smith a piece of paper with the position on it, and Smith in turned walked down to the wireless office and gave it to Marconi operator Jack Phillips. He asked Phillips to send out a call for assistance. As Bride would later report, Smith said, *"Send a call for assistance...[send] the regulation international call for help, just that."*

While Phillips sent the CQD (the distress signal), *"...we joked while he did so. All of us made light of the disaster...The humor of the situation appealed to me, and I cut in with a little remark the made us all laugh, including the captain. Send 'S.O.S.' I said, it's the new call, and it may be your last chance to send it..."* reported Harold Bride.

■ 12:05 a.m., Monday, April 15, 1912: Just 25 minutes after the collision with the iceberg and 30 minutes after Cyril Evans on *Californian* shut down his wireless system, the first call for assistance was sent out by Phillips:

CQD...MGY, CQD...MGY. 41° 46' N, 50° 14' W.

(CQD stood for "Come Quick, Danger" and was the international distress signal. Although the present day SOS was also in use in 1912, having been adopted just a few years before, it was not universally used yet.

Phillips was using the more universal CQD to start with. MGY was *Titanic's* call sign.)

Several ships and the land station at Cape Race all heard the message, but all of them heard a different location due to atmospheric interference. However, they got the correct location on the next transmission.

CARPATHIA

At noon on Thursday, April 11, about the time *Titanic* was steaming into Queenstown, the Cunard Liner *Carpathia* departed New York bound for several Mediterranean ports with 743 passengers.

■ *Carpathia* had only one wireless operator, twenty-one year old Harold Cottam. Cottam worked whatever hours were required to keep up with the messages inbound or outbound from the passengers. By midnight Sunday, he had been on duty for seventeen hours with only a short lunch break. Cottam was tired and ready to go to bed, but he was waiting for confirmation of a message he had sent to the liner *Parisian*. While listening for the reply through his headphones, Cottam removed his shoes and some of his clothes.

Still waiting for *Parisian*, Cottam switched over to the Cape Cod land station to see if there was anything interesting going on, and heard Cape Cod transmitting some commercial messages to *Titanic*. Because *Titanic* wasn't responding, Cottam copied several of the messages, figuring he would transmit them to *Titanic* in the morning.

It was now well over a half hour after Cottam had planned to shut down for the night, but because he was still waiting for a reply from the *Parisian*, Cottam switched over to *Titanic's* frequency. Hearing nothing being transmitted, he sent the following message, using *Carpathia's* call letters MPA:

"I say, old man, do you know there is a batch of messages coming through for you from MCC (Cape Cod)?"
Phillips: (MGY), broke into Cottam's message: *"Come at once. We have struck a berg. It's a CQD, OM [Old Man]. Position 41° 46' N, 50° 14' W."*
Cottam: *"Shall I tell my captain? Do you require assistance?"*
Phillips: *"Yes. Come quick."*

Carpathia was 58 miles away from *Titanic*.

Above: *Carpathia's* wireless operator Harold T. Cottam. *National Archives*

Left: Captain Arthur H. Rostron of *Carpathia*. *National Archives*

The *Carpathia*. *National Archives*

■ Cottam grabbed his jacket, ran up to the bridge, and reported the message to the watch officer First Officer H.V. Dean. Dean, pushing Cottam ahead of him and down the stairs, burst into Captain Arthur H. Rostron's cabin without knocking.

Rostron, having just gone to bed and irritated by the intrusion, demanded to know what was happening. Dean told Cottam to repeat the message.

> Cottam: *"Sir, I have just received an urgent distress call from Titanic...she requires immediate assistance...she has struck an iceberg and is sinking. Her position is 41° 46' N, 50° 14' W."*
> Rostron: *"Are you certain?"*
> Cottam: *"Yes, sir."*

Rostron went to the chart room and quickly figured out the course, distance and time to *Titanic*. *Carpathia* should be at *Titanic's* side in about four and one-half hours, or around 4:45 am if she steamed at her maximum rated speed of 14.5 knots.

■ **12:05 a.m.**: On the bridge of *Titanic*, Smith, Ismay, Andrews and some of the officers were discussing the status of the ship. In the 25 minutes since striking the iceberg, all five of the forward holds were filling up with water, and water was already appearing on F deck.

■ Down in the mailroom the five postal clerks struggled to move some of the 3,430 sacks of mail up one deck to the post office on G deck. Once the water started flooding that deck, they gave up the attempt and concentrated moving 200 sacks of registered mail up to the empty passenger cabins on D deck.

■ Back up on the bridge, Smith gave the order to uncover the lifeboats, assigning Chief Officer Wilde the responsibility, who immediately delegated the work to Second Officer Lightoller. Lightoller went to lifeboat 4 on the port side and started removing the canvas cover while waiting for some crewmen to show up. He then proceeded to each boat as additional crewmen came up, giving instructions with hand signals because of the noise from the escaping steam coming from the funnels.

■ Harold Bride reported about this time that, *"The Carpathia answered our signal, and we told her our position, and said we were sinking by the head...in five minutes the operator returned and told us Carpathia was putting about and heading for us..."*

■ **12:10 a.m.:** Captain Rostron ordered *Carpathia* turned north-west at full-speed. All off duty firemen, trimmers and stokers were ordered to their work stations to help feed the boiler fires. Before too long, *Carpathia* would be steaming in excess of 17 knots, almost 20 percent faster than it had ever steamed before.

Next, Rostron ordered four extra lookouts posted and had every officer on the bridge looking for icebergs.

All unnecessary equipment and the ships heating system was turned off so that all steam could be fed into the engines.

As *Carpathia* steamed north toward the ice field, the temperature started dropping. With the heat turned off, many of the sleeping passengers began to inquire about the cold, but they were told that the lack of heat was just a temporary problem. For some passengers this was the first indication they had that something unusual was taking place.

Meanwhile, Rostron ordered that all of *Carpathia's* boats be readied for launching, at which time he told his officers that the reason for this was *Titanic* had struck an iceberg and was sinking.

Rostron then issued a whole series of orders:

Every crewman was to report to duty at his normal duty station, and each was to be fed and served all the hot coffee he wanted to help keep him awake and warm.

Crew members from the steward's department were to gather up all of the blankets, towels and extra crew's clothing to hand out to survivors and to prepare all the public areas with beds.

The cooks were to prepare hot coffee and food for survivors.

All Third Class passengers were to be placed into one section of the Third Class area so that there would be room for *Titanic's* survivors.

All empty cabins and all officers' cabins, including Rostron's, were to be readied. All cabins with passengers but with empty beds were to be identified so that the empties could be utilized.

There were three ship's doctors on board *Carpathia*, an English, Italian and Hungarian. Each was told to prepare for the arrival of survivors, one doctor for the First, Second and Third class passengers.

After the lifeboats were readied, all gangway doors were opened and all stewards, pursers and extra crewmen were to remain by them to help people onto the ship. At each gangway, the crew slung a chair which could be lowered so that survivors could sit in it while being lifted onto the ship.

The crew readied canvas bags and cargo nets to be used to haul aboard.

Ladders for survivors to climb up on and powerful lights were hung over the sides.

Oil buckets were lined up at the forward toilets. If the seas were rough, oil would be poured into the toilets and dumped into the water to help calm it.

■ As steam was diverted from the cabin heat to the engines, even more passengers started to complain about the cold. Shortly, they would also notice the increased speed and that the ship seemed to be pounding through the water. Some would even notice that they were steaming in a new direction. Stewards were placed in every corridor to answer questions without giving out too much information and they asked all of the passengers to remain in their cabins and keep the corridors clear.

■ While Rostron was preparing his ship, wireless operator Cottam sat at his system monitoring messages. He had a steward available who passed every message to Rostron on the bridge.

■ 12:50 a.m.: Cottam copied a message to *Olympic* which was more than 500 miles away: *"I require immediate assistance."* At 1:10 a.m. another message to *Olympic: "We are in collision with berg. Sinking head down. Come as soon as possible. Get your boats ready."* At 1:25 a.m.: *"We are putting the women off in small boats."* At 1:35 a.m.: *"Engine room getting flooded."*

■ 1:45 a.m.: *"Engine room full up to the boilers."* This was the last message Cottam would hear directly from *Titanic*.

■ Meanwhile, *Carpathia* churned through the crystal clear and cold night air. All officers and lookouts were now straining to see the ever increasing number of icebergs looming up out of the dark. *Carpathia* dodged and weaved through them, many bigger than the ship itself.

Care had to be taken now. Colliding with an iceberg would do neither the over 1,000 passengers and crew on *Carpathia* nor the survivors from *Titanic* any good.

Carpathia was now making 17.5 knots. At this speed, it would reach *Titanic's* reported position at around 4:00 am.

For Captain Arthur Henry Rostron, the ship *Carpathia*, and its crew, it was now *Carpathia* to the rescue.

CHAPTER 12

NOT ENOUGH LIFEBOATS

After *Titanic* struck the iceberg and Captain Smith ordered the engines stopped, all the steam in the boilers was vented through the escape valves in the funnels. The resulting noise was so loud that it prevented any sort of conversation on the deck and was the one item that seemed to awaken most of the passengers and crew who had not already been awakened by the collision itself.

Second Officer Lightoller reported, *"...The ship had been running under a big head of steam, therefore the instant the engines were stopped the steam started roaring off at all eight exhausts, kicking up a row that would have dwarfed the row of a thousand railway engines thundering through a culvert..."*

There wasn't anything like a public address system or a warning bell to notify the passengers. Once Smith ordered the uncovering of the lifeboats, officers and crew were sent throughout the passenger areas, knocking on each door until someone was awakened. In many cases, the crew forced the doors open.

■ In the First Class areas, the order was to put on warm clothing and a life belt and report to the boat deck. Second Class passengers were told to report to the dining saloon. Third Class passengers faired poorly in the warning. Mostly the stewards just used their pass key and threw open the cabin doors, pulled the life belts off the top of the shelf where they were stored, dumped them on the floor and told everyone to get up and put their life belt on. Those who could not understand English were left to their own devices to figure out what it was the stewards were telling them. Additionally, conversation throughout the ship was difficult because of the noise from the escaping steam.

Since most of the crew were in some sort of dormitory or multi-person rooms, the crew chain-of-command was used to awaken them. As they were encountered, all deck hands and Seamen were ordered to the Boat deck to help with the launching of the lifeboats. The saga of the lifeboats was about to begin.

LOADING THE LIFEBOATS

Note: Survivors did not keep track of the actual times. Times shown are based upon a combination of survivor records and official reports. However, the loading sequence is correct.

■ Shortly after the collision, Colonel Archibald Gracie decided to go up to the Boat deck, but he didn't see anything or anyone. Returning to his cabin, he ran into his friend Clinch Smith who showed him a piece of ice he had picked up off the forward edge of A deck. Gracie then returned to his cabin and dressed in his warmest clothes, thinking he might be spending some time out on the deck.

■ Down in cabin C91, First Class passenger Margaret Graham heard her governess, Miss Elizabeth Shutes, ask an officer in the corridor if there was any danger. The officer replied, *"No, I think we can keep out of the water a bit longer."* Margaret was trying to eat a chicken sandwich, but her hand started shaking so hard the chicken kept falling out of the sandwich.

■ During the first half hour after the collision, or until about 12:10 a.m. most of the normal shipboard activities kept on, with the lookouts being replaced at 12:00. Even the dining room stewards were busy setting the tables for breakfast.

■ Down in the third class areas, people generally remained in or near their cabins awaiting further orders. Without someone to tell them where they should go, they just remained where they were.

■ Meanwhile, up on the Boat deck and public rooms, First and Second Class passengers were wandering all over the place, talking, swapping stories or asking questions. They were pretty much unconcerned that the ship might actually sink.

■ On the boat deck, according to Lightoller, *"...All the Seamen came tumbling up on the boat deck in response to the order 'All hands on deck'..."*

■ Down at the First Class Purser's Office on C deck, many of the passengers lined up to retrieve their valuables.

"The passengers by this time were beginning to flock up on the boat deck, with anxious faces, the appalling din [from the escaping steam] only adding to their anxiety in a situation already terrifying enough in all conscience..." Second Officer Lightoller.

■ Major Arthur Peuchen was in his cabin C104 when the collision occurred. He was awake and dressed anyway, so he went up the Grand Staircase to the Boat deck. After watching some of the boats being uncovered, he went back to his cabin and dressed in his warmest clothing. He then left his cabin, locking it behind him. On the desk was a tin box containing over $300,000 in securities.

■ **12:20 a.m.**: The lifeboats were uncovered and the officers were back on the bridge awaiting further orders from Captain Smith. Lightoller asked Chief Officer Wilde if the boats should be swung out. Wilde replied, *"No."*

■ **12:25 a.m.**: Forty-five minutes after *Titanic* stuck the iceberg, Captain Smith finally gave the orders to swing out the boats and begin loading the passengers.

"...having got the boats swung out I made for the Captain, and happened to meet him near by on the boat deck...'Hadn't we better get the women and children into the boats, sir?' He heard me and nodded a reply. One of my reasons for suggesting getting the boats afloat was, that I could see a steamer's steaming lights a couple of miles away on our port bow. If I could get the women and children into the boats, they would be perfectly safe in that smooth sea until this ship picked them up...My idea was that I would lower the boats with a few people in each and when safely in the water fill them up from the gangway doors on the lower decks, and transfer them to the other ship..." Second Officer Lightoller.

To accomplish this, Lightoller later reported: *"...I told the Bosun's Mate to take six hands and open the port lower-deck gangway door, which was abreast of No. 2 hatch. He took his men and proceeded to carry out the order, but neither he or the men were ever seen again..."*

■ Up in the First and Second Class areas, the pending disaster was already having its effect on some of the passengers and crew. Many of them took to the now opened and available liquor cabinets in order to prepare themselves for whatever lay ahead.

■ **12.25 a.m.**: Colonel Gracie was wandering through the corridors on C deck looking for blankets that could be given to the people who soon would be leaving in the lifeboats when he encountered squash racket instructor Fred Wright on the stairway. Remembering that he had an appointment the next morning with Wright, Gracie jokingly asked him *"Hadn't we better cancel that appointment for tomorrow morning?"* Wright agreed, but he didn't tell Gracie that the water was already to the ceiling of the squash racquet court down on G deck.

■ **12:30 a.m.**: Some of the passengers were beginning to mingle around the lifeboats up on the Boat deck, but the noise of the steam still escaping and the freezing cold was too much for many of them, so they moved indoors into the First Class Entrance or the gymnasium. Among the group in the gymnasium were Colonel and Mrs. Astor. He was sitting there, using his penknife to slice open a life belt to show Madeleine Astor what was inside it. Shortly, the Astors moved down to A deck to wait for lifeboat 4 to be lowered.

■ On A deck, one deck below the Boat deck and directly under lifeboat 4 on the port side forward, a small group of some very influential passengers had been rounded up by their stewards and were waiting for the boat to be prepared for lowering. Having them wait on A deck kept the passengers out of the cold because this deck is the one that had been glassed in to keep the spray out: this was the last-minute design change Ismay had ordered.

Waiting in this group were the Astors, Wideners, Ryersons, Thayers and several other family groups along with their maids, valets and other servants. Here these captains of industry, millionaire's all, waited patiently for the boat to be lowered from the deck above. None of them were dressed warmly because they were the first to be aroused from their cabins. Most of them sent their maids and valets back to their cabins to gather up warmer clothing and blankets. All had on their life belts, and later the women would be seen wearing some of their finest fur coats while the men were in their warmest jackets.

Officer Lightoller ordered lifeboat 4 swung out and lowered to A deck, but once the boat was there, it was found that the newly installed screened windows couldn't be opened without a special tool. There was no one available to go search for a crewman who had the necessary tool, so Lightoller told the passengers to wait and he would be back. Wait they did.

■ Deep down in the hull, the water in the first five compartments was raising at the rate of one and one-half feet per minute. The bow of *Titanic* started to take on a noticeable dip, and people walking down any stairway facing forward noticed an odd sensation as the stairs tilted forward. There was also beginning to be a slight list to the port, although most people at this time didn't notice it.

Not believing the ship was sinking, the Third Class matron locked herself into her cabin, stating, *"I am going to stay where I am safe."* That was the last time she was seen alive.

■ Down in the Third Class common areas, many of the Catholic Irish passengers gathered together to pray and await their fate. Several Third Class passengers had already found their way through the maze of corridors and had arrived on the Boat deck. Most of the others, though, were still waiting for someone to come and tell them were they should go.

"...The usual order was given, 'Women and children first.' That order was carried out without any class distinction whatever. In some cases we had to force women into the boats as they would not leave their husbands..." Seaman Joseph Scarrott.

■ For First or Second Class male passengers, much of the determination of whether they got into a lifeboat or not was based upon which side of the ship they happened to be on. First Officer Murdoch generally oversaw the launching of the starboard side boats and when they were ready to launch, if there weren't any women or children around, he allowed any male in who was close by, including extra crewmen, on board. However, on the port side, Second Officer Lightoller carried out his orders to the letter: no men were allowed onto the boats except whatever crew was needed to man them. If the boats weren't full and there were still men standing by, they weren't allowed to enter the boats.

■ 12:40 a.m.: The horrible sound of escaping steam finally came to a sudden stop as the steam in all the boilers except in Boiler Room 1 was finally bled off. Once that happened, the ships orchestra, lead by Wallace Hartley, set up in the forward First Class Entrance and played music while the passengers mingled around. Later, the orchestra would set up on the starboard side of the Boat deck outside the gymnasium and play through the night.

12:45 a.m.: Lifeboat 7

■ One hour and five minutes after striking the iceberg, the first lifeboat to be lowered was lifeboat 7 on the starboard side across from the entrance to the gymnasium. This lifeboat was designed to hold 65 persons but was launched with exactly 28 (12 male and 12 female First Class and one male Second Class passenger plus three crewmen). Included in this boat were the newly-weds Mr. and Mrs. Dickinson Bishop, Miss Margaret Hays and her little Pomeranian dog, Mr. James R. McGough, the French aviator Mr. Pierre Maréchal, the "Baron von Drachstedt", (Mr. Alfred Nourney) and two of the lookouts, Archie Jewell and George Hogg. Also among the passengers was Mrs. Catherine Crosby who was escorted to the boat by her husband Edward. At the time the boat was being loaded, men weren't being allowed on, so Mr. Crosby kissed his wife good-bye then stepped back. Later, when men were allowed to board, Mr. Crosby was nowhere to be found, and he died that night.

■ There wasn't any reported confusion during the launching of lifeboat 7. There also weren't many people around to put into the boat because at this point hardly anyone thought the ship would sink. Other than Captain Smith, Ismay and Andrews, probably none of the officers even knew of the danger they were in. It doesn't appear that they were told until too late, if at all.

Lifeboat 7 and most of the subsequent ones were lowered so that the top of the boat was even with the gunwale of the ship. *"About five minutes later the boats were lowered and we were pushed in...My husband was pushed in with me and we were lowered with twenty-eight people in the boat...Somewhat later five people were put into our boat from another one...we had no compass or light..."* Mrs. Dickinson H. Bishop.

Lifeboat 7 was ordered to hang around the gangway door, which it did for awhile, but shortly the crewmen rowed it down the length of the ship and then about 200 yards away from the starboard side. Later it was rowed further away to avoid the anticipated suction as the ship sank. The twenty-eight people in lifeboat 7 would spend the next 90 minutes in a front row seat, watching the drama of the sinking of the *Titanic* happen before them.

■ **12:45 a.m.**: Back on the docking bridge above the Poop Deck, quartermaster George Rowe had spent the last hour wondering what was going on and trying to keep from freezing. Since he had seen the full masted sailing ship/iceberg pass the starboard side, he had seen little and heard less due to the escaping steam. Suddenly, he noticed a lifeboat full of passengers being rowed along the side of the ship. Rowe then called the bridge to report to Fourth Officer Boxhall that there was a lifeboat in the water! Boxhall told Rowe to report to the bridge and bring a load of signal rockets with him.

■ **12:45 a.m.**: Boxhall fired the first rocket, one hour and five minutes after the collision. Each rocket would shoot up to about 800 feet then explode with a bang and scatter 12 white stars. Shortly before he fired the first rocket, Boxhall could see the lights of another ship in the distance and with his binoculars he could even see its masthead lights. The rockets were fired to attract the attention of the ship that Boxhall and shortly several other officers and crewmen could see in the distance to the north off the port bow.

"We were firing rocket distress signals, which explode with a loud report a couple hundred feet in the air. Every minute or two one of these went up, bursting overhead with a cascade of stars..." related Second Officer Lightoller.

■ Actually, Quartermaster Rowe was firing a rocket about every five minutes or so, eight in all. Boxhall and Rowe could now see the other ship approach, close enough that they could see both the red and green marker lights without their binoculars. Seeing both lights meant the ship was approaching them and it would have to be less than five miles away to see the lights without the binoculars.

Other members of the crew, including Captain Smith, also saw the ship. It was just a few degrees off the port bow and Smith estimated to be only five miles away too. Eventually, just the red port light could be seen, which meant the ship had turned to starboard.

Because the other ship was estimated to be only five miles away, Boxhall tried to raise it with the Morse lamp, but there was no response.

Soon only the stern lamp of the other ship was showing. This meant that it was actually moving away. Given that *Titanic* was stopped and drifting with the current, the other ship appeared to have approached *Titanic* then turned around and steamed off.

■ 12:45 a.m.: While Boxhall, Rowe and Captain Smith were watching a ship that seemed to be moving, back on the Boat deck Second Officer Lightoller thought he saw a ship, this one not moving, off the port bow (in the same direction the others had seen the moving ship). This stationary ship is the one Lightoller kept telling the crews of the lifeboats to row toward.

The identity of this ship, if it ever existed, is one of the mysteries of the tragedy. If it did exist, it would not have been *Californian* which was much further away, stopped and surrounded by the icefield.

■ 12:45 a.m.: Down in Boiler Room 5, the crew had already shut down the dampers so they wouldn't explode when the water reached them. The ship's pumps were pumping the water out of the room almost as fast as it came in and additional hoses had been strung through the watertight doors which were partially opened to allow easier passage between the compartments.

Leading Fireman Fred Barrett, now working in Boiler Room 5 after having been driven from number 6, had pulled the grating off a portion of the floor to make some adjustments to the valves below. The room was full of steam and smoke and visibility was limited. Several crewmen were working in it, and engineer Jonathan Shepard went rushing across the deck and fell into the opening where the grating should have been and broke his leg. Barrett and several others moved Shepard into a corner out of the way while they continued to work.

■ 12:45 a.m.: Shortly after the crew moved Shepard, the entire bulkhead between Boiler Rooms 6 and 5 collapsed. Boiler Room 5 almost instantly filled with water, drowning everyone in the room except for Barrett, who was able to once again climb up the escape ladder ahead of the water.

The bulkhead that collapsed is the one next to the coal fire that had smoldered for two weeks. There is speculation that the bulkhead collapsed because it was weakened by the fire.

■ 12:45 a.m.: Chief Baker Charles Joughin returned to his cabin to obtain some liquid refreshment and ran into Dr. William O'Loughlin who had the same idea.

■ 12:45 a.m.: Seaman John Poingdestre had been working on the Boat deck but decided to return to his cabin down on E deck forward to pick up his boots. Before he started back up to the deck, the entire wooden wall between his cabin and the Third Class area next to it crashed in with a wall of water behind it. Poingdestre had to struggle for several minutes to get out of the water and up to the next deck.

In the gymnasium Mrs. and Mrs. Lucian Smith and Mrs. and Mrs. Henry Sleeper Harper were chatting away, watching some of the other passengers work the mechanical horses.

12:55 a.m.: Lifeboat 5

■ Lifeboat 5 was the second boat launched, also from the starboard side. Although the lifeboat was capable of holding 65 passengers, there were between 35 and 41 people on board. (The actual number of passengers on most of the lifeboats is open to dispute because once launched, several boats traded passengers or picked people up out of the water. Also, some people died on the boats and there was no official counting of passengers by boat when they were rescued. In the dark and the haste to load the lifeboats, no one bothered to count the people in them or to take their names.)

There were approximately 13 male, 14 female and one child First Class passengers and two female and about six male crew members that were accounted for. Among the passengers were Mr. and Mrs. Beckwith, Mrs. Washington Dodge and her son Washington Jr., Dr. Henry Frauenthal and his brother Isaac and Mrs. Charles Stengel. Miss Helene Ostby left her father behind, and Mrs. Anna S. Warren left her husband.

Also on board was Edward Calderhead, who had just helped dump fellow passenger Margaret Brown into lifeboat 6 on the port side, then crossed to the starboard side of the ship to get into this boat. Among the crew members was Quartermaster Alfred Olliver and Third Officer Pitman, who was ordered into the boat by Murdoch to assist with the boats being lowered into the water.

■ J. Bruce Ismay decided to help load this boat, and just before it was lowered he called out, *"Are there any more women before this boat goes?"* There was no answer. However, a woman walked up and Ismay said, *"Come along, jump in."* She replied, *"I am only a stewardess."* Ismay responded, *"Never mind - you are a woman; take your place."*

Ismay was still hanging around the lifeboat and as it was slowly being lowered, yelled out *"Lower away! Lower away!"* at Fifth Officer Harold G. Lowe, who was working hard to safely launch the boat. The young officer probably did not know who Ismay was, and replied angrily, *"If you'll get the hell out of the way I'll be able to do something! You want me to lower away quickly? You'll have me drown the whole lot of them!"* Ismay was apparently disheartened by this and quickly left the area.

■ Standing on the deck watching lifeboat 5 being lowered were Dr. Frauenthal and his brother. Dr. Frauenthal's wife was in the boat and he decided to join her, so the two brothers jumped in when the boat was about four feet below the deck. The good doctor landed on top of Mrs. Annie May Stengel and dislocated two of her ribs, knocking her unconscious. This was a double blow for Mrs. Stengel because she too had said good-bye to her husband on the deck. However, Mr. Stengel would later manage to get onto lifeboat 1 and be re-united with his wife on *Carpathia.*

Mrs. Warren's husband had actually entered the boat with her, but he stepped out to help assist the other women and was not able to rejoin his wife.

Mrs. Washington Dodge and her son Washington Jr. said good-bye to Mr. Dodge who stood back while the boat was launched. During the night Mrs. Dodge and her son were transferred to lifeboat 7. In the morning there would be a joyous reunion as Mr. Dodge was found on *Carpathia,* having gotten into lifeboat 13.

■ Third Officer Pitman was put into the boat in order to have it row around to pick up passengers out of the water, but instead it was rowed out about 200 yards where the boat waited. Pitman later wanted to row back in to pick up passengers but all of the women started complaining about that idea. "...after it sank, Mr. Pitman then said to pull back to the scene of the wreck. The ladies started calling out 'Appeal to the officer not to go back. Why should we lose all of our lives in a useless attempt to save others from the ship'...we did not go back." reported Steward H.S. Etches.

12:55 a.m.: Lifeboat 6

■ Lifeboat 6, the first boat launched from the port side was lowered into the water with between 24 and 28 people (16 female and one male First Class passengers, two First Class servants, one Third Class male passenger and at least four crew members including two women.) Considerable drama took place on this lifeboat.

Among the passengers were Margaret "Molly" Brown, Helen Churchill Candee and Madame Berthe de Villiers. The crew included lookout Frederick Fleet and Quartermaster Robert Hichens, who was placed in command.

■ Mrs. James Baxter would leave her 24-year old son behind, while Mrs. Tyrell Cavendish would exchange a long, lingering kiss with her husband before he placed her into the boat. Mrs. Edgar Meyer, Mrs. Martin Rothschild and Mrs. William Spencer would also lose their husbands. Recently married Mrs. Lucien Smith would lose her husband, too, while Marjorie and Madeleine Newell would leave their father on the deck.

Molly Brown had assisted some other women into the lifeboat and was walking away from it to round up other women. As the lifeboat began to descend, two of her friends, Edward Calderhead and James McGough, picked her up and dumped her over the railing. Molly fell four feet into the bottom of the boat. McGough and Calderhead then went over to the starboard side. McGough got into lifeboat 7 and Calderhead into lifeboat 5.

■ There were just two seamen on the lifeboat and as the boat was being lowered, the women started calling up to the deck to send down more men to help with the rowing. There weren't any seamen left in the area, so Second Officer Lightoller was trying to decide what to do when Major Arthur Peuchen called out, "If you like, I will go." Lightoller replied, "Are you a seaman?" and Peuchen responded, "I am a yachtsman." Lightoller then replied, "If you are sailor enough to get out on that fall...you can go down." Peuchen climbed out eight feet to the fall line then sixty feet down to the boat. Just prior to making his descent, Peuchen had been speaking with Charles Hays, who said, *"Peuchen, this ship is good for eight hours yet. I have just been getting this from one of the best old seamen, Mr. Crosby..."*

A few minutes earlier, Edward Crosby had been in his cabin telling his wife, *"You'll lie there and drown!...This ship is badly damaged!"* By now, Crosby had gotten his wife and daughter onto lifeboat 7 and he was helping women enter lifeboat 6. He would not survive.

■ Both Major Peuchen and Mrs. Candee reported seeing about 100 stokers and firemen come up from below decks. They were met by one of the officers who ordered them all back down. They complied, just like soldiers following the orders of their officers.

As she was entering the lifeboat, Mrs. Candee slipped on an oar and fell into the boat, breaking her ankle.

■ Several passengers told of a stowaway in the boat: an Italian boy (and the term *Italian* was used derisively). However, it seems that in an attempt to find more seamen for the boat, Lightoller grabbed the first male he found and tossed him into the boat. This person turned out to be a Third Class passenger with an already broken arm, and the passengers thought he was a stowaway.

■ With only three men on the boat—Hichens manning the tiller, Fleet and Peuchen trying to row—it was impossible for the two men to make any headway by themselves and Hichens refused to help. Molly Brown then grabbed an oar as did one of the Newell sisters. They helped row the boat away from the side of the ship.

Every survivor in lifeboat 6 complained about the conduct of Quartermaster Hichens. Several times one of the ship's officers would try to call the boat back, but Hichens said, *"No, we are not going back to the boat: it is our lives now, not theirs,"* reported Major Peuchen. He also claimed that Hichens said, *"there was no use going back—that there were only a lot of stiffs there."* Mrs. Candee reported that, *"Hichens was cowardly and almost crazed with fear all the time."*

Molly Brown reported that when asked to help row the boat, Hichens said no, that it wasn't his duty to do so. Sometime during the night the boat picked up a half frozen stoker from another boat. Hichens protested when the women were wrapping him up in blankets and furs to keep him warm. Hichens moved to prevent it, but Molly Brown told him that if he did, *"he [Hichens] would be thrown overboard...it wouldn't be necessary to toss him in, for if she had moved in his direction, he would have tumbled into the sea, so paralyzed was he with fright,"* reported Mrs. Helen Candee.

So, lifeboat 6, with its load of women serving as its rowing crew moved out into the night with room for another forty people, despite the protests of several women who wanted to go back.

1:00 a.m.: Lifeboat 3

■ Lifeboat 3, another 65 passenger boat on the starboard side, was lowered with between 38 and 40 people in it. There were ten First Class males and eight females, one child, one First Class male and five female servants and at least thirteen crewmen (ten firemen, one pantryman and two seamen. This boat was under the command of Able Bodied Seaman George A. Moore.

Among the people in lifeboat 3 were Mrs. James Cardeza, her son Thomas, her maid and Thomas' manservant; Mr. and Mrs. Henry Sleeper Harper, their dragoman and Mr. Harper's Pekinese dog Sun Yat Sen; Mr. and Mrs. Frederick Spedden and their child, Mrs. Spedden's maid and the child's nurse. Mrs. Thornton Davidson was the daughter of Mr. and Mrs. Charles Hays, and while Mrs. Charles Hays would leave her husband behind, Mrs. Davidson would lose both her husband and father. All the male passengers got in after the women had been loaded.

■ Standing on the deck helping load the passengers into lifeboat 3 were Thornton Davidson, Charles Hays, Charles Case and Washington A. Roebling. As the boat was lowered, there was still room, so Murdoch offered to let the men board it. All four stood back and went elsewhere to help where they could. Mrs. Hays later reported seeing the four of them standing together as the boat was rowed away. All four were lost.

■ Henry Sleeper Harper and his wife were returning from a long vacation and research trip in Egypt. For whatever reason, maybe for his own amusement, Harper hired a dragoman (an Egyptian interpreter), Hamad Hassah to accompany him to New York.

■ All the firemen congregated at the bow of the boat except Seaman Moore who manned the tiller. None of the firemen knew how to row a boat, (which is interesting because many of the women in other boats knew how and helped row) and shortly two of the four oars were lost in the water. Lifeboat 3 drifted all night and the few times anyone suggested returning to pick up people out of the water the idea was immediately rejected by the crewmen who were afraid the boat would be sucked under. Throughout the night, the crewmen kept lighting matches and holding them up, but after the ship sank, they couldn't see any other boats. When the lights of *Carpathia* were spotted in the morning, someone lit a newspaper and later Mrs. Davidson's straw hat to attract attention.

In the morning as the sun started to come up, the immense ice field could be seen, and little six-year-old Douglas Spedden called out, *"Oh, Muddie, look at the beautiful North Pole with no Santa Claus on it!"*

1:10 a.m.: Lifeboat 8

■ Lifeboat 8 on the port side was launched. In keeping with Lightoller's requirements, no male passengers were allowed on board. There were seventeen First Class women and six First Class servants plus four crewmen on board: 27 people in a boat with a capacity of 65. Able Bodied Seaman Thomas Jones was in charge of this boat.

No less than six of the women left their husbands behind and two more their fathers. Eighteen year old Mrs. Victor Penasco lost her husband of less than two weeks. Also losing husbands were Mrs. Alexander Holverson, Mrs. Frederick Kenyon and Mrs. Thomas Pears. Losing a husband and father were Mrs. Emil Taussig and daughter Ruth and Mrs. George Wick and her daughter Mary.

■ Among the other people in lifeboat 8 were the Countess of Rothes, her maid and her cousin Miss Gladys Cherry; Mrs. William Bucknell and her maid (Mr. Bucknell was the founder of Bucknell University in Pennsylvania, but he wasn't on the ship); Miss Ellen Bird, maid to Mrs. Isador Straus; and Miss Sarah Daniels, maid to Mrs. Hudson J.C. Allison.

■ Standing together on the deck as the boat was being loaded was Macy's Department Store owner Isador Straus and his wife Ida Straus, their maid Miss Ellen Bird and Colonel Archibald Gracie. When Mrs. Straus was asked to enter the boat, she replied, *"No! I will not be separated from my husband. As we have lived, so will we die. Together."* When it was suggested that, because of his advanced age no one would object to his entering the boat with his wife, Mr. Straus replied, *"No. I do not wish any distinction in my favor which is not granted to others."* The Strauses ordered their maid Ellen Bird to enter the boat, then they went down to A deck and sat down on chairs to watch the activity going on around them. Sometime later they were seen going back to their cabin and that is probably where they died.

"...on the deck I passed Mr. and Mrs. Straus leaning up against the deck house, chatting quite cheerily. I stopped and asked Mrs. Straus 'Can I take you along to the boats?' She replied 'I think I'll stay here for the moment...and they went down together..."
Second Officer Lightoller.

"I found another couple sitting on a fan casing, I asked the girl, 'Won't you let me put you in one of the boats?' She replied with a frank smile, 'Not on your life. We started together, and if need be, we'll finish together..." Second Officer Lightoller.

■ None of the women had anything much good to say about the four male crewmen on their boat. None could row, and the two bedroom stewards on board didn't even know to put the oars into an oarlock before rowing. It was up to Mrs. J. Stuart White to show them how to do so.

Eventually, the women took over the oars, primarily to get away from the anticipated suction, but also because they were under orders to row to a light off in the distance. Once reaching what was believed to be a ship, they were to discharge the passengers and return for more. The rowing also helped keep them warm. At some point, the Countess of Rothes took over the tiller, and her cousin, Miss Gladys Cherry, rowed all night. By the time *Titanic* sank, they were so far away they didn't even see it.

1:10 a.m.: Emergency Lifeboat 1

■ Emergency lifeboat 1 was the small 40 passenger boat on the starboard side next to the bridge wing. There were exactly twelve people on this boat: four First Class male and one female passenger, one servant and seven crewmen. This was the boat in which Sir Cosmo and Lady Lucy Duff Gordon and her maid escaped. Lookout George Symans was in charge.

■ First Officer Murdoch was trying to get this boat launched for a couple of reasons. It was closest to the bow and the bow was sinking ever lower. Shortly the water would begin to cover the forward well deck (C deck) and this boat needed to be launched so that the davits could be freed up to attach collapsible C, setting on the deck, and later collapsible A which was on the roof of the officers quarters. So the davits had to be used for three boats, which is why Murdoch loaded seven crewmen into the boat. Their orders were to drop into the water and pick up anyone who jumped in or crawled down the falls.

As the boat was starting to be lowered, the Duff Gordons walked up and Sir Cosmo asked Murdoch, *"May we get in that boat?"* Murdoch replied, *"With the greatest pleasure,"* and helped Lady Duff Gordon and her maid Miss Laura Francatelli get into the boat. Sir Cosmo and two other male passengers who were standing by were also allowed to board. Lifeboat 1 was then lowered away.

Instead of waiting around looking for other people, the crew began to row away from the ship and pulled up about 200 yards away. There the lifeboat and its passengers waited while everyone watched the activity. No one recommended they go back to pick anyone up: none of the crew wanted to assume responsibility for it, fearing they would be swamped. Lookout Symons, in charge of the lifeboat, said nothing.

During the night crewmen R.W. Pusey heard Lady Duff Gordon tell her maid Miss Francatelli, *"You have lost your beautiful nightdress,"* and Pusey replied, *"Never mind, you have saved your lives; but we have lost our kit."* Because of this comment, Sir Cosmo offered to replace the kits (personal effects) of all the crewmen on lifeboat 1, which he did sometime in the future.

Unfortunately, this act of kindness caused one of the biggest scandals concerning the passengers because it was later asserted that Sir Cosmo was paying off the crew with a bribe *not* go back to pick up survivors in order to save his wife and himself. Although not true, once the newspapers printed this story, the Duff Gordons would spend the rest of their lives defending themselves against it.

■ **1:10 a.m.:** *"...I met the Purser, Assistant Purser and the Senior and Junior Surgeons...there was only time to pass a few words, then they all shook hands and said 'Goodbye'..."* Second Officer Lightoller.

■ **1:15 a.m.:** To prevent a rush on the lifeboats, Third Class male passengers had been held behind the locked gates in their section of the ship. Third Class Steward John Hart later said that at 1:15 the gates were opened so these passengers could make their way to the Boat deck. Nobody showed them how to get there, however. Later reports said that many of them climbed up on the deck crane, crawling along the crane's boom, then dropping down on A deck.

1:20 a.m.: Lifeboat 10

■ Lifeboat 10, on the port side of the Boat deck, was lowered. By this time, one hour and forty minutes after *Titanic* had struck the iceberg, almost everyone was aware that the ship was in grave peril. Finding people to get into the boats was becoming much easier. Passengers in the lifeboats already launched would later say that the tops of the propellers could be seen as the bow continued to sink. Water was pouring into the forward well deck, where it had free access to flow throughout the forward part of the ship. Lifeboat 10 left with around 55 people on board, ten short of its capacity.

Every surviving passenger commented that, at this time anyway, there still wasn't any panic on board the ship.

■ At the time lifeboat 10 was being launched, there were no male passengers on board because of Second Officer Lightoller's restrictions. Thus, there were around 41 women and 7 children on board with all three classes about equally represented. Able Bodied Seaman Edward J. Buley was in charge.

Among the passengers on this were Mrs. Mark Fortune and her three daughters, but left behind was her husband and a son. Most of the remaining passengers left behind a husband or father.

■ Lifeboat 10 was Chief Baker Charles Joughin's assigned boat, but he was so busy helping other passengers that he wasn't able to get into the boat before it was launched. Seaman Frank Evans was one of the crewmen on the boat, and he reported that Joughin, *"was getting the children and chucking them into the boat. Mr. Murdoch and the baker made the women jump across into the boat about two feet and a half...He threw them* [the children] *on to the women and he was catching children by their dresses and chucking them in."*

Later, Evans reported, *"One woman in a black dress slipped and fell. She seemed nervous and did not like to jump at first. When she did jump she did not go far enough, but fell between the ship and the boat. She was pulled in by some men on the deck below, went up to the Boat Deck again, took another jump, and landed safely in the boat."*

■ As lifeboat 10 was being lowered past A deck, Third Class passenger Mr. N. Krekorian (referred to in different reports as an "Armenian" or as a "crazed Italian") jumped into the boat. Some passengers later thought he was hiding under the seats before the boat was launched, but he apparently jumped. In any case, he survived the jump.

When the boat reached the water, the weight of the boat and the total lack of any wave action prevented the crew from releasing the falls on the boat. Normally there would be enough slack in the falls as the boat crested a wave to allow the release to work. Consequently, the boat remained tied up to the ship until someone found a knife to cut the falls.

Lifeboat 10 pulled away about 200 yards and shortly later tied up to three other boats under the direction of Officer Lowe. Because this boat was essentially full, there wasn't any attempt to pick up survivors.

1:20 a.m.: Lifeboat 9

■ Lifeboat 9 was lowered from the starboard side of the ship with between 48 and 56 people in it. This left room for another ten or so. Word was passed that no men were allowed until all the women in the area were loaded. Madame Leontine Aubert, the mistress of Benjamin Guggenheim, was on this boat along with Miss Marion Wright.

Boatswain's Mate Albert Haines was in charge. In all, there were a few First Class and Third Class, but mostly there were Second Class passengers.

After all the women that could be found were loaded, Murdoch allowed whatever men were around to board. Gambler George Bradley (Brayton) entered the lifeboat, as did at least nine other male passengers. Finally, Murdoch ordered any of the crewmen standing around to get in and about 15 of them did. Even then, the boat was lowered with room available for more.

■ One elderly lady waiting on the deck was ordered to board and several of the crewmen tried to assist her, but she caused quite a commotion and broke away. She was last seen going back inside the ship.

■ By this time, *Titanic* had developed a noticeable list to starboard. The boats hanging on their falls were swinging away from the ship, and it was becoming difficult for the passengers to navigate the gap. Consequently, Murdoch and others would stand with one foot in the boat and one on the deck rail to help assist the women into the boats.

■ The novelist Jacques Futrelle escorted his wife May Futrelle to the side of the lifeboat. When she objected to leaving, he told her, *"For God's sake, go! It's your last chance! Go!"* Mrs. Futrelle was still standing on the deck when one of the officers forced her into the boat. Mr. Futrelle was lost.

■ After the boat was lowered into the water, it took a while until someone could find a knife to cut the lashings for the oars. Once free, lifeboat 9 was rowed out about 100 yards. No attempt was made to go back to pick up others, but for the next hour or so the crew rowed toward the light of another ship they thought they saw in the distance.

1:20 a.m.: Lifeboat 11

■ By now everyone realized that those boats still remaining would have to be loaded more fully. All the boats launched so far had rowed off, and none were coming back to pick up additional people. Starboard lifeboat 11 with a capacity of 65 people was launched with 70 people, with a good mix of second and third class passengers and crew. Quartermaster Sidney Humphreys was in charge.

Lifeboats 11 and 13 were loaded at almost the same time from A deck, and a human chain made up of stewards was created to pass women and children into the boats. One of these children was six-year old Nina Harper whose father Reverend Harper wrapped her up in a blanket and handed her off to her aunt Miss Jessie Leitch as she was entering the boat. Reverend Harper remained behind and was lost.

■ Mrs. Nellie Becker and her three children were all on the deck together. During the confusion Mrs. Becker, her four-year old daughter and one-year old son were loaded into the boat, but twelve-year old daughter Ruth was left behind on the deck. Mrs. Becker was beside herself with grief all night, and it wasn't until she was on the *Carpathia* that she found Ruth, who had managed to get onto lifeboat 13.

■ Eight year old Marshall Drew later recounted, *"The lowering of the lifeboat seventy feet into the sea was perilous. Davits, ropes, nothing worked properly so that first one end of the lifeboat was tilted up and then far down. I think it was the only time I was scared."*

■ One of the more tragic events in this night of tragedy was the saga of the Allison family: First Class passenger Mr. Hudson Allison, his wife Bessie, their two-year-old daughter Helen and one-year-old son Hudson Trevor. Also part of the Allison group was a maid, Sarah Daniels, Trevor's nurse Mrs. Alice Cleaver, cook Mildred Brown and chauffeur George Swane.

Shortly after *Titanic* struck the iceberg, Alice Cleaver, who was sharing a room with the Allison children, wrapped baby Trevor up in a blanket and took him up to the Boat deck without telling anyone where she was going. She was joined by Mildred Brown and they managed to get into lifeboat 11. During the ensuing confusion Mr. and Mrs. Allison and the servants looked all over the ship for Alice and Trevor. At some point Sarah Daniels also got off the ship. By the time the Allisons finally figured out that Trevor was safe with Alice, there weren't any boats left. The Allisons were last seen setting on A deck behind the windows with their daughter. Little Helen was the only child from First or Second Class who was lost. Mr. Allison's body was later found, and he was buried in Canada. Young Trevor died when he was 18 and is buried next to his father.

Alice Cleaver was initially hailed as a heroine for saving Trevor, but the families of Hudson and Bess would always condemn her for leaving the rest of the family to die on the ship.

■ Another bizarre incident occurred on this boat. Eighteen-year old Leah Aks was standing near Madeleine Astor on A deck with her 10-month old son Philip "Filly" Aks. Mrs. Astor gave Leah a shawl to wrap the baby in.

While lifeboat 11 was being loaded, someone thought Leah was trying to rush the line and she was held back. Then, someone grabbed the baby out of her arms and tossed him into the boat. Passenger Elizabeth Nye caught baby Philip much like a football and held onto him all night. No one knew who the baby belonged to, and Leah didn't get on the boat. Fortunately, Leah Aks managed to get into lifeboat 13 and was saved.

The story doesn't end here. Once on board *Carpathia*, Elizabeth Nye wouldn't give up the baby to Leah because she didn't know who the mother was. Eventually Captain Rostron would have to settle the dispute when Leah Aks was able to identify a birthmark on the baby, and Filly would be returned to his mother.

■ Because this boat was seriously overcrowded, many of the passengers had to stand all night. There was a considerable amount of squabbling and complaining among the women about this. Many of them would later also register complaints about the crewmen who were smoking in front of them.

Obviously, the survivors in lifeboat 11 didn't attempt to pick up anyone else. It was enough work for the crewmen just to pull the boat away from the ship before it sank.

1:25 a.m.: Lifeboat 13

■ Just a few minutes after lifeboat 11 was launched, lifeboat 13 on the starboard side was lowered with between 60 and 64 people on board. There was only one First Class passenger, Dr. Washington Dodge, who would meet up with the rest of his family on *Carpathia*. Also aboard was Miss Ruth Becker who had gotten separated from her mother and brothers. They were on lifeboat 11.

Another second class passenger was Lawrence Beesley who had wanted to find a good vantage point when *Titanic* arrived in New York so he could see its massive size in its entirety. His view instead would be from its starboard side as it sank. Beesley would later write one of the best accounts of the sinking of the ship.

■ Among the Third Class passengers was Mr. Eugene Daly who had played "Erin's Lament" on his Irish pipes as *Titanic* steamed away from the coast of Ireland. (There is some confusion about which boat Daly was on as he was reported to be on lifeboat 13, lifeboat 15 and on collapsible B). Other Third Class passengers included Johan Svensson, a fourteen-year old boy traveling alone who was denied boarding on two boats prior to getting onto lifeboat 13, and Leah Aks, whose baby had been taken away from her and tossed into lifeboat 11.

■ Altogether there were about 30 Third Class passengers in lifeboat 13. There were also about 25 crewmen on the boat. Leading Fireman Frederick Barrett, having escaped from both boiler room 6 and then boiler room 5 as they flooded, got up to A deck and managed to get into lifeboat 12 where he was placed in charge. Barrett had been soaked by freezing water twice in the past 90 minutes, and once he was in the open boat, he was so cold he couldn't continue to command it, so someone else took over. One of the women wrapped Barrett up in a piece of canvas to keep him from freezing to death.

■ After having gotten his family loaded into lifeboat 5, Dr. Washington Dodge was standing near lifeboat 13, assisting other passengers. His steward was also helping load the boat and told Dr. Dodge, *"You had better get in here then."* He got behind the doctor and pushed him into the boat and then followed him in as it was being lowered.

■ As the boat neared the water, several people noticed a huge discharge of water coming out of the side of the ship right below the boat. The water was from the pumps down inside the hull still pumping water out of the ship. If the lifeboat was lowered down into the discharge, the boat would have been sunk in just a few moments.

The passengers called up to the deck to stop lowering the boat. The oars were used to push the boat further away from the ship while the boat was lowered into the water. While all this was happening, lifeboat 13 drifted backwards from the splash caused by the discharge, so the falls now couldn't be released and had to be cut. If this wasn't enough of a problem, lifeboat 13 had drifted directly underneath lifeboat 15 which was now being lowered right on top of it.

Once again the passengers had to call out to the deck to stop lowering lifeboat 15 while the falls were cut with a knife. Once the falls were cut, lifeboat 13 was rowed away.

■ **1:25 a.m.:** Quartermaster Rowe fired his eighth and last distress rocket.

■ **1:25 a.m.:** Benjamin Guggenheim and his servant Victor Giglio returned to their cabins and changed into their best evening clothes. Guggenheim shed his warm clothing and lifebelt, telling his steward that *"We've dressed up in our best and are prepared to go down like gentlemen."*

1:30 a.m.: Lifeboat 15

■ Lifeboat 15 was the last regular lifeboat launched from the starboard side off A deck. Lifeboat 15 contained one First Class male passenger, about 40 third class passengers (almost an equal number of male and female passengers with about six children) and about 25 crewmen and one female crewmember. By this time *Titanic* had acquired a slight list to port which meant that it was easier to load the passengers from A deck.

Few of the survivors on this boat left any recollections about the launch. Fireman Frank Dymond was in charge, and his testimony centered on how quiet the passengers on the decks were as they watched the last boat on that side of the ship lowered away.

Because the boat was full, the crew rowed away from the ship about 500 yards and waited while it sank.

■ **1:30 a.m.:** *"...The Chief Officer [Wilde] came over and asked did I know where the firearms were?...and into the First Officer's cabin we went...where I hauled them out still in all their pristine newness and grease..."* Second Officer Lightoller.

1:30 a.m.: Lifeboat 12

■ Lifeboat 12 was launched at this late time with only somewhere between 30 and 40 people on board. Once again there were no male passengers on the boat, and Lightoller launched it half full when there were no women in the vicinity instead of allowing any men on board. Most of the people came from Second Class, there being only about five Third Class passengers and two crewmen on the boat when it was launched. Able Bodied Seaman John Poingdestre was in charge of lifeboat 12.

As the boat was being lowered, one Third Class male jumped in from A deck. Seaman Fredrick Clench, the only other crewman on the boat, said he saw the man jump in and then disappear under the seats where he hid until the boat was rowed away. Shortly, lifeboat 12 joined up with lifeboats 14 and 4, and some of those passengers were transferred to lifeboat 12.

With only two crewmembers on board, there wasn't any attempt to pick up people in the water.

1:30 a.m.: Lifeboat 14

■ Lifeboat 14 was launched from the port side with around sixty people on board and was commanded by Fifth Officer Lowe who was ordered into the boat by Second Officer Lightoller. Most of the passengers were women from Second Class although there were several from First Class and Third Class.

■ First Class passenger Mrs. Alexander Compton and her daughter Sara were in this boat, but they left Sara's brother Alexander Jr. behind. Most of the other women passengers left a male family member behind.

■ *"My father never said anything...he put my mother and me into a lifeboat...then he walked away..."* Passenger Edith Brown.

■ While loading this boat, Officer Lowe fired his revolver along side the ship into the water. This was the first boat loaded where passengers were starting to fear that they might be left behind. Lowe later reported, *"...as we were coming down past the open decks, I saw a lot of Latin people all along the ship's rails. They were glaring more or less like wild beasts, ready to spring. That is why I yelled out to 'look out.' and let go, bang! right along the ship's side...."* This statement and many by Lowe and other survivors all show a large amount of prejudice toward anyone who wasn't obviously English.

■ Lowe rounded up lifeboats 10, 12 and 4, tied them all together and moved the survivors around to help level out the loads.

"We divided the passengers of our boat amongst the other four...we rowed away amongst the wreckage as we heard cries for help coming from that direction. When we got to it the sight we saw was awful. We were amongst hundreds of dead bodies floating in lifebelts..." reported Seaman Joseph Scarrott.

■ As Lowe was transferring people among the boats in order to free up one to go back to pick up people in the water, he asked for volunteers to go back to the wreck and *"...it was at this time that I found the Italian. He came aft and had a shawl over his head, and I suppose he had skirts. Anyhow, I pulled the shawl off his face and saw he was a man. He was in a great hurry to get into the other boat and I got hold of him and pitched him in* [to the other boat]*...he was not worth being handled better..."* Edith Brown would later relate that Lowe told the passenger, *"I've a good mind to shoot you, you might have capsized the boat..."*

■ It was after this transfer of passengers that Lowe went out and pulled four people out of the water, including First Class passenger William Hoyt, who later died from the cold.

■ After transferring the passengers and while looking for survivors in the water, Lowe came upon a body strapped onto a door. This small person turned out to be Japanese passenger Mr. Masabumi Hosono who had tied himself to the door and, by all appearances, was already dead. When he didn't answer when called, Lowe said, *"What's the use? He's dead, likely, and if he isn't there's others better worth saving than a Jap!"* In any case, he was hauled into the boat and a couple of the women rubbed him down and warmed him up. Shortly, Mr. Hosono stood up, stretched his arms, stamped his feet and within a few minutes apparently regained most of his strength. When one of the crewman became too tired to continue rowing, Hosono pushed him aside and rowed the rest of the night. Later, Lowe would say, *"...I'm ashamed of what I said about the little blighter. I'd save the likes o' him six times over if I got the chance."* Unfortunately, when he arrived home in Japan, Mr. Hosono would be ostracized for having survived.

■ Toward dawn, Lowe came across collapsible A and removed the survivors from it because that boat was about to sink.

1:35 a.m.: Lifeboat 16

■ Somewhere between 50 and 56 people were in lifeboat 16 when it was launched from the port side by Second Officer Lightoller. There were no male passengers on this boat, and most of the crew were women from the Stewards Department.

The majority of the passengers were Third Class women and children, although "Winnie" Troutt from Second Class did end up on this boat. Most of the women left their husbands on the deck. Master-at-Arms Joseph Bailey was in charge, and he had to climb down the falls to get into the boat. There were only four male crewmembers on this boat.

■ One of the stewardesses was Violet Jessop who was now living through her second shipwreck. Miss Jessop had been on *Olympic* when it was involved in the collision with HMS *Hawke*. Miss Jessop would survive the sinking of *Titanic* and would continue to work for White Star Line. Five years later in 1917, Jessop would be working as a nurse on *Titanic's* other sister ship *Britannic* when that ship would be sunk by a mine in the Aegean Sea. Thus, Violet Jessop would have the dubious honor of serving on all three of the "*Olympic*" class ships when they met with disaster.

■ Another crewman, Fireman John Priest, was also on all three ships and survived. During World War I, Priest served on two merchant ships that were also sunk, which meant that four ships he had served on sank from under him and another seriously damaged. He had to retire because the word was out that he was unlucky and no one would serve on the same ship with him.

■ Lifeboat 16 later tied up to lifeboat 6 to transfer passengers to help balance the loads. Although there was some room on the boat, no attempt was made to go back to pick up anyone else.

1:40 a.m.: Lifeboat Collapsible C

■ It was now exactly two hours since striking the iceberg, and the last of the boats were being prepared for launching. It was now time for collapsible C to be launched from the same davits that lifeboat 1 had been launched from, and this was the last boat to be launched on the starboard side. The list to port was now enough that, as it was being lowered, the lifeboat had to be pushed away from the side of the ship to keep from rubbing its canvas sides against the rivet heads.

With one notable exception, all the passengers were from the third class areas, about 40, all women except for a couple men and about six crewmen. The one exception was the President of the White Star Line.

■ The boat was only partially filled when Quartermaster George Rowe arrived and a call was made for more women and children. When none stepped forward, the mass of men waiting nearby started to move toward the boat, and Chief Purser Herbert McElroy fired his pistol into the air twice hold them back. It worked. Shortly, a few more women came up from below decks, and First Officer Murdoch ordered the boat lowered so that collapsible A on the roof of the officer's quarters could be gotten ready. By this time the group of men had moved off and as the boat was lowered, two male passengers, William Carter and Bruce Ismay, stepped into it.

■ Ismay, after having helped with lifeboat 5, went down toward the bow to help load collapsible C that had been attached to the davits. As it was starting to be lowered, Ismay just stepped into it and took a seat. Most of the people on the boat observed this although at the time few knew who he was. Chief Officer Wilde, First Officer Murdoch and Chief Purser McElroy also observed Ismay get into the boat, but since none of them survived, it can only be imagined what they thought when they saw the owner of the company, the person who had decided that more lifeboats would not be needed, take a seat in one of the few lifeboats available.

■ The crew thought they saw a light off in the distance and rowed all night to get to it, and by daylight collapsible C was over five miles from where *Titanic* sank. Also around daylight, five stowaway men from Third Class were found under the seats of the boat.

1:45 a.m.: Emergency Lifeboat 2

■ Emergency Lifeboat 2 on the port side forward, with a capacity of about 40, was launched with between 19 and 25 people in it. There were four crewmen on this boat including Fourth Officer Boxhall. The rest of the people were evenly divided among First and Third Class passengers, all women or children except for one Third Class male who got on the boat with his family.

■ Prior to the official loading of the boat, a whole group of crewmen, estimated to be about 25 or more, had already gotten into it. Second Officer Lightoller, carrying a pistol in his hand saw them and shouted, *"Get out of there, you damned cowards! I'd like to see every one of you overboard!"* Everyone scrambled out of the boat, and the women were loaded. Lightoller and Boxhall oversaw the loading and launching of the boat. Lightoller was in a hurry because he wanted to get collapsible D hooked up to the davits and launched. By now the water had climbed over the top of the bow and the ship was both far down (over 60 feet) by the head and had a substantial list to port. (A few minutes earlier there was a sharp list to starboard, so apparently the water in the ship was causing it to list in each direction alternately.)

Murdoch ordered Boxhall into the boat, and Boxhall brought along a box of small green rockets. There was also a small lantern on the boat, the only boat to have one. Boxhall and the other seaman on the boat, Frank Osman, had to do the rowing so they enlisted First Class passenger Mrs. Walter Douglas to man the tiller which she did all night. Murdoch had ordered Boxhall to row around to the starboard side to pick up people in the water, but by the time they got around the ship, suction from water flowing into the open portholes prevented them from getting close enough to pick anyone up.

■ Boxhall attached the lighted lantern to the end of a pole and had one of the women passengers hold it up high so it could be seen. Throughout the night Boxhall also fired off his little rockets, and it was these rockets that the crew of *Carpathia* would see and guide on as they came upon the wreckage in the morning.

1:55 a.m.: Lifeboat 4

■ The last regular lifeboat to be launched was lifeboat 4. This is the boat that was going to be the first one launched almost 90 minutes earlier before being forgotten by the crew after it was discovered that the passengers couldn't be loaded from A deck because of the glass-and-screened windows for which no one had a tool to open.

For over thirty minutes the Astors, Carters, Ryersons, Thayers and Wideners, along with their servants had all waited on A deck for someone to come back with the tool needed to open the window. Around 1:00 a.m. steward George Dodd finally sent them all up to the Boat deck via the small crew stairway to wait, figuring that because all the other boats were being loaded from the Boat deck, this lifeboat would be raised back up so they could load from there.

And so they waited while around them all the other boats were loaded and launched. They watched the rockets being fired and listened to the orchestra play. Meantime, lifeboat 4 was still resting next to A deck below.

After lifeboat 2 had been launched, Lightoller came back to number 4 and discovered that it hadn't been launched and that the passengers were on the boat deck and the boat was on A deck. So he ordered the passengers back down to A deck where, by now, someone had found the tool needed to crank open the windows. With the ship now having a serious list to port, lifeboat 4 was too far away from the ship to get into, so grappling hooks and wire was used to secure the boat to the side of the ship.

A small ladder was found and, with Lightoller straddling the gap with one foot on the ship and one in the boat, the women and children climbed the ladder, crouched to get through the window and stepped into the lifeboat outside. They were stepping from the bright lights on the ship into almost total darkness.

■ First into the boat was Madeleine Astor. Colonel Astor helped her up the steps, then asked Lightoller if he could join her because she was in a *"delicate condition."* Lightoller said no, not until all the women were loaded. Colonel Astor stood back and helped with the other women.

■ The Ryerson family came next and Arthur Ryerson noticed that his wife's maid didn't have a lifebelt, so he took his off and put it on her. Mrs. Ryerson led her two daughters and son to the window, but Lightoller told her, *"That boy can't go!"* Arthur Ryerson replied, *"Of course that boy goes with his mother—he is only thirteen."* Lightoller let him pass, but announced to all who were near, *"No more boys."*

■ Mrs. Willam E. Carter and her son and daughter were escorted into the boat by Mr. Carter. Once they were on board the lifeboat, Mr. Carter quickly moved to the starboard side of the ship and stepped into collapsible C with Bruce Ismay. The Carter's had a grand reunion on *Carpathia*.

■ Mrs. John Thayer and Mrs. George Widener both kissed their husbands and sons good-bye and boarded the boat. After the rest of the available women passengers were loaded, lifeboat 4 was lowered the few remaining feet to the water, which was now only about one deck below. It was discovered that there weren't any sailors on the boat, so Quartermaster Walter Perkis and Seaman William McCarthy were ordered to slide down the falls and get into the boat.

Mrs. Ida Hippach and her daughter were in the boat. Eight years earlier Mrs. Hippach had lost two sons in the fire that destroyed Chicago's Iroquois Theater.

As the boat was rowed away, the passengers could all see John Jacob Astor, the two Thayers, the two Widener men and Arthur Ryerson standing together in a group, waving at the boat and all deep in their own thoughts. At some point, Colonel Astor went down to F deck aft to where the dog kennels were and let all the dogs out. Madeleine Astor would later say that as the ship started to go under, she could see Colonel Astor's Airdale dog "Kitty" running around on the Boat deck.

■ Quartermaster Perkis had orders to row to the aft gangway hatch to pick up people, and enroute two crewmen slid down the falls of lifeboat 16. One was able to get into the boat but the other fell into the water and was fished out and pulled into the boat.

Within the next few minutes, six more men were pulled from the water but one of them, Steward Sidney Siebert, died from exposure on the boat and another, Seaman William Lyons, died on *Carpathia*.

In all, lifeboat 4, capable of holding 65, would have about 40 people in it.

2:00 a.m.: Colonel Archibald Butt, Francis Millet, Clarence Moore and Arthur Ryerson retired to the First Class Smoking Room on A deck aft, sat at their usual table and played one last hand of cards while they waited for the end. About 2:10 they left, none to be seen again.

2:05 a.m.: Lifeboat Collapsible D

■ By now it was over two hours and twenty minutes since striking the iceberg. Collapsible lifeboat D was attached to the davits where lifeboat 2 had been, and this was the last lifeboat that could reasonably be launched. Collapsibles A and B were still tied down on top of the officer's quarters, and without a crane there wasn't any good way to launch them.

There was room enough for 49 people in collapsible D, and there were still over 1,500 people on *Titanic*. Even then, collapsible D was launched with only about 40 people in it. In order to keep people from storming the boat, a human chain was formed by the crewmen on deck, and they allowed only women and children through.

Although only women were supposed to be allowed into this boat, First Class passenger Frederick Hoyt saw his wife into the boat then jumped into the water near where he though the boat might pass. As the lifeboat was rowed by, Hoyt was hauled into the boat where he sat shivering in the cold for the rest of the night. Theater owner Henry Harris escorted his wife to the edge of the chain and when told he couldn't go any further, kissed his wife and said, *"Yes, I know. I will stay."*

■ Two small boys were brought to the edge of the chain by their father and passed through to the boat where some of the women wrapped them up to keep them warm. The father told the people in the boat that his name was "Mr. Hoffman" traveling to New York. He then stepped back. Nobody knew it at the time, of course, but the boys were Edmond and Michel Navratil, and the father was Michel Navratil who was kidnapping his children from his estranged wife in France.

Since Hoffman (Navratil) didn't survive, no one knew who the two small boys were. The newspapers picked up the story and published a photograph of them which was reprinted in newspapers throughout Europe. Eventually their mother, still in France, saw the photograph and made her way to New York where she was re-united with her kidnapped and lost children.

■ Colonel Archibald Gracie showed up with two of the women he had been "protecting," Mrs. John M. Brown and Miss Edith Evans. Colonel Gracie was stopped at the line but the two women got through just as the boat was being lowered away. Miss Evans told Mrs. Brown, *"You go first. You have children waiting at home."* and then helped Mrs. Brown over the rail. Mrs. Brown got into the boat but then it was too far down for Edith Evans to get into it, so she remained behind to die with the men who also remained on the deck.

■ Down on A deck, First Class passengers Hugh Woolner and Bjornstrom-Steffanson had been helping people into boats for two hours and now the deck was deserted. They walked forward through the door to the open Promenade Deck and decided it was time to take their chances in the water which was already over the tops of their shoes anyway. They got onto the railing to prepare to dive in when, just a few feet below them, they saw collapsible D descending toward the water. They decided to make a jump for it, and Steffanson jumped into the bow of the boat, land-ing on his head. Woolner followed, but missed and ended up half in, half out, hung over the side. He was pulled in just as the boat hit the water.

Quartermaster Arthur Bright was in charge of collapsible D. Once the boat was in the water, everyone rowed or paddled to get as far away from *Titanic* as possible for, by now, water was up to the bridge and the stern was completely out of the water. They didn't want to be sucked under when the ship went down.

■ **2:05 a.m.:** Captain Smith went into the wireless room and told Marconi operators Phillips and Bride that their work was done and to save themselves. Both would stay on duty for another 12 minutes while Phillips sent another message. On his way back to the bridge, Smith told several crewmen, *"It's every man for himself."*

■ **2:10 a.m.:** A steward saw Thomas Andrews in the First Class Smoking Room, alone, with his lifebelt laying on a table. Andrews, with arms folded across his chest, was staring at a painting titled "Plymouth Harbor" by Norman Wilkinson. Andrews was not seen again.

■ **2:10 a.m.:** Wallace Hartley and the three remaining members of the orchestra, now wearing jackets and lifebelts, began to play their final piece of music. Hartley had always said that his favorite piece of music was *"Nearer, My God, to Thee"* and wanted to have it played at his funeral. Hartley probably called out to play this favorite song of his even though it wasn't on the "approved list" of pre-numbered pieces.

Survivors would differ as to which piece of music the orchestra played, with three different possibilities: *"Nearer, My God, to Thee"*, *"Autumn"* or *"Songe d'Automne"* It will never be firmly established which it was. In any case, with the water now rushing up the Boat deck, Hartley and the or-chestra played their final piece.

2:15 a.m.: Collapsible Lifeboat B

■ The only two lifeboats left were collapsible B on the port-side roof of the officer's quarters and collapsible A on the starboard side. *Titanic* was sinking rapidly now and anyone who was available was working to get the boats un-lashed and moved off the roof.

After the lashings were cut, several dozen men managed to push col-lapsible B off the roof, but it landed on the Boat deck upside down. Although they tried to right it, the boat weighed too much and there was-n't enough time. As the bridge went under water, a wave pushed the boat over the railing into the sea. The boat was still upside down. The wave also washed Second Officer Lightoller, Sixth Officer Moody and dozens of other people overboard with the lifeboat.

■ As they were struggling in the water, people started to climb onto the bottom of the boat, and there were a few people on it when the forward funnel fell over and just missed the lifeboat but crushed dozens of people under it. The wave that the impact of the funnel created washed everyone off the lifeboat and pushed it about twenty yards away.

Lightoller later reported that after he was in the water, *"I was driven back against the blower, which is a large thing which faces forward to the wind and which then goes down to the stoke hole: but there is a grating there and it was against this grating that I was sucked by the water, and held there under water. There was a terrific blast of air and water and I was blown out clear... Colonel Gracie, I believe, was sucked down in identically the same manner... caused by the water rushing down below as the ship was going down."*

■ Marconi operator Harold Bride found himself *under* the lifeboat with only his head above water. As more people got onto the lifeboat, it kept sinking lower, and at some point Bride swam out from under the boat and tried to get on but was prevented from doing so by the people already on the boat. He then swam around to the other side and found someone who knew him and was let onto the boat.

■ After having been sucked into the blower holes—twice each—both Lightoller and Archibald Gracie managed to get on top of collapsible B. Also there was young Jack Thayer; First Class passenger Algernon Barkworth wearing an enormous fur coat that kept him afloat and alive; Harold Bride and about thirty other men. There were no women because everyone on it had to get on it by their own devices, and everyone had to climb out of the freezing water.

■ The story of collapsible B is one of the more dramatic of the night. The water temperature was 28 degrees and the air temperature was 31 degrees. The men on the upside-down boat all climbed out of the water which meant they were all soaked. They huddled together throughout the night. At first, several other people were able to get onto the boat, but it was soon seriously overcrowded and newcomers had to be pushed away. While many of the men in the center section of the boat were standing, those on the bow and stern were kneeling and using wooden planks to try to paddle away from both the sinking ship and the mass of humanity that was trying to climb onto their boat.

"Hold on to what you have, old boy. One more would sink us all" someone on the boat shouted to one of the swimmers in the water. *"That's all right, boys; keep cool. Good luck, God bless you"* replied the swimmer as he swam away.

■ Chief Baker Charles Joughin also managed to get onto this boat after holding onto its side and treading water for well over ninety minutes. Joughin didn't freeze as most of the other people in the water did. His size provided a lot of body fat, and prior to entering the water he had consumed most of a bottle of Scotch which helped keep him warm.

■ Although the sea had been flat calm all night, toward the morning there was a slight swell and collapsible B rolled with it, each time letting a little more air escape from under the sides of the boat, and as the air escaped, the boat sank lower. Several men on the lifeboat died during the night and they were allowed to slide off to make more room for the others. One of the dead was probably John Phillips, the Marconi operator. At least several people said they saw him there, but if he was, his body was allowed to slide off, too.

■ **2:15 a.m.:** The wave that swept over the bridge probably also claimed the life of Captain Edward J. Smith. Although there are a lot of stories of Smith later turning up in the water, the bridge is the last place anyone actually saw him. In all likelihood, Smith was standing on the bridge when the wave crashed over it. Also seen standing on the port bridge wing at this time was John Jacob Astor.

■ **2:15 a.m.:** The forward funnel had stabilizing wires attached to various parts of the deck. Some of the wires were attached to the other side of the forward expansion joint. As the front of the ship was filling with water, the joint expanded and the resulting tension burst the stabilizing wires. The forward funnel then fell over forward and to the port side, crushing the port side bridge wing and killing everyone under it, including Astor, whose body was later found crushed beyond recognition and covered with soot. The resulting wave of water is what washed everyone off collapsible B and pushed the boat further away from the ship.

"I was just lending a hand when a large wave came awash of the deck. The wave carried the boat off. I had hold of an oar-lock and went off with it. The next I knew I was in the boat...and the boat was upside down, and I was under it...I was under water. How I got out from under the boat I don't know. There were men all around me—hundreds of them. The sea was dotted with them, all depending on their lifebelts..." Harold Bride.

2:15 a.m.: collapsible Lifeboat A

■ The last lifeboat, collapsible A, had been pushed off the top of the officers' quarters, and it landed upright on the Boat deck. Several crewmen tried to attach it to the falls of lifeboat 1, but the ship was sinking too fast and finally a few people jumped into the boat while the rest were washed away by the same wave that floated collapsible B off the port side deck when the bridge went under. Most survivors were surprised to see that this boat survived at all. It was tangled up in all the loose ropes and cables laying around the deck. Somehow, it floated free and several more people managed to climb into it.

The boat was actually floating when a couple of crewmen cut the falls away. It was filling up with people who were climbing out of the water when the forward funnel fell over. The wave washed everyone out of the boat and filled it with water. The canvas sides were also down, so it had little buoyancy. However, several men did get on board, and they helped several others, including the only woman on the boat, Mrs. Stanton (Rosa) Abbott, who lost her two sons when the ship went down. During the night a dozen of the men died, but the bodies of three of them were left on board.

2:15 a.m.: As the stern rose ever higher, every item inside *Titanic*—furniture, dishes, beds, lamps, boilers, engines, people—all began to slide toward the bow of the ship in one continuous roar.

In his excellent book *A Night to Remember*, Walter Lord gives a fascinating description of this slide of objects:

> There has never been a mixture like it—29 boilers...the jeweled copy of the Rubáiyát...800 cases of shelled walnuts...15,000 bottles of ale and stout...huge anchor chains (each link weighed 175 pounds)...30 cases of golf clubs and tennis rackets for Spalding...Eleanor Widener's trousseau...tons of coal...Major Peuchen's tin box...30,000 fresh eggs...dozens of potted palms...5 grand pianos...a little mantel clock in B-38...the massive silver duck press...And still it grew—tumbling trellises, ivy pots and wicker chairs in the Café Parisien...shuffleboard sticks...the 50-phone switchboard...two reciprocating engines and the revolutionary low-pressure turbine...8 dozen tennis balls for R.F. Downey & Co., a cask of china for Tiffany's, a case of gloves for Marshall Field...the remarkable ice-making machine on G deck...Billy Carter's new English automobile...the Ryerson's 16 trunks, beautifully packed by Victorine.

■ **2:15 a.m.:** Still the stern rose higher, the three huge propellers now towering above everyone in the water and the after-decks crawling with people trying to avoid the inevitable.

On the aft well deck, Father Thomas R. Byles had about a hundred people gathered around him and was hearing confessions until the end. He had to hold onto a piece of machinery to keep from falling off the tilting deck.

■ **2:17 a.m.**: Marconi operator Jack Phillips sent his last transmission, then he walked out of the wireless office to the port side and stepped into the water that rushed up the boat deck and into the cabin.

■ **2:18 a.m.**: The engineers, who had remained in the very bottom of the ship while struggling to maintain power for the lights and thus sacrificed themselves, finally lost the battle as the lights flickered once then went out forever. The entire engineering crew, all 35 of them, went down with the ship.

■ **2:20 a.m.**: The ship was almost vertical in the water, then that portion behind the after expansion joint suddenly broke off and settled back slightly as the forward three-fourths of the ship started its descent toward the bottom of the sea, the remaining funnels breaking as they came into contact with the water.

"When the Titanic upended to sink," reported Marshall Drew, *"all was blacked out until the tons of machinery crashed to the bow...As this happened the hundreds and hundreds of people were thrown into the sea. I shall never forget the screams of these people as they perished in water said to be 28 degrees..."*

"I hung on by the rail and then let myself drop into the sea. the distance to the water was quite 75 feet, and I thought I was never going to get there. When I did come into contact with the water, it was like a great knife cutting into me. My limbs and body ached for days afterwards..." reported storekeeper Frank M. Prentice.

■ The after part of the ship which appeared to have broken off was still attached at the keel, and as the forward part of the ship sank, it pulled the after portion upright, almost 200 feet of the ship, into a vertical position. There it remained for a few seconds, stationary, as bulkheads collapsed and it lost its buoyancy, then the stern portion started to slide into the sea.

■ Chief Baker Joughin stood on top of the railing at the very back of the ship (where the fictional Rose and Jack stood in the film *Titanic*). Joughin, using the flagstaff as a support, reported that that ship went down much as an elevator does. A big bubble of trapped air burst to the surface, and as the stern went under, Joughin just stepped off it into the water. He didn't even get his hair wet.

■ **2:20 a.m.:** Five minutes after the last lifeboat floated off the ship and two hours and forty minutes after striking the iceberg, *Titanic* disappeared beneath the surface of the North Atlantic Ocean.

CHAPTER 13

RESCUE

Throughout the hours while the lifeboats were being loaded and the various dramas were taking place on the decks of *Titanic,* Captain Arthur H. Rostron and the crew of *Carpathia* were speeding north at over 17 knots, far beyond its rated speed, to rescue the survivors.

All of the preparations had been made, and now it was time to wait: 1:00 a.m., 2:00 a.m., 3:00 a.m., 4:00 a.m., and still *Carpathia* steamed on. With the air and water temperature both below freezing, time was of the essence. Rostron hoped that *Carpathia* would arrive at *Titanic's* location before the ship sank.

Life in the Boats

■ **2:18 a.m., April 15, 1912:** The lights of *Titanic* flickered once then went out forever. Two minutes later, the stern of *Titanic* disappeared under the surface of the ocean. A total of 698 passengers and crew had been put aboard the lifeboats, and another fourteen were picked up out of the water, seven of whom later died. In the twenty lifeboats were 712 people while over 1,500 more were fighting for their lives and dying in the freezing water.

It was absolutely black with the only light coming from the stars. During the two hours of launching the boats, most of them had become scattered all over the sea, and daylight would show that some of them were more than five miles away. Dawn would also show that the boats were just small objects surrounded by dozens of mountainous icebergs, including one that looked like a huge rock and had black and red paint all along one side of it.

■ After the stern slid into the sea there was a small ripple of water: no big suction to pull all of the boats down, nothing much to even disturb the surface of the calm sea. Just a slight gulp that didn't even create a wave. Because the fires in the boilers had been put out two hours earlier, none of them exploded when they were submerged in the water.

There were, however, fifteen hundred people thrashing around in the water, all calling out for help, loudly in the beginning and then growing fainter until within twenty minutes or so there was silence or as one survivor reported, *"twenty boats and a quiet sea."*

"...and finally the ghastly noise of the people thrashing about and screaming and drowning, that finally ceased. I remember saying to my mother once, 'how dreadful that noise was' and I'll always remember her reply 'yes, but think back about the silence that followed it'...but all of a sudden the ship wasn't there, the lights weren't there and the cries weren't there..." – passenger Eva Hart.

■ Twelve-year-old Ruth Becker was on lifeboat 13. She knew her mother and siblings were on another boat so she wasn't overly concerned about them. Years later she wrote, *"it* [the lifeboat] *was filled to standing room with men and women in every conceivable condition of dress and undress. It was bitter cold—a curious, deadening, bitter cold. And then with all of this, there fell on the ear the most terrible noises that human beings ever listened to—the cries of hundreds of people struggling in the icy cold water, crying for help with a cry that we knew could not be answered..."*

■ Also on lifeboat 13 was Leah Aks, and Ruth Becker reported, *"Standing on one side of me was a little German lady. She was crying and I asked her why. She told me—through an interpreter standing near—that her little six-weeks-old baby had been taken away from her...and put into another boat. The baby was wrapped so heavily in blankets that she was afraid it would be taken for baggage and thrown in the ocean..."*

■ One would think that a lifeboat would be permanently equipped with some sort of emergency equipment—food, water, compass, lights, oars. However, most only had oars and many of those were lost by inexperienced crewmen. Only one lifeboat had a lantern. Before the boats were loaded, some of them were supplied with loaves of bread brought up from the storeroom by the bakers. It was bad enough that the survivors had to watch the world's largest ship sink before their eyes, but until or even if a rescue ship arrived, they were stranded in the middle of the North Atlantic Ocean with absolutely nothing except the clothes they were wearing and the lifeboat they were sitting in.

■ Because most of the surviving officers had never gotten the word, few, if any of the survivors knew that any sort of rescue ship was steaming toward them. The only boat that knew for certain was overturned collapsible B because both Lightoller and Marconi operator Bride were on it and they both knew. Other than these few survivors, the people in all the other boats could only wait through the night, hoping that daylight would bring rescue.

■ Once he had sorted things out on his boat, Fifth Officer Lowe in lifeboat 14 started rounding up some of the other boats, figuring he could move some of the passengers around and then have an empty boat with which to go back to pick up people swimming in the water. He gathered up lifeboats 10, 12, and 4 and all four were tied together. Lowe then transferred the 55 people in his lifeboat to the other four and accepted some experienced oarsmen to help him row.

Transferring passengers was work enough to drive Lowe crazy: it was 2:30 in the morning, pitch black and the passengers were hopping from boat to boat in the middle of the ocean. Lowe was losing his patience and he starting to swear a lot, shouting to one of the hesitant women, *"Jump, damn you, jump."* His language didn't endear him to many of the ladies, and several later complained about it, some even starting a rumor that he was drunk. Lowe enjoyed that little rumor because, as everyone who counted knew, Lowe was a lifelong teetotaler.

Eventually he got everyone moved around, and at 3:00 Lowe set off to look for survivors in the mass of wreckage and humanity that was all that was left of the *Titanic.*

There was little to find. In the dark Lowe and his crew could hear people calling for help, but locating them was almost impossible. In all, only four people were pulled from the water and one of them later died. It was a grand, but fruitless attempt to find more survivors, but at least Lowe went back. He was the only one who did.

■ In lifeboat 1 with only 12 people in it, Fireman Charles Hendrickson told the other people, *"It's up to us to go back and pick up anyone in the water,"* but no one spoke up. When Hendrickson said it again, Sir Cosmo Duff Gordon said he didn't think they should try it because the boat would be swamped, so lifeboat 1 drifted around in the water only a few hundred yards from the people in the water.

Fourth Officer Boxhall asked the women in lifeboat 2 if they should go back but they all said no, so his boat also drifted in the night.

In every one of the lifeboats a similar act was played out. Someone would suggest going back, but the suggestion was refused and nothing was done.

■ There were eighteen lifeboats capable of picking up survivors and only 14 people were hauled out of the water: collapsible D picked up one passenger (Mr. Hoyt, whose wife was on that boat); lifeboat 4 picked up eight who just happened to be in the right place at the right time; Lowe picked up four in lifeboat 14 and one was picked up by collapsible A.

■ By now it was after 3:00 a.m. and the sea was quiet. Almost all of those in the water were dead, most soon would be frozen stiff. The adrenaline generated during the past few hours while *Titanic* was sinking started to take it's toll on the survivors in the boats. Most were in shock and few yet realized or knew that family and friends were lost forever. It hadn't really occurred to them yet.

■ With boats scattered all over the ocean and only one equipped with a lantern, it was impossible to see other boats so Fourth Officer Boxhall started firing off his little green flares, figuring that other boats would see them and row his way. Although he didn't know that *Carpathia* was enroute, firing the rockets would help guide any ship in the vicinity to them.

■ Several other boats joined up over time: lifeboat 16 tied up to 6 and transferred a stoker to help with rowing. Other boats met up and transferred passengers around. Mrs. Washington Dodge was in lifeboat 5 and kept pleading with everyone to go back to pick up some of the people in the water. They refused and Mrs. Dodge decided she didn't want anything to do with them anymore, so when lifeboat 7 rowed by, she switched boats.

■ Throughout the night, the survivors coped as best they could under the circumstances, most lost in their own thoughts, just waiting for whatever the immediate future would bring.
Surrounding all the boats was a sea full of debris: everything that could float off the decks as *Titanic* went down did so. Cork, wooden doors and deck chairs, paneling, furniture, chunks of timber, lifebelts and bodies. There were also icebergs in the area and in the quiet night water could be heard splashing against them. Some of the lifeboats even bumped into icebergs in the dark.

■ With the exception of the engineering crew, the crewmen who drowned in boiler rooms 6 and 5 when they flooded, and the staff of the á la carte restaurant who had been locked into their cabins below decks, most of the 1,500 people who died were probably on one of the open decks when the ship sank, and their bodies were floating around the lifeboats. The current would quickly pick them up and within a few hours, the bodies would be drifting away in all directions, many up against the icebergs which would hold them there for days.

■ Second Officer Lightoller recalled that the sensation of being in the 28 degree water *"was that of a thousand knives being driven into the body,"* and few of the people in the water lived more than 20 minutes. The one notable exception was Chief Baker Joughin who had enough alcohol in his system to keep him alive for well over 90 minutes.

Since only collapsible A and collapsible B were close enough for any of the swimmers to reasonably get to, that is where they headed. Neither was a good choice with B being upside down and A almost swamped. The best and strongest swimmers had the best chance of making it, but in the cold, even they didn't last long.

■ The survivors in all the lifeboats except B and A were reasonably well off for the short term, and those standing on top of B at least had an officer who took control and had knowledge that help was soon at hand. The twenty-odd men and one woman standing on collapsible A, which was awash with ice water up to everyone's knees, had nothing to sustain them. Mrs. Abbott, the only woman on the boat, had actually been on the Poop Deck when the stern went under, and what little suction there was pulled her and her two sons down. She somehow managed to get to the surface and onto collapsible A, but she spent the night not knowing the fate of her sons or of herself. One of the passengers, Edvard Lindell, managed to get onto the boat and someone else tried to pull his wife on board, but she slipped away and was lost. When Mr. Lindell was told what had happened, it was already too late because he had frozen to death.

As reality started to set in, some of the women hailed each passing boat calling for their husbands or sons or friends and in lifeboat 6 Madame de Villiers kept calling for her son. She was imagining things because fortunately for her, her son hadn't even been on the ship.

■ Cold started to affect a lot of the survivors, and Mrs. Charlotte Collyer was so cold and numb she fell over, catching her hair in an oarlock which resulted in a good portion of it being pulled out by the roots. Most of the firemen, stokers and trimmers who had been on duty down in the boiler rooms were only wearing sleeveless shirts and short pants, and these men suffered terribly from the cold. The rest of the people in the various boats tried to help keep them warm as best they could, often giving up a portion of what little they had to help.

A crewman gave Mrs. Washington Dodge the stockings off his feet, explaining, *"I assure you, ma'am, they are perfectly clean. I just put them on this morning."*

■ Many of the women helped with the rowing or manning of the tiller, partly because they were needed and partly because it helped keep them warm. On lifeboat 8, however, Mrs. J. Stuart White appointed herself as the keeper of the light. She had a cane with a built-in light, and she waved it about all night, helping no one and confusing most. She became so animated that one of the crewmen threatened to toss the cane into the sea.

■ As the night wore on, as if there wasn't enough to concern themselves with, the survivors on most of the boats broke out in petty squabbles. Some complained about the men who smoked, Mrs. Washington Dodge complained about the people who wouldn't go back, and in lifeboat 11, *Titanic's* masseuse, Maud Slocombe threatened to toss overboard a woman who kept setting off an alarm clock.

■ Over in lifeboat 4, Major Peuchen and Quartermaster Hichens quarreled all night, Peuchen wanting to give orders and Hichens not wanting to take them. Things got so out of hand that Molly Brown finally had to step in and threaten to toss Hichens into the water if he didn't shut up. He did, wrapping himself in the boat's sail where he spent the rest of the night sulking away.

■ Passenger Millvina Dean later told of "*...another woman whose husband was left behind was only concerned that she'd lost her feather bed...she didn't say anything about her husband, just that her feather bed had gone...*"

■ One survivor remembered, "*...We sang as we rowed, all of us...and we were still singing when we saw the lights of the Carpathia. Then we stopped singing, and prayed.*

■ Throughout the night, Boxhall in lifeboat 2 kept firing his little green flares and at 2:30 a.m., ten minutes after *Titanic* slipped beneath the waves, one of these flares was seen far in the distance by the crew of *Carpathia*, speeding toward the spot where *Titanic* went down.

■ **3:00 a.m.:** Captain Rostron on *Carpathia* ordered the firing of rockets every 15 minutes to let the survivors know that help was coming.

■ **3:30 a.m.:** Someone on a lifeboat noticed a rocket from the *Carpathia* and yelled out, and on several of the other boats people saw it too: a flash of light off in the horizon followed by a distant boom. Some thought it was lightning and Hichen's thought it was a falling star, but it was enough to give everyone hope that help was on its way. Soon it could be seen: a large steamer coming up, firing rockets and showing several rows of bright lights along the side.

■ **3:35 a.m.**: *Carpathia* was at the location where *Titanic* should have been had the coordinates Boxhall worked out not been off by several miles. If afloat, *Titanic* should have been seen, but all that the crew on *Carpathia* could see were the outlines of many icebergs. Off in the distance, a small green light could be seen low in the water, so Rostron had the ship slow down and the engine room alerted for a quick stop.

■ Within a few minutes all the boats had seen the steamer. In lifeboat 3, someone put a match to a newspaper and then to Mrs. Davidson's straw hat. Boxhall in lifeboat 2 burned his last flare, and Mrs. White in lifeboat 8 waved her cane with the light in it.

■ **4:00 a.m.**: Rostron ordered the engines stopped. There was a lifeboat only 300 yards ahead showing a small green light, and Rostron didn't want to run it down. Rostron ordered "dead slow ahead" to move up to the boat and blew the ship's whistle to let the people in the boat know they had been seen. Rostron wanted to bring the lifeboat up on *Carpathia's* port side, but an iceberg was in the way, so the ship was turned and the lifeboat approached on the starboard side.

■ **4:10 a.m.**: The women on lifeboat 2 started climbing up the side of *Carpathia* with the assistance of crewman on the ship and Fourth Officer Boxhall.

Boxhall was asked to report to the bridge by Rostron, and when Boxhall arrived, soaked and shivering, he told Rostron that *Titanic* had sunk at 2:20, less than two hours before.

Shortly, most of the passengers on *Carpathia* knew what was going on, and they poured out of their cabins and lined the decks of the ship, searching in the dark for more lifeboats. Because of the dark and the fear of running down unseen lifeboats, *Carpathia* remained stationary and the lifeboats had to row to the ship until the morning became light enough to see. Then *Carpathia* slowly moved through the ice, going from boat to boat, picking up the soaked and mournful survivors.

The sad little fleet of row boats, all that remained of the world's largest and most luxurious ocean liner, slowly moved closer to *Carpathia*, their survivors now cheered by the prospect of rescue.

■ Those women who couldn't climb up the ladders were hauled up in slings and chairs while the children were brought up in ash bags.

Overloaded collapsible D draws near the *Carpathia*. *National Archives*

Lifeboat 6 approaches the side of *Carpathia*. *National Archives*

Everyone was met on the deck and taken below where they were warmed up and given food and drink.

Young Ruth Becker reported she was so cold she couldn't move. She was put into a sling and tied in because she couldn't hold on.

■ Shortly, the first light of dawn started a beautiful new day. Many commented on how the icebergs, some hundreds of feet high, looked pink and yellow in the morning sun. Seaman Joseph Scarrott later told, *"...the day was just beginning to dawn. We then saw we were surrounded with icebergs and field ice. Some of the fields of ice were from sixteen to twenty miles long..."*

Young Marshall Drew related that *"When I awoke [in the lifeboat] it was broad daylight as we approached the Carpathia. Looking around over the gunwale it seemed to me like the Arctic. Icebergs of huge size ringed the horizon for 360 degrees..."*

■ After Fifth Officer Lowe in lifeboat 14 had made his attempt to save the people in the water, he had spent the next hour rowing around from boat to boat to check on conditions, having left a little group of lifeboats, boats 4, 10, 12 tied together for mutual support.

■ Once the *Carpathia* was in sight, Lowe hoisted the sail on lifeboat 14 and set off to reach the rescue ship, later stating, *"Not all sailors are boatmen, and not all boatmen are sailors."* when asked how he knew enough to set a sail. Shortly, Lowe came up on collapsible D which was low in the water and didn't have enough crew to row. Lowe tied a rope to collapsible D and towed it along.

Then Lowe spotted the swamped collapsible A well over a mile off, looking as if it would sink at any moment. Over half the thirty people who had been on it during the night had frozen to death while standing in water half way up to their knees. Lowe sailed over to collapsible A and transferred the dozen remaining survivors, including Mrs. Rosa Abbott, to lifeboat 14. He then removed the sea plugs so the boat would sink. Left on board were the bodies of three men.

■ Over on collapsible B, Second Officer Lightoller was calling "lean to the left" and "lean to the right" every time a wave rocked the little boat, trying to keep what little air was left under it from escaping under the sides. Shortly after the sky was bright enough to see, Lightoller saw Lowe's little group of boats, and he began blowing his whistle.

■ About the time Lowe was hitching up to collapsible D, the little flotilla he had left behind was making its way toward *Carpathia* when Quartermaster Perkis in lifeboat 4 and Seaman Clinch in lifeboat 12 heard an officer's whistle blowing in the distance. They then noticed, off in the dark to the west and about half a mile away what looked like a bunch of men standing on top of one of the funnels that had broken off the *Titanic*.

Perkis and Clinch immediately untied from the other two boats and rowed over to the little group of men who, as they got closer, could be standing on top of an overturned boat. Collapsible B was really low in the water now, most of the men were almost knee deep in it. When lifeboat 4 pulled up along side, it nearly washed everyone off. Lightoller supervised the transfer, one-by-one, of all the people on his boat into lifeboats 12 and 4. Young Jack Thayer crawled into lifeboat 12 so cold and stiff that he didn't even notice his mother huddled in lifeboat 4. Lifeboat 12 was now seriously overloaded, so Lightoller took command of it and slowly steered it towards *Carpathia*.

■ The little fleet of small boats now started to converge upon *Carpathia*, some rowing toward it until daylight when *Carpathia* was able to steam toward the boats. At 4:45 a.m. lifeboat 13 tied up, and at 5:15 lifeboat 7 pulled up. One of the very few happy reunions happened when Dr. Washington Dodge got off lifeboat 7 and met his wife and son who had been on lifeboat 13.

■ **6:00 a.m.:** Lifeboat 3 pulled up along side the *Carpathia*. Miss Elizabeth Shutes recalled that she was so weak that she had to be lifted up by a sling. One of the passengers on *Carpathia* was Louis Ogden, and he was watching the activities from the deck when an old friend, Henry Sleeper Harper, climbed on board along with his wife, dog and dragoman.

■ **6:15 a.m.:** Collapsible C pulled up next to the *Carpathia* and the first person off the boat was Bruce Ismay. When asked if he wanted to go below decks for something hot to eat or drink, he replied, *"No, I don't want anything at all...If you will leave me alone, I'll be much happier here...No, wait, if you can get me in some room where I can be quiet, I wish you would."* With that, Dr. Frank McGhee, the ships senior doctor, led Ismay to his own stateroom where Ismay sequestered himself for the rest of the trip.

Ismay's self-imposed isolation certainly didn't do him any favors in the world of public opinion. It was bad enough he had gotten into a lifeboat, but now it appeared he wanted special privilege. He would be pilloried for his actions, and from this·day forward, J. Bruce Ismay was a ruined man.

■ Also climbing off this boat was William Carter who knew he had put his family on a lifeboat but didn't know which one. Carter would now stand on the deck watching each approaching boat.

■ **7:00 a.m.**: Fifth Officer Lowe brought lifeboat 14, still towing collapsible D along side, and off loaded his passengers. He then carefully put the sail and mast away so the boat could be used again, if necessary.

■ Lifeboat 4 eventually pulled up and William Carter saw his wife and daughter but not his ten-year-old son. Carter shouted down to the boat, *"Where's my boy?"* Little William Jr. looked up and replied, *"Here I am, Father."* He had been wearing a girl's hat and his father hadn't recognized him.

The Thayers, mother and son, found each other on *Carpathia*, but they would not find Mr. Thayer.

■ By 7:00 a breeze had come up and the water was getting choppy. By 8:15 all the boats had been brought alongside except lifeboat 12 which was seriously overloaded: 74 people were in a boat designed to hold 65. Slowly Rostron moved the *Carpathia* closer to the lifeboat, and at 8:30 lifeboat 12 tied up to *Carpathia* and started unloading its passengers. It was all completed by 8:45, and the last person to board *Carpathia* was Second Officer Lightoller.

Passenger Ruth Becker: *"That was the saddest time of all... so many of the women who had been put into lifeboats by their husbands—and told they would meet each other later—realized that they would never see each other again..."*

With all 20 of *Titanic's* lifeboats now accounted for, 18 having come up with passengers and collapsible B sunk and collapsible A cast adrift with three bodies on it, Rostron knew he had all the survivors he would find. *Carpathia* made a couple of swings through the area where he thought *Titanic* had gone down, but there weren't any survivors. In fact, there wasn't much of anything, just a few deck chairs and other junk and only one body.

■ Rostron counted heads and found he had 705 survivors and one body from *Titanic*, the body being that of Edvard Lindell who had been brought along from collapsible A. Within hours, three of the survivors, all men plucked out of the water, would die.

■ Rostron had to make an immediate but easy decision about where to go with his survivors. He didn't have enough supplies on his ship to continue on, so he ordered *Carpathia* turned around and made its new destination New York City. Before doing so, he ordered thirteen of *Titanic's* lifeboats be brought on board, and all but lifeboats 4, 14, 15 and collapsible's A, B, C and D were winched up and stowed. Possibly Rostron was ·

thinking that he might need them later, or that there might be some senti-mental reason for keeping them. Possibly he was thinking of the survivors, who, according to the insurance rules of the time, would only be able to collectively collect the value of any recovered material.

■ Before *Carpathia* left the scene, *Mount Temple*, answering *Titanic's* dis-tress messages, arrived. Rostron asked the captain of *Mount Temple* to con-tinue the search. Then *Carpathia* started steaming around the icefield. It would take four hours and 56 miles before she got out of the field to begin the sad trip home. One more ship came up then, snooped around a bit, then headed for Boston. This ship was the *Californian*.

■ At 4:00 p.m. Rostron had the engines on *Carpathia* stopped, and a brief service was held in the main lounge. When that was completed, Father Roger B.T. Anderson oversaw the burial-at-sea of four bodies: Edvard Lindell and the three unknown survivors who died after rescue. It was so cold and windy that most of the passengers remained inside. When the burial was over, Rostron restarted the engines and *Carpathia* started the long trip home.

CHAPTER 14

A SAD AWAKENING

On April 15th at 1:20 a.m. local time at *The New York Times* offices in New York City, a wireless message was received from the Cape Race, Newfoundland land station that read:

"...At 10:25 o'clock tonight the White Star Line steamship *Titanic* called 'CQD' to the Marconi station here, and reported having struck an iceberg. The steamer said that immediate assistance was required."

Further inquiry by the editors of the newspaper showed that several other ships, *Virginian, Baltic* and *Olympic,* had received the message and were steaming toward the site of the *Titanic.* The *Virginian,* shortly before passing out of wireless range, reported that it had received a message that had suddenly been cut off.

The morning edition of *The New York Times* ran the headline:

NEW LINER TITANIC HITS AN ICEBERG;
SINKING BY THE BOW AT MIDNIGHT;
WOMEN PUT OFF IN LIFEBOATS;
LAST WIRELESS AT 12:27 A.M. BLURRED.

■ Throughout the morning of Monday, April 15, all sorts of messages were being received in New York. The offices of the International Mercantile Marine were inundated with visitors and phone calls. Around noon a message was received from Cape Race that reported the kind of news that made everyone happy:

ALL TITANIC PASSENGERS SAFE
VIRGINIAN TOWING THE LINER INTO HALIFAX

■ The IMM New York Manager and White Star Line Vice President P.A.S. Franklin accepted this great news and arranged to have an express train readied to take family members to Halifax and then bring the passengers back to New York.

White Star then sent telegrams out to many of the families:

ALL TITANIC'S PASSENGERS SAFE
LINER BEING TOWED TO HALIFAX

■ That afternoon *The New York Times* reported in its afternoon city edition that *Titanic* had foundered with great loss of life. This headline was printed without confirmation but based upon some assumptions. Little did the editors know how right they were.

■ Around 2:00 p.m. another message from an unknown source in "mid-ocean" reported that *Carpathia* and *Parisian* were making for New York with all passengers safely transferred and *Parisian* towing the *Titanic*. Since the ships were coming to New York, the express train that was now enroute to Halifax was stopped and then ordered to New York.

On top of Wanamaker's Department Store in New York City was the most powerful radio station on the eastern seaboard, and at 4:30 p.m. on Monday, twenty-one-year old David Sarnoff went on duty. At 4:35 p.m. he received a faint signal from the *Olympic*, almost unreadable because of jamming by other stations, that said that *Titanic* had foundered at 12:47 a.m. New York time and that about 675 people, the only known survivors, were headed to New York on the *Carpathia*. It was news that stunned the world. (Sarnoff went on to become one of the biggest and well known names in radio and early television.)

■ On *Carpathia*, once the last of the survivors had been brought aboard, Rostron and Ismay met in Dr. McGhee's quarters, and Ismay gave Rostron a message to send to P.A.S. Franklin in New York, that read:

"Deeply regret advise you Titanic sank this morning after collision with iceberg, resulting in serious loss of life. Full particulars later. Bruce Ismay."

■ Harold Cottam got the message but did not send it right away. Then, Ismay drafted up another one and had it sent to Franklin, which was sent immediatly:

"Very important you should hold Cedric daylight for Titanic's crew. Answer. YAMSI."

■ What Ismay, using a poorly disguised name was trying to accomplish was to have the White Star Line ship *Cedric* held up in New York for an extra day, figuring that the surviving crewmen could be put on it immediately and sent home. This message got sent before the one that told of *Titanic's* sinking, and this also caused much confusion in New York.

■ By Monday afternoon the word was out that *Titanic* had gone down with a great loss of life. On *Carpathia*, Harold Cottam was handed a complete listing of all of the survivors and told to send the list. On top of Wanamaker's Department Store, David Sarnoff was trying to copy down the list but there was so much static and other traffic breaking in that he was having a real problem trying to get the names right. In addition, Cottam had been working for over 24 hours by now, and he was extremely fatigued.

■ Second Office Lightoller rounded up Harold Bride who was recovering from his ordeal. His feet were bandaged because of frostbite and he, too, was tired, but Bride offered to spell Cottam. For the rest of the trip, Cottam and Bride took turns processing messages and transmitting names.
    Cottam and Bride, with Rostron's approval, made an early decision that they would not acknowledge any incoming messages received from newspapers or private individuals because there was just too much to do. With 700 names to transmit and outgoing messages from the survivors, there was more than they could handle. They even refused to acknowledge a message from President William Howard Taft who was inquiring about his friend Archibald Butt.

■ With everyone screaming for information and none forthcoming, President Taft ordered the US Navy warship *Chester* to steam out to meet up with the *Carpathia*. *Chester*, with a better wireless set than *Carpathia*, was supposed to find out what was going on and then relay that information. When it arrived near the *Carpathia*, *Chester* was all but ignored. No one was going to know anything until *Carpathia* pulled into New York. Eventually, Taft ordered all wireless stations to cease transmission except *Carpathia*, *Chester* and David Sarnoff's station on top of Wanamaker's.

■ By Wednesday April 17, the names of most of the survivors were finally known as the names were sent then resent, some several times. Many of *Carpathia's* messages were forwarded on by *Olympic* to England and *Chester* to New York, so by now everyone had an idea of the scope of the disaster. *Carpathia* was now expected to arrive in New York by around 10:00 p.m. Thursday April 18.

■ While on board the *Carpathia*, the survivors organized a committee and collected $15,000 to be given to the crew of *Carpathia* on its next trip to New York City as thanks for coming to the rescue. The committee also obtained a silver loving cup that would be given to Rostron on a later trip.

Cunard Line, owner of the *Carpathia*, refused to allow the crew to accept the money, instead turning it over to charity for the survivors. White Star later tried to pay Cunard for the expenses incurred in rescuing the survivors and bringing them back to New York. Cunard refused this, too, stating that this was a humanitarian gesture. Cunard, however, did pay all the crewmen on *Carpathia* an extra month's pay for their efforts. White Star, meanwhile, stopped paying the surviving crew members the moment *Titanic* sank, and never offered them anything for their ordeal.

■ Thursday evening the 18th was cold and wet, but people started to line up near the Cunard pier at 6:00. Normal customs regulations were suspended, and the press and public was barred from the Cunard pier itself. Only immediate family were allowed onto the pier. Hundreds of New York City policemen were called out to control the crowd. By 9:00 there were more than 40,000 people in the streets around the pier waiting for the arrival of the *Carpathia*.

■ Shortly after 9:00 p.m. *Carpathia* appeared out of the dark and gloom, surrounded by a flotilla of boats of all sizes and shapes. Some were loaded with family members but most were full of reporters who were having a collective coronary as they fell over each other trying to get some information from the survivors.

There had been an injunction placed on reporters to remain away from the *Carpathia*, but some managed to bribe their way onto the pilot boat. Once the *Carpathia* slowed to allow the pilot to board, several of the newsmen tried to get on the ship but were forced back by crewmen. One did manage to get aboard, but he was prevented from talking to the survivors.

Carpathia managed to outrun most of the small boats and as the ship passed by the Statue of Liberty, rain started coming down hard with lighting and thunder accompanying the ship. Over on the Battery, 10,000 people waited in silence as *Carpathia* passed by.

■ The Cunard pier was at the foot of Fourteenth Street, and that is where another 30,000 people waited. However, instead of pulling into the Cunard pier, *Carpathia* steamed past it to the White Star Line pier at the foot of Nineteenth and Twentieth Streets. There, *Carpathia* stopped long enough to unload the thirteen lifeboats, all that remained of the *Titanic*, into the White Star dock.

Finally, at 9:30 p.m. *Carpathia* was pushed into the Cunard pier and the First Class and Second Class passengers were allowed to get off to meet the friends and family who had come to greet them.

■ Most of these passengers had arrangements made to get home, some even by private train. Mrs. Charles Hays, whose husband had been the president of the Grand Trunk Railroad, boarded a private train. Mrs. John Thayer and her son and Mrs. George Widener each had their own trains to take them back to Philadelphia. Mrs. Thayer had lost her husband and Mrs. Widener both her husband and son.

■ Many others took waiting cars to some of the hotel rooms reserved by White Star Line.

Ruth Becker later recalled that *"...Mother went shopping...and bought us clothes to wear...The hotel made us honorary guests and would take nothing for food and lodging...When we boarded the train to Indiana, Mother took me aside and said, 'Ruth, don't you dare tell anybody that we are survivors of the Titanic disaster.'...But, when we got on the train, we were showered with cookies and gifts for my little brother and sister from the passengers..."*

■ By 10:30 p.m. all the First and Second Class passengers were gone, as was most of the throng of people and all the reporters. Then, at 11:00 the Third Class passengers were let off. Most of the 174 passengers were absolutely destitute with no money, no belongings, many with no where to go. White Star Lines and several private relief organizations, including the American Red Cross, put the survivors up and helped them arrange transportation to their destination.

■ The very last–except one–to depart was *Titanic's* crew, which was placed on the Red Star Line ship *Lapland.* There they remained until they were allowed to go home.

Most of the crew was in as bad a shape as the survivors: all had lost everything and their pay ended at the moment the ship sank.

■ The last survivor to leave *Carpathia,* fifteen minutes before it was to resume its much delayed trip to the Mediterranean on Saturday, April 20, was Marconi operator Harold Bride. Bride was still working two days after the *Carpathia* docked, catching up on all the messages that hadn't been sent. Carried ashore on the shoulders of two of *Carpathia's* officers, Bride was taken to a hospital to recover from his frostbitten feet.

The iceberg, photographed by a passenger on *Carpathia*. *National Archives*

CHAPTER 15

RECOVERY OPERATIONS

During the afternoon of Monday, April 15 as the news was becoming more depressing about the lack of survivors, the White Star Line chartered the cable ship *Mackay-Bennett* out of Halifax to return to the area where *Titanic* sank and recover as many of the bodies as possible. The undertaking firm of John Snow and Company were hired to oversee the arrangements.

■ With the proper supplies on board including tons of ice, tools, 100 coffins, an all-volunteer crew who was being paid double, *Mackay-Bennett* steamed out of Halifax at noon on Wednesday, April 17, a day before *Carpathia* docked in New York.

■ Once the word was out to all of the ships crossing the Atlantic that *Titanic* had sank, most of the other steamship captains steamed many miles out of the way to avoid the wreckage in order not to distress their own passengers.

One ship, the *Bremen*, actually steamed through the wreckage and the crew sighted more that 100 bodies.

One of the Bremen's passengers, Mrs. Johanna Stunke, told reporters later, *"We saw the body of one woman dressed only in her night dress, and clasping a baby to her breast. Close by was the body of another woman with her arms tightly clasped around a shaggy dog... We saw the bodies of three men in a group, all clinging to a chair. Floating by just beyond them were the bodies of a dozen men, all wearing lifebelts and clinging desperately together..."*

■ At 8:00 p.m. on Saturday, April 20, *Mackay-Bennett* arrived on the scene and the recovery operation began the next morning.

Fifty-one bodies were recovered the first morning. All valuables were removed and a complete description of body was made. However, many of the bodies were in bad shape after having been in the water for over a week.

That night 24 bodies, almost all of crewmen and none identifiable, were placed in canvas bags and weighted down with iron grates. The rest were embalmed for their return to Halifax. There was a brief service which Engineer Frederick Hamilton described in his dairy that night:

For nearly an hour the words 'For as much as it hath pleased. . . we commit this body to the deep' are repeated and at each interval there comes, splash! as the weighted body plunges into the sea, there to sink to a depth of about two miles. Splash, splash, splash.

■ The fourth body brought on board was an unidentified child about two years old. He was the only child ever recovered, and he is buried in Halifax.

■ John Jacob Astor's body was found, smashed to a pulp and covered with soot. He was identified by his monogrammed clothing, watch and diamond cufflinks.

■ As bodies were identified—many by the clothing they wore or items in their pockets—their names were sent back to shore via wireless. The rest would await identification back in Halifax.

While the *Mackay-Bennett* was picking up bodies, reports kept coming in from all over by ships finding bodies, wreckage and more icebergs. Virtually anything that could float off *Titanic* was found in the next couple of weeks.

■ On April 21st the captain wired for help and on the 22nd the ship *Minia* left Halifax with more coffins and supplies. By the end of April 23rd, there were 80 bodies on *Mackay-Bennett*. The next day 87 more were found. *Minia* arrived on the 26th.

■ On the afternoon of the 26th, *Mackay-Bennett* started for Halifax. She had recovered 306 bodies and had returned 116 of them to the sea. Of the remaining, 100 were in coffins and the rest were placed in canvas bags. Class structure was maintained. The remains of crew members were stored on the open deck and iced down with no embalming or preparations made. Second and Third Class passengers were placed in canvas bags and for the most part unidentified. First Class passengers were embalmed and placed in coffins, and most of them were identified.

■ *Minia* was only able to recover 15 bodies before bad weather set in. One of those was of Charles M. Hays. Most of the rest of the bodies drifted into the Gulf Stream and were lost forever.

■ Upon the return of the *Mackay-Bennett* to Halifax, the 190 bodies were unloaded at the coaling wharf. Sailors and police managed to keep the curious away except for one photographer. He had his camera confiscated.

■ In Halifax, a curling rink was set up as a morgue and the rest of the bodies were embalmed. They were arranged in cubicles so family or friends could come in to try to identify them. The bodies were kept for two weeks and Death Certificates prepared. Cause of death on each one was "Accidental Drowning, SS Titanic, at sea." Technically, "Accidental Drowning" was not correct: most of those who died in the water froze to death.

Those not taken away for burial were buried at one of three cemeteries in Halifax based upon either their known or assumed religion. There were mistakes. "Mr. Hoffman", the real Michel Navratil, was not claimed by his wife and although Catholic, he is buried in the Jewish cemetery.

■ Much of the town turned out for the burial of the small boy and hundreds wanted to take responsibility for his burial, but in the end the crew of the *Mackay-Bennett* asked for and was given the honor. They paid for a marker for the child with the inscription:

Erected to the Memory of an Unknown Child Whose Remains Were Recovered after the Disaster to the Titanic, April 15, 1912.

■ Throughout the weeks, four more bodies were found by another recovery ship, the *Montmagny* and on May 14 *Algerine* found another.

Finally, in late May, the *Oceanic*, enroute to New York, came upon collapsible A still floating with the three bodies left behind by Lowe when he rescued the survivors off it. *Oceanic* picked up the bodies and the boat and took them all back to New York.

■ In all, 328 bodies were recovered, 119 of which were buried at sea. Of the 209 returned to Halifax, 59 were removed by family members and the remaining 150 were buried in Halifax. Of these, 128 were never identified and they are buried under numbered headstones with room left for a name if they are ever identified.

CHAPTER 16

LORD OF THE CALIFORNIAN

When wireless operator Cyril Evans on the Leyland Line steamship *Californian* shut down his wireless at 11:35 p.m. on April 14, he went to bed without rewinding the detector, a mechanical device which allowed incoming messages to be received. Evans figured he would rewind it in the morning, something he usually did. Five minutes later, *Titanic* struck the iceberg. Twenty-five minutes later at 12:05 a.m., Marconi operator Jack Phillips on *Titanic* sent his first CQD message calling for assistance. Cyril Evans was, by this time, asleep.

The story of what did and did not transpire on board the *Californian* during the next few hours is one of those great stories of missed opportunities. It brought out some of the most obvious omissions in the rules of the sea: unmanned wireless systems, distress rockets being ignored, subordinates unwilling to take a risk, a ship's captain who ignored the warnings and who was also unwilling to get out of bed. All of these things happened, yet, when we put these events into the context of the society and laws of the time, Lord and his crew did not do anything wrong.

■ **10:20 p.m.**: Captain Lord ordered the engines reversed and let *Californian* drift to a stop just short of a large ice field. The ship was surrounded by icebergs. Lord checked and logged the position of *Californian* as 42° 5' N, 50° 7' W. The ship was pointed north-east.

■ **10:30 p.m.**: Lord saw what looked like a steamer coming up from the east, but Third Officer Charles V. Groves thought it was just a star.

■ **10:45 p.m.**: Lord pointed out the light, which now appeared to be a steamer coming up from the south and the east, to his chief engineer.

Captain Stanley Lord of the *Californian.*
Washington Evening Star

Wireless Operator Cyril Evans. *New York American*

The *Californian.*

The *Californian.*

■ **10:55 p.m.:** Lord asked Cyril Evans if he knew of any other ships in the vicinity. When Evans replied that *Titanic* was the only ship around, Lord told him that the ship he had seen wasn't *Titanic*. However, Lord told Evans to contact *Titanic* and tell them about the ice. Evans' message is the one that Jack Phillips broke into, telling him to, *"Keep out! Shut up! You're jamming my signal. I'm working Cape Race."*

■ **11:30 p.m.:** The other ship was much larger and closer now, and Lord could see the starboard green marker light. He estimated that the ship was only five miles away. Lord asked Groves to watch the ship, and then Lord left the bridge. Groves thought the ship was about the same size as the *Californian*. Also, it looked as if it had masts: in other words, a sailing vessel, possibly steam powered.

■ **11:35 p.m.:** Evans shut down the wireless and went to bed.

■ **12:00 a.m.:** Lord decided to retire and told his replacement, Second Officer Herbert Stone, to notify him if the other ship, directly off the starboard side of the *Californian*, came any closer. Although not underway, the bow of the *Californian* was now swinging with the current, and the ship was facing almost due east. This put the other ship due south of the *Californian*.

■ **12:10 a.m.:** Fireman Ernest Gill, on deck after his 8-midnight watch below, saw the lights of a large steamer off the starboard side and about 10 miles away, he thought. Gill went down to his bunk and told his mate that the ship was going full speed.

■ **12:15 a.m.:** Groves, now off duty, decided to stop by the wireless room to listen in on some of the messages. He wore the headphones for awhile, heard nothing, and then left. Groves did not know that Evans had not rewound the detector. During the fifteen minutes between 12:15 and 12:30 Jack Phillips on *Titanic* sent a total of 10 distress messages.

■ **12.30 a.m.:** Gill went back up on the deck for a cigarette. About ten minutes later, he saw a white rocket off the starboard side, about ten miles away. Thinking it was a shooting star, he waited for awhile and less than 10 minutes later he saw another one, this time a rocket for sure. Later Gill reported, *"It was not my business to notify the bridge...I turned in immediately after."* He did not hear a rocket explode or any escaping steam, either.

When Second Officer Stone reported to the bridge, he too saw the steamer. Told to watch its actions by Lord, Stone kept an eye on it and noticed eventually that it's red port side light was showing, which means it was also facing east, the direction in which it had come. It had turned around.

■ **12.35 a.m.:** Lord checked with the bridge to see if the other ship had moved. Stone reported that it had not and that several attempts to reach it via Morse had failed.

■ **12:45 a.m.:** Stone reported a flash in the sky directly over the other ship. He too thought it was a shooting star. Then, a few minutes later he saw another flash. These were the same flashes Gill had seen. Within the next fifteen minutes, Stone saw three more flashes. It appeared to Stone that there was another ship between *Californian* and the ship firing the rockets.

■ **1:15 a.m.:** Stone notified Captain Lord, down in his cabin, of the signal rockets he had seen. Asked if they were private signals, Stone told Lord he didn't know, only that they were white. Lord ordered Stone to keep signaling and *"...when you get an answer let me know..."* Stone continued to signal and Lord went back to bed.

■ **1:50 a.m.** By now Stone had seen eight rockets, the last one about 1:25 a.m. *Carpathia* was now facing almost west-south-west and the other ship, still stationary, was to the south-west, still with its port side red light showing.

■ **2:00 a.m.:** The other ship started to steam away to the south-west, the red light disappeared and soon all that was visible was the stern light. (Could it be that the ship he was watching actually was sinking, and the light was the stern light just before the power failed?)

Stone then sent Apprentice James Gibson down to tell Lord that the other ship was leaving. Gibson later reported that he woke Lord, told him the ship was leaving and told him of the eight rockets. Lord then asked, *"Are you sure there were no colors in them?"* Gibson returned to the bridge and Lord went back to sleep. Stone didn't go down to see Lord because he couldn't leave the bridge and, besides, Lord was known as a very stern captain and it was better to send the new guy down to wake up Lord then to do it himself.

Lord would later relate that he didn't remember the conversation although he did remember Gibson coming into his cabin.

■ **4:30 a.m.:** Lord was awakened by the officer of the watch, Chief Officer G.V. Stewart. It was still dark out.

■ **5:15 a.m.:** It was getting light now, and Stewart saw a four-masted ship off to the south-west. Concerned that it might be in trouble, he told Lord that Stone said he had seen the ship fire rockets during the night. Lord had finally decided that it was safe to navigate through the ice field to the west, and he had Evans awakened to check with the ship to find out if it needed any help.

■ **5:20 a.m.:** Evans rewound the detector, turned on his set, sent a request for someone to wireless back that his transmitter was working. He immediately received a message from *Virginian* reporting that *Titanic* had sank during the night and its position at the time of the sinking. The message was given to Lord who calculated that the *Californian* was about 19 miles away from where the *Titanic* went down. Lord ordered his ship to steam through the ice field then turn south toward the disaster site. Once through the ice, *Californian* steamed at full speed, 13.5 knots.

■ **7:30 a.m.:** *Californian* passed *Mount Temple* which was stopped in the area that *Titanic* had said it struck the iceberg. There wasn't any wreckage. *Californian* continued south, passed another ship that didn't have a wireless, and then sighted the *Carpathia* on the east, or far side of the ice field. After confirming that *Carpathia* was picking up survivors (the last lifeboat was picked up at 8:50), Lord passed back through the icefield and pulled up along side just as *Carpathia* began it's trip to New York.

■ After looking for survivors for a few hours, Lord ordered *Californian* underway for Boston.

■ On the face of it, it doesn't look like Captain Lord or his crew did anything wrong. At least, that is what Lord would always say. And he might be right. There were three major things that transpired that his detractors used against him, and Lord had an answer for each:

1) The wireless system was shut down for the night. This is correct, and it's also not an issue. Only a very few ships, large ones such as *Titanic* and *Olympic*, had more than one wireless operator. There were no US or international laws that required more, especially since the purpose of the wireless was for the use of the passengers. With only one operator, there were going to be times when the system wasn't working. The fact that Evans went to sleep or that he didn't rewind the detector does not have any bearing on this issue. He was following the accepted procedures of the time.

2) Neither Lord or the rest of the officers responded to the rockets fired by the crew of *Titanic*. This is also true, and Lord could argue this position too. Many ships in 1912 weren't equipped with wireless and the usual method of communications between them at night, as had been the case for well over 100 years, was by the use of rockets. Especially white rockets. In fact, the British Board of Trade regulations in effect at the time stipulated that whaling vessels, which often worked in fleets, were to use white rockets to communicate. Why white? Because intra-company communications (such as from one White Star Line ship to another White Star Line ship) were supposed to use colored rockets to communicate. There were no BOT regulations that rockets were to be used to signal distress. Also, *Californian* was in a known whaling area and had seen several whaling vessels the day before. The white rockets could very well have been whaling ships communicating with each other.

3) Lord slept through the night while *Titanic* sank a few miles away. So the guy was tired. His ship was stopped by an icefield, he had a competent set of officers on watch and the only other ship in the vicinity appeared to be stopped by the icefield too. It was all rather routine.

■ Books have been written about whether Lord was incompetent or in any way responsible for the great loss of life by not coming to the aid of *Titanic*. Some of the issues that have been brought up are:

1) There is much speculation about how far apart the two ships were (it varies from five to 25 miles) and whether they could even see each other. Without a pair of binoculars, from the bridge of *Californian* the officers could only see an object about eight miles distant at water level, but a ship the size of *Titanic* could have been seen about 15 miles distant. Based upon *Californian's* reported and logged position and that of Boxhall's reported position, the two ships would have been almost 20 miles apart with a great deal of ice between them, some of the icebergs being over 200 feet high. There is also evidence that *Titanic* was almost six miles further away from *Californian* because Boxhall's reported position was almost surely wrong. At 25 plus miles, the two ships would have been out of sight of each other.

2) There has always been speculation that another ship was actually between the *Californian* and the *Titanic* and that this may be the ship that the officers on both vessels actually saw. There is good evidence that there was another vessel, the Norwegian sealing ship *Sampson*. This ship, much smaller than *Californian*, was known to be in the area and it didn't have a wireless set. It was also a three masted sailing ship with a steam engine, which matches what both Second Officer Lightoller on *Titanic* and Third Officer Groves on *Californian* thought they saw in the distance.

Lightoller and Boxhall reported that they had seen a ship, a four masted sailing ship, come toward them about five miles away (they could see both the red port and green starboard lights) then saw the ship turn to port and finally reverse course.

There are enough similarities between what the crew of the two ships saw to believe that another ship, probably the *Sampson,* was between them that night. Also, the First Officer of the *Sampson* made a confidential report to the Norwegian government that the ship was close enough to *Titanic* to see its lights and the distress rockets. However, this report wasn't released until 1962.

So, if the *Sampson* was close enough to see the rockets and the lights, it had to have been between *Titanic* and *Californian,* but it didn't do anything either. Why not? *Sampson* was illegally hunting seals and already had a good catch. The captain of the ship was concerned that he would get caught, and he thought that the rockets were being fired to signal his position to another ship that might try to apprehend him. So *Sampson* left the area, weaving in and out of the ice until morning when Lord saw it nearby, heading east.

■ No one will ever solve the riddle about *Californian* and whether it was in a position to help the survivors of *Titanic.* It is known that even in the daylight, it took Lord well over two hours to get to the site of *Carpathia.* Whether the trip could have been made in the dark in time to save anyone in the water is doubtful.

■ Should Stanley Lord have been accused of criminal neglect or gross negligence? Probably not. Maybe he should have been more concerned about what was going on with the rockets, but rockets weren't unusual. To say he knowingly failed to go to the aid of *Titanic* isn't fair. Did Lord have a lapse in judgment? Probably. Could *Californian* done anything to save some of the people on *Titanic?* Doubtful. Should Lord have been made the scapegoat for the disaster, been vilified by the press and public? No.

■ The sinking of *Titanic* was a huge disaster and there needed to be a another live scapegoat besides Ismay. Stanley Lord happened to be in the wrong place at the wrong time.

"...the collision...was due to excessive speed..."

CHAPTER 17

AFTERMATH

At noon, April 10, 1912 the RMS *Titanic* departed Southampton, England bound for New York City with 2,234 people on board. Five days later, 705 of them were survivors on the Cunard Steamer *Carpathia*. The remaining 1,529 had died, either of drowning or freezing to death in the cold North Atlantic Ocean.

Following is a breakdown of the losses by class and gender:

	MEN		WOMEN		CHILDREN	
	SAVED	LOST	SAVED	LOST	SAVED	LOST
FIRST	57	127	141	4	7	1
SECOND	14	154	79	15	23	0
THIRD	75	395	76	95	26	54
CREW	189	681	18	3		
TOTAL	335	1357	314	117	56	55

THE AMERICAN HEARINGS

■ Although news of the disaster was known fairly quickly in both the United States and England, it was two days before confirmation of the extent of it was received by White Star Line and thus the rest of the world. Ismay's message to P.A.S. Franklin, drafted the morning of April 15, wasn't sent by Harold Cottam until the afternoon of the 17th.

■ It didn't take long for the United States Senate to respond to the tragedy.

Early on the morning of Wednesday, April 17, United States Senator William Alden Smith of Michigan, by now having guessed the extent of the disaster, managed to get President William Howard Taft to appoint him as the head of a Senate committee to study the disaster.

Smith had his committee picked and managed to be in New York City in time to meet the *Carpathia* when it arrived on Thursday night. Armed with enough official paperwork to hold all the crewmen as well as the ship's officers and Bruce Ismay in New York, Smith set to work to find out what happened. The American inquiry began the day after *Carpathia* arrived in New York, and Bruce Ismay was the first person called as a witness.

Smith was not necessarily trying to find out what happened and why it happened. He was more concerned about who was going to pay damages to the survivors and the families of the lost. Smith's arch-enemy was J.P. Morgan. If Smith could establish negligence on the part of White Star Line, then he would win the right for the survivors and families to sue Morgan for damages.

■ In 1898 a law called the Harter Act was passed which allowed individual passengers to sue for damages if it could be established that a steamship company knew of any negligence before an incident but had not acted to address the negligence. Otherwise, under international law, if negligence could not be established, the passengers could only claim a portion of the material that had been salvaged from the wreck: in other words, the only value left of the *Titanic* were the 13 lifeboats that Rostron had brought to New York.

The Harter Act only applied to American owned ships, which is why the whole relationship between the International Mercantile Marine, White Star Line and *Titanic* was important. Although manned with a British crew and built in Ireland, *Titanic* was *owned* by an American company and was *enroute* to an American port.

■ The Senate hearings lasted 17 days, (things happened quickly in those days) starting in New York City on April 17 and ending in Washington DC on May 25. The testimony totaled 1,145 pages. A total of 82 witnesses were called, including 53 British subjects and 29 American residents. In addition to Ismay, the surviving ship's officers and the two Marconi operators Cottam and Bride, 29 crew members were called. The detained crew members were actually prevented from returning home to England when the rest of the crew departed on *Lapland* on Saturday, April 20 and they did not get to leave for a few more days.

Smith and his committee, in spite of a total lack of knowledge of things related to ships and the sea, managed to conduct a fairly comprehensive investigation. Many newspapers and even his peers called Smith a moron and worse because of his lack of knowledge, but in the end the committee identified several things that went wrong and needed changing. The committee didn't agree, however, that anyone at IMM, White Star Line or Bruce Ismay could be held at fault for the disaster.

■ William Alden Smith presented his findings to the entire United States Senate on May 28 and called for three resolutions:

1) To present a medal to Captain Rostron from President Taft on behalf of the people of the United States.
2) To examine and re-evaluate all maritime legislation.
3) To investigate the laws and regulations concerning construction and operation of all ocean going ships.

■ The outcome of the American inquiry resulted in great praise for Rostron and his crew on *Carpathia* while Captain Lord of the *Californian* was thoroughly condemned. More importantly, laws were passed to override the British Board of Trade's lifeboat requirements so that now all ships would have to meet the following requirements: carry enough lifeboats to hold all passengers and crew; be equipped with survival material for all people on board; insure all lifeboats have adequate manning and trained crews; hold a lifeboat drill for each person on each voyage. (Even then, some of the British newspapers complained about the restrictions, but there was no avoiding the reality that if a ship intended to enter an American port, it had to abide by American laws.)

Additionally, all ships that carried passengers would have to be equipped with a wireless system, the crew who manned them could not favor the transmission of one company over another and the wireless would have to be manned 24 hours per day.

THE BRITISH HEARINGS

■ The British government had its own set of hearings. While the American hearings were designed more to determine *who* was at fault, the British hearings were geared more to *why* and *how* the disaster to *Titanic* happened. The British inquiry was called the Mersey Commission because it was headed up by Lord Mersey.

When *Lapland* arrived in England, the remaining *Titanic* crew was immediately detained and each member interviewed before being allowed to leave. Although most were interviewed and released the day they arrived in England, many had to wait overnight before they were interview and released.

The Mersey Committee hearings started on April 30 and ended on July 30. Dozens of people were questioned and the 25,600 questions filled 960 pages of text. *Olympic* was used to simulate tests, and huge models of *Titanic* were built as props. Other than Bruce Ismay, only two civilians were called to testify: Sir Cosmo and Lady Duff Gordon were asked to explain their actions that night in not going back to pick up people in a boat only one quarter full and if they had paid off the crew of the boat not to go back.

The Mersey commission found fault:

"...the collision...was due to excessive speed...that a proper watch was not kept...that the ships boats were properly lowered but insufficiently manned; that the Leyland liner Californian might have reached Titanic if she had attempted to do so...and that there had been no discrimination against third class passengers in the saving of life."

■ The majority of the 684 crew members lost were from Southampton, so when the remaining 160 Southampton survivors arrived there in two groups over two days, over 50,000 people met them at the train station when they arrived. Hundreds of families and entire city blocks had lost their principle wage earner. For months and years local charities would be aiding families who were now destitute.

COMPENSATION

■ Because of the Merchant Shipping Act of 1894, White Star Line was held liable for all freight losses, about $600,000, most of which was covered by insurance.

■ Claims by Americans for loss of life and property were in the millions of dollars, the smallest being the United States Postal Service for $41.00. The largest property claim was filed by Mrs. Charlotte Cardeza for her lost luggage to the value of $177,352.74. The largest claim for loss of life was filed by Mrs. Henry B. Harris for $1,000,000.

Because American law limited compensation for losses to the salvage value of the ship (the thirteen lifeboats), the owners of *Titanic* filed suit in American courts to limit the liability to American law. The only other requirement, by law, was to compensate the families of passengers who *did not survive* for the cost of the tickets they had purchased. Survivors wouldn't be paid anything because, well, they survived and they did finish their trip.

■ The sum of the liability under American law was $97,772.02 and the claims filed were worth $16,804,112. Because British law allowed claimants to gain more in a lawsuit, eventually most of the lawsuits were transferred to Britain.

■ In 1916, four years after the disaster, the courts finally settled all the lawsuits: a total of $663,000 was divided among all claimants.

HERO'S AND VILLAIN'S

Every man and woman who stepped back and gave a seat to someone else was a hero in this story, although probably none of them would have considered themselves a hero. By the standards of the early 20th Century, that is what people did. Women and children first. Probably in today's society it would not be that way.

There were other heroes too: the engineering staff that remained at their job deep inside the ship to the very end to keep the lights burning; the Marconi operators who worked up to three minutes before the ship went down. Even the people in the lifeboats were heroes in their own right.

■ The true hero of this story is Captain Arthur H. Rostron of *Carpathia*. He was honored as such by both the American and British governments and by the public as a whole. Medals, loving cups and all sorts of gadgets would be handed to him, and for the rest of his life he would be known as Rostron of the *Carpathia*.

■ There were villains in this story, too: White Star Line, the International Mercantile Marine, Harland & Wolff—all for not building a sound ship or for not putting on enough lifeboats.

J. Bruce Ismay would return to England as a hero of all things because the British public thought he had been treated badly by the American press and public. Ismay was a ruined man, however, and he would spend most of the rest of his life in seclusion.

■ The true villain in the *Titanic* disaster, according to both the American and British governments, to the newspapers and the citizens of both countries, was Captain Stanley Lord of the *Californian*, the one ship that everybody thought was close enough to save most of the victims and did nothing.

■ The real villain, however, was complacency. It was the Guilded Age, the end of the Victorian Era, the climax of the industrial revolution. Man could build anything now, and nothing man or nature could devise could destroy what man could build. The largest, most luxurious ship ever built didn't need enough lifeboats to accommodate every person on board because this ship couldn't sink. The lifeboats were needed only to save people on other ships who were in danger. Wireless operators worked for the passengers first and the ship second. They weren't needed for the safe navigation of the ship.

The *Titanic* disaster marked the end of an era. Suddenly people weren't so sure anymore. Maybe Nature could control man, and maybe man didn't have all the answers. Things seemed to be out of control, out of balance. And in two years, the entire world would be at war.

THE FUTURE

■ Even before *Carpathia* reached New York, it suddenly occurred to everyone that there was, in fact, room on all of the liners to put enough lifeboats for everyone on board. When *Olympic* next steamed out of Southampton, it was carrying 64 of them.

■ Within a year, *Olympic* would go back to Harland and Wolff's Belfast shipyard for complete upgrading. The double bottom would now extend above the waterline and the watertight bulkheads would go all the way to C deck, the first open deck. A ship-wide signaling system would be installed.

■ *Titanic's* other sister ship, *Gigantic*, would undergo similar upgrades, and its name was changed to *Britannic*.

■ In the United States, a new North Atlantic ice patrol was established.

■ In May, 1940 Sir Winston Churchill put out a call for every available boat, yacht and skiff on the south coast of England to make their way to the coast of France to extract the British and French Army from Dunkirk. One 58-foot private boat in particular, manned by a three man crew, set out to help.

Never having had more than 21 people on it, the owner and his crew decided to do their part to save their country at a time of its greatest peril.

It made the trip and when it returned to England, the little boat disgorged 130 British soldiers who had been crammed into every nook and cranny. This time, 66 year old retired Second Officer Charles Herbert Lightoller wasn't going to be accused of not filling up a lifeboat.

■ Colonel Archibald Gracie's health failed to recover and he didn't survive a year. He wrote a small book titled *The Truth About the Titanic* in late 1912 and died shortly thereafter.

■ Sir Cosmo Duff Gordon was never convicted of having done anything wrong and he was exonerated by his government. Not being one to squabble with the newspapers, he never answered any of the questions he was asked. His trip on *Titanic* was a mixture of bad luck and even worse taste. He died in 1931.

■ Lady Lucile Duff Gordon died in 1935, always defending her husband's actions. Her fashion business died along with the millions who died in the trenches during World War I.
■ Lawrence Beesley also wrote a book, published in 1912 titled *The Loss of the S. S. Titanic: Its Story and Its Lessons.* He would live until 1967.

■ Helen Churchill Candee would become a well known author and world traveler. She lived to be 90 years old.

■ "Winnie" Troutt beat out Mrs. Candee. She died in 1984 at the age of 100.

■ None of the surviving *Titanic* officers was ever given command of his own ship. Lightoller retired in the mid-1920's and died in 1952. Fifth Officer Lowe died in 1944 after having served in the Royal Navy during World War I. Third Officer Pitman remained at sea for many years and died in 1961.
Fourth Officer Boxhall defended until his death the position he had worked out for *Titanic* the night it sank, not that being off a few miles would have made much difference. When he died in 1963, his ashes were scattered over the spot where *Titanic* sank.

■ Jack Thayer became the Vice-president of the University of Pennsylvania. He took his own life in 1945 when he was 50 years old.

■ J. Bruce Ismay would forever be called a coward by most people although some of the British public were dismayed by the way he was treated in the United State Senate hearings. Within a year he had to resign as Chairman White Star Line. This was followed shortly after by his resignation from the IMM. Although the public felt there was a moral obligation to go down with his ship, to do so would have just added another name to the casualty list. Ismay died in 1937.

■ Stanley Lord, Captain of the *Californian,* spent the rest of his life defending his actions that night. He soon lost his job with the Leyland Line and ended up taking smaller commands for the remainder of his life. His career effectively ended with the *Titanic.* Lord died in 1962, and to this day his family is still trying to get his name cleared.

■ Arthur H. Rostron, in turn, had done the right thing and that night made his career. Eventually he was given command of *Mauretania* and remained there until 1926. He was then made Commodore of the Cunard Line and retired in 1931. Rostron died in 1940.

■ A good number of the women survivors, many who lived into the 1970's and beyond, found they could never talk about their experiences without crying and several wouldn't talk about the *Titanic* at all.

■ In Cherbourg, France, the tender *Traffic* was scuttled in 1940 before German troops occupied the port. Raised and used by the German Navy, it was sunk by the Royal Navy in 1941.

■ The other Cherbourg tender, *Nomadic* was a floating restaurant in the River Seine in Paris near the Eiffel Tower. It was still in use in the late 1990's.

■ *Olympic* had a distinguished career before it was scrapped in 1935. Among other actions, it rammed and sank a German U-boat during World War I.

■ *Britannic,* once named *Gigantic* and then renamed before it was completed, was launched in April 1914, two years after *Titanic* sank. Immediately pressed into wartime service, *Britannic* became a hospital ship. In September 1916, it struck a mine in the Aegean Sea and sank in less than an hour. There were plenty of lifeboats this time and warm water. Only 38 people were lost, most during the initial explosion.

■ Sufficient lifeboats weren't always going to be the answer though. In 1915 the RMS *Lusitania* was torpedoed by a German U-boat in the waters off Queenstown, Ireland. *Lusitania* sank in 18 minutes and claimed the lives of over 1,200 people. There were ample lifeboats, there just wasn't time to launch them.

■ The *Californian* was torpedoed and sunk by a German U-boat in 1917 and the *Carpathia* in 1918.

"...keep one's hands on the whitewash brush."

CHAPTER 18

A FEW MORE FACTS...

■ The iceberg *Titanic* struck was photographed by several people on *Carpathia* and other ships. Although there were dozens of large of icebergs in the vicinity, this one was identifiable because of the black and red paint smeared along its side.

■ All 35 engineers remained at their stations and died there. King George V later decreed that all British marine engineers wear the insignia of their rank next to a royal purple background to remember their brave colleagues on *Titanic*.

■ First Officer William Murdoch's decision to order Quartermaster Hichens to turn the ship "hard-a-starboard," was probably the wrong one. Had *Titanic* rammed the iceberg head-on, the first four compartments probably would have been crushed and some of the people in the bow may have died, but the ship would have remained afloat long enough for rescue ships to come to the aid of the surviving passengers and crew.

■ Although most people were impressed with the size of *Titanic*, some felt is was too big and carried too many people.

■ The unknown child, mentioned in an earlier chapter, who was re-covered and buried in Halifax, was later tentatively identified as Gosta Paulson. Gosta had been traveling with his mother and two siblings. As it turns out, he was buried as an unknown in a grave only a few feet from his mother. Neither of his siblings survived.

■ Bagpiper Eugene Daly's brother and sister were with him on *Titanic*, and both survived.

■ None of the nine-man Harland & Wolff Guarantee Group survived the sinking.

■ The British Postal Service assigned the number "7" to *Titanic*. The number was handstamped on all correspondence handled on the ship. After the disaster, the number was officially retired.

■ Some of the surviving British crewmen who were awaiting transportation back to England were invited to work behind the counter of the Woolworth store in New York, and they were allowed to keep all the money they collected from sales.

■ On April 15, within hours after *Titanic* sank, there was an eclipse of the sun visible throughout most of Canada.

■ First Officer Murdoch was engaged to be married and the wedding was scheduled one week after *Titanic* was supposed to complete her maiden voyage. Murdoch's fiancé lived another 58 years and never married.

■ Reported as lost on *Titanic* was a fireman named Thomas Hart. His mother was officially notified of his death. On May 8, Hart walked into his mother's house. He had lost his identification papers in a bar and was too embarrassed to return home. Whoever took Hart's papers used them to secure a job on *Titanic* and was lost. The imposter has never been identified.

■ Captain Stanley Lord apparently gave little thought to the *Titanic* disaster until 1958, when the movie *A Night to Remember* portrayed Lord and the *Californian* as having been close enough to help but having done nothing. In 1959, Lord entered the office of the British Mercantile Marine Service Association and announced, *"I'm Lord of the Californian."* Initially, no one knew what he was talking about. Lord spent the remaining three years of his life trying to get a new hearing to clear his name.

■ Passenger William Stead, who told his dinner companions about the Egyptian mummy with the curse that had killed everyone who came into contact with it, died that night. The story holds that the mummy was actually on *Titanic* and its curse is what caused the ship to sink. There was no mummy on the ship, but the story is making the rounds on the internet.

■ What really happened to Captain Edward J. Smith? Several accounts by survivors placed him on the port side of the bridge shortly before a wave washed over it. If so, he may have been crushed when the forward funnel tumbled over, killing several people in the water including John Jacob Astor.

There are about a dozen different stories about Smith's last moments, including one in which he supposedly swam to a lifeboat with a small baby in his arms, handed it to the passengers in the boat, and swam away to his death. Since all the surviving babies were accounted for by those who saved them, this story is untrue.

■ Second Officer Lightoller once said of the British hearings, *"In Washington it was of little consequence, but in London it was very necessary to keep one's hands on the whitewash brush."*

■ Steward P. Keene reported, *"...One of the engineers got horribly jammed when the doors in the bulkheads were closed. His injuries were terrible, and, as there was no chance of releasing him, he implored that he might be shot to be put out of his misery. This, I have been told, was done..."*

Most likely Steward Keene's story is not true, at least the portion about putting the victim out of his misery. Other than the guns carried by the ship's officers, no others are known to have been carried on board. Also, no one ever stepped forward to confirm the story.

■ There was a rumor that workers were actually trapped inside the hull during construction because of the speed in which the ship was built. Some thought this spelled doom for the ship. The story is false.

■ The hull number for *Titanic*, assigned by the British government, was 390904. When some of the working-class Catholic employees in Belfast saw this in a mirror image, they saw the words "NO POPE." This was enough for them to stop construction. Management had to assure the workers that the number was just a coincidence. However, some felt this also spelled doom for the ship.

■ Did one of the officers shoot himself? Several survivors testified that they saw one of the officers put a revolver to his head and shoot himself shortly before the ship sank. No one could agree about who it was, if in fact it did happen.

If one of the officers did shoot himself, who could it have been? Since Lightoller, Boxhall, Lowe and Pitman survived, that leaves Captain Smith, Chief Officer Wilde, First Officer Murdoch, Sixth Officer Moody and Purser McElroy.

Smith didn't have a pistol and there are no accounts that Moody was issued one that night. Many accounts have speculated that Murdoch took his own life because he felt responsible for the collision as he was the watch officer at the time, but it seems that everyone who knew Murdoch felt he would not have taken his own life. Purser McElroy was seen in the water by three survivors. That leaves Wilde as the only other known person who had a pistol that night.

Little is known about Wilde. Few of the survivors knew who he was and for the most part, the surviving officers didn't remember seeing him after they started launching the lifeboats. So, if one of the officers did shoot himself, it seems it would have been either Murdoch or Wilde, but it will never be known for sure.

■ The name "Titanic" was sanded off the thirteen surviving lifeboats on Friday, April 19. The following day the boats were hoisted up to the second floor of a warehouse and stored, later to be joined by collapsible A. Eventually, the total value of the lifeboats was set at $4,520. In time, they were moved and then lost to history. Probably they were placed upon another White Star Line ship.

■ It seems that Sir Cosmo and Lady Lucy Duff Gordon just couldn't do anything right. The day after they were rescued by the *Carpathia*, the Duff Gordons arranged to have a photograph taken of them and the ten other survivors on lifeboat 1, all sporting big smiles. Considered tacky at best, the photograph added fuel to subsequent stories circulating about Sir Cosmo having paid off the crew to not go back and pick up survivors.

■ In 1898, 14 years before the *Titanic* sank and nine years before the ship's design was even conceived, author Morgan Robertson published a book called *Futility*. It was a story about a huge passenger liner that met disaster after a collision with an iceberg on its maiden voyage.

The name of the fictitious ship in *Futility* was *Titan*. All the dimensions of the *Titan* were spelled out in the book. Notice the similarities:

	Titan	*Titanic*
Length	800 feet	882.5 feet
Top Speed	25 knots	25 knots
Number of passengers	2,000	2,200
Registered	British	British
Displacement	70,000 tons	66,000 tons
Propellers	3	3
Lifeboats	24	20
Watertight bulkheads	19	15
Time of voyage	April	April
Side striking the iceberg	starboard	starboard

Robertson died in 1915, having lived long enough to see his fictitious story come frightenly true.

■ In August, 1912, Madeleine Astor gave birth to a boy, John Jacob Astor V.

■ One of the survivors in lifeboat 7 was actress Dorothy Gibson. Exactly one month after the *Titanic* sank, Gibson co-wrote and starred in a silent movie called *Saved from the Titanic*. In the movie, she wore the same dress that she wore the night the real *Titanic* sank.

■ In 1913 the racehorse Craganour was disqualified after having won the English Derby. No one complained about the horse having won, but the race's stewards awarded the win to the second place finisher. Only later was it revealed that B. Ismay was the owner of the horse. This B. Ismay turned out to be Bower Ismay, younger brother of J. Bruce Ismay. The widespread feeling in the English racing community was that no horse owned by the Ismay family should win their most important award.

■ Molly Brown died in 1932. She was never called "Unsinkable Molly Brown" while she lived. It wasn't until 1960 when the Broadway musical *The Unsinkable Molly Brown* opened that Molly Brown became "unsinkable."

■ In 1848 the seaport town of Cobb, Ireland changed its name to Queenstown in honor of Queen Victoria. In 1922, Queenstown was once again renamed Cobb.
In 1915 then Queenstown was propelled into the front page of world events when Lusitania was sunk off Queenstown and the ship's survivors were taken there.

GLOSSARY

This glossary is provided to help readers understand some of the nautical terminology used in this book.

Aft: toward the back of the ship.
Amidships: the middle portion of the ship.
Astern: toward the back of the ship.
Barge: a small flat-bottomed, unpowered floating platform that was pushed or towed into position. Used to carry coal, equipment or other bulk items.
Berth: the place where a ship is docked at a wharf *or* a place to sleep (such as bed).
Bilge: the inside of the double bottom of the ship.
Boat deck: topmost deck on the ship, where lifeboats were stored and launched from.
Boatswain: a junior officer who commands the anchor and deck crew.
Bow: the front of the ship.
Bridge: where the ship is guided from and where the captain of the ship commands from. Usually the highest or close to the highest deck on the ship.
Bulkhead: a wall between two compartments.
Capsize: if a ship becomes unbalanced with too much weight on one side, the ship will tip over toward that side. Generally, this is the most common occurrence when a ship sinks.
Capstan: a revolving cylinder used for hoisting weights by winding in a cable or chain.
Collier: a barge used to transport coal to the side of a ship.
Collapsible (Englehardt boat): a boat made with canvas sides and a wooden bottom. Stored on ship with the sides folded down, it was the crew's

responsibility to build up the side supports before launching the boat. There were four of these on *Titanic*.

Corridor: a hallway or passageway

Compartment: a room.

Crow's Nest: a small platform high on the foreword mast, used by the look-outs to stand on.

Davit: a small crane used to lower the lifeboats, two being required for each boat.

Deck: the nautical term for the floor.

Displacement: the volume of water displaced by a boat which is one of the measures of a ship's size. The amount of water a ship displaces must exceed the actual weight of the ship.

Docking bridge: an open platform running the width of the ship on top of the poop deck that contained equipment to communicate with the bridge. Used primarily when in port to help with docking the ship.

Drydock: enclosed area where water is pumped out of to allow construction or repair of a ship.

Fall: ropes attached to boats and the davits, used to lower the boats.

Fireman: a person who tended the fires in the boilers.

First Class: the best accommodations on the ship, obviously with various levels of 'upgrade'. First Class passengers paid the highest rate and received access to all of the amenities.

Forecastle (fo'c'sle): a small raised deck at the bow of a ship.

Forepeak: the most forward compartment of the ship.

Forward: toward the front (bow).

Funnel: another name for smokestack. Technically ships don't have smoke-stacks, they have funnels.

Galley: kitchen where food is prepared.

Gangway: a door in the side of a ships hull.

Graving Dock: a drydock a ship is placed into, used to do the fitting out of a new ship.

Greaser: a crewman whose primary job was to apply grease to all the moving parts of the engines.

HMS: initials for His (or Her) Majesty's Ship, for vessels of the Royal Navy.

Hull: the enclosed frame of a ship.

Joiner: a crewman who was a carpenter or cabinetmaker.

Keel: the lowest part of the ship *or* the lowest structural member upon which the rest of the ship is constructed.

Knot: a unit of speed (1.15 miles per hour) *or* distance (2,000 yards).

List: if the weight of a ship becomes unbalanced, the ship will tilt to one side or the other.

Lough: (as in Belfast Lough): a bay or an inlet of the sea.

Marconi: the brand name of the wireless telegraph unit carried on *Titanic*, owned and staffed by the Marconi Company.

Masthead light: a bright white light located at the top of the mast.

Orlop (deck): lowest actual deck of a ship, the deck above the tank top on *Titanic*.

Poop Deck: a raised deck at the very stern (rear) of the ship.

Port: if standing on the deck of a ship looking forward, port is the left side of the ship.

Promenade deck: a public place for the passengers to go for a walk. Each class had it's own promenade deck.

Quartermaster: a junior officer responsible for the navigation of the ship. On *Titanic*, they were the one's responsible for manning the ships wheel.

RMS: in the early part of the 20th century, initials for Royal Mail Steamer *or* Royal Mail Steamship.

Reciprocating engine: a high-pressure steam-driven engine with pistons that turn a crankshaft which then turns a propeller.

Second Class: a class of accommodations better than Third Class but not as good as First Class. Second Class passengers were afforded many amenities that Third Class passengers weren't.

Sidelights: a large light located on the side of the bridge, colored red for port and green for starboard. These allow other ships to determine the course, speed and distance at night.

Starboard: if standing on the deck of a ship looking forward, starboard is the right side of the ship.

Steerage: (or Third Class): the part of the ship allocated to the cheapest and largest class of accommodations, placed in the lowest portions of the ship, usually in the stern near the steering apparatus. The accommodations were often a berth in a dormitory-type room.

Stern: the rear of the ship.

Stoker: a crewman who fed coal into the ships furnace, usually with a shovel-like tool.

Third Class: see Steerage.

Tiller: lever used to turn a ships rudder.

Transverse bulkhead: bulkheads going across the width of the ship.

Trimmer: a member of the crew who distributes coal from the coal bunker to the stoker who shovels it into the boiler fires.

Upper deck(s): the topmost decks on the ship that are exposed to the open air.

Well deck: a part of the upper deck that sits slightly lower than the decks around it. There were two well decks on Titanic, one fore and one aft. These were the Third Class promenade areas.

BIBLIOGRAPHY

BOOKS

Ballard, Robert D. *The Discovery of the Titanic.* New York: Warner, 1987.

Beesley, Lawrence. *The Loss of the SS Titanic.* Boston: Houghton Mifflin, 1912.

Bullock, Shane F. *A Titanic Hero: Thomas Andrews, Shipbuilder.* Baltimore: Norman, Remington 1913.

Davie, Michael. *Titanic: the Death and Life of a Legend.* London: Bodley Head, 1986.

Eaton, John P. and Charles Haas. *Titanic: Destination Disaster.* New York: W. W. Norton, 1987.

Eaton, John P. and Charles Haas. *Titanic: Triumph and Tragedy.* New York: W. W. Norton, 1988.

Gracie, Archibald. *The Truth About the Titanic.* New York: Kennerly, 1913.

Hoffman, William and Jack Grimm. *Beyond Reach: The Search for the Titanic.* New York: Beaufort, 1982.

Kuntz, Tom. ed. *The Titanic Disaster Hearings: The Official Transcripts of the 1912 Senate Investigation.* New York: Pocket Books, 1998

Lightoller, Charles Herbert. *The Titanic and Other Ships.* London: Nicholson and Watson, 1935.

Lord, Walter. *A Night to Remember.* New York: Holt, Rinehart and Winston, 1955.

Lord, Walter. *The Miracle of Dunkirk.* New York: William Morrow, 1976.

Lord, Walter. *The Night Lives On.* New York: William Morrow, 1986.

Pellegrino, Charles. *Her Name, Titanic.* New York: Avon Books, 1988.

Simpson, Colin. *The Lusitania.* Boston: Little, Brown and Company, 1972.

Wade, Wynn Craig. *The Titanic: the End of a Dream.* New York: Penquin, 1979.

Winocour, Jack, ed. *The Story of the Titanic as told by its Survivors.* New York: Dover Publications, Inc., 1960.

PERIODICALS

Ballard, Robert D. "How We Found *Titanic.*" *National Geographic,* (December 1985).

Carrothers, John C. "Lord of the *Californian.*" *United States Naval Institute Proceedings* 94

(March 1968).

Carrothers, John C. "The *Titanic* Disaster," *United States Naval Institute Proceedings* 88 (April 1962).

Lord, Walter: "Maiden Voyage." *American Heritage,* December 1955.

DOCUMENTS

Great Britain, Parliamentary Debates (Commons), 5th series, 37–42, April 15–October 25, 1912.

U.S. Congress, Senate, *Hearings of a Subcommittee of the Senate Commerce Committee pursuant to S. Res. 283, to Investigate the Causes leading to the Wreck of the White Star Liner "Titanic."* 62nd Congress, 2nd session, 1912. S. Doc 726 (#6167).

U.S. Congress, Senate, *Loss of the Steamship 'Titanic': Report of a Formal Investigation...as conducted by the British Government, Presented by Mr. Smith,* 62nd Congress, 2nd session, 20 August 1912, S. Doc. 933 (#6179).

U.S. Congress, Senate, *Report of the Senate Committee on Commerce pursuant to S. Res. 283, Directing the Committee to Investigate the Causes of the Sinking of the 'Titanic' with speeches by William Alden Smith and Isador Rayner,* 62nd Congress, 2nd session, 28 May 1912, S. Rept. 806 (#6127).

INTERNET SITES

Discovery Channel Online:
   http://www.discovery.com/area/science/titanic/titanicopener.html
Encyclopedia Smithsonian:
   http://www.si.edu/resource/faq/nmah/titanic.htm
In Memoriam: RMS *Titanic*
   http://www.wwa.com/~dsp/titanic
Molly Brown House:
   http://mollybrown.com
Titanic Diagram:
   http://members.aol.com/lorbus
Titanic Historical Society:
   http://titanic1.org

New from Lee W. Merideth . . .

GREY GHOST
THE STORY OF THE AIRCRAFT CARRIER HORNET

(Available Summer 2001)

(Includes a Self-guided tour of the Aircraft Carrier
Hornet Museum in Alameda, California)

The United States Navy's most decorated combat ship, the USS *Hornet* (CV-12), holds the record for the number of enemy ships and aircraft destroyed during World War II. During a span of fifteen months, *Hornet's* pilots shot down 668 enemy planes, destroyed 742 more on the ground, and sank or damaged 486 ships totaling 1,269,710 tons. After being decommissioned for a brief period, *Hornet* was brought back into service, modernized three times, and saw service in Vietnam. She also served as the Prime Recovery Vessel for the Apollo 11 and Apollo 12 moon missions.

Decommissioned again in 1970 after 26 years of stellar service, *Hornet* languished in reserve and disposal status for almost another three decades until a dedicated group of volunteers saved the gallant old ship from the cutter's torch in 1997 and moved her to the former Alameda Naval Air Station,

California, for conversion into a floating museum. Now, future generations can walk her decks and ponder the sacrifices made by thousands of her former crewmen to preserve the freedoms we enjoy today.

Lee Merideth is a docent at the Aircraft Carrier Hornet Museum and is the author of the best selling *1912 Facts About Titanic* (1999).

Although there are several excellent histories and coffee table-style books available on the history of the *Hornet*, Mr. Merideth did not believe there was a suitable book for either casual visitors or experts on the subject; *Grey Ghost* is the result of that belief.

In addition to being a complete history of the *Hornet*, *Grey Ghost* also covers the development of aircraft carriers, the history of the six previous ships named *Hornet*, and the story of the seventh *Hornet* (CV-8), which carried Jimmy Doolittle and his raiders on their bombing mission over Tokyo in April 1942.

Grey Ghost also contains a detailed and fascinating self-guided tour of the Aircraft Carrier Hornet Museum at Alameda Point, California. In addition, *Grey Ghost* boasts numerous drawings and text sections entitled "How it Works," which explain how the ship's various systems operate, such as the 5" gun, elevator, the engine room, and how steam is generated to drive the engines that turn the propeller shafts. After leading hundreds of tours of the gallant ship, author Lee Merideth realized that what visitors really wanted and needed were explanations about how aircraft carriers work.

The remaining portion of the book serves as a self-guided tour of the Hangar Deck, Second Deck, Flight Deck and Island.

ELEVATOR DIAGRAM

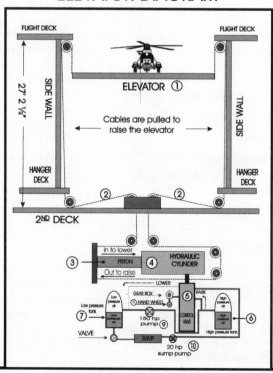

GREY GHOST
THE STORY OF THE AIRCRAFT CARRIER HORNET

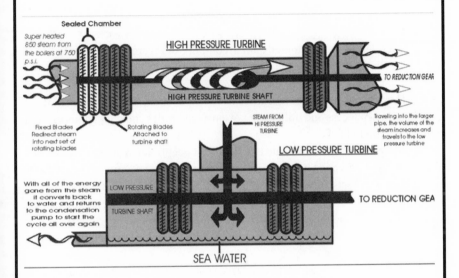

Specifications: 240 pages, 6" x 9", soft cover, 30 photographs, 12 drawings. Acid-free 50-lb. natural stock. $15.00 each, postage-paid.

All books ordered directly from the publisher will be signed and personally inscribed upon request.

Historical Indexes Publishing Company, Dept. T-1, P O Box 64142, Sunnyvale, CA 94088

(Please make out your check or money order to Historical Indexes)

Lee Merideth is available to speak to your group or answer your questions. Write or email him at historyindex@earthlink.net

About the Author

Lee W. Merideth is the acclaimed author-compiler of several historical magazine indexes, including *Civil War Times and Civil War Times, Illustrated 30-year Index* (1989) and the mammoth two-volume *Guide to Civil War Periodicals* (1991 and 1995). These combined 110,000 entries have helped thousands of students of the Civil War better access and utilize their extensive libraries and collections of Civil War-related periodicals.

In addition to the Civil War, Lee has been deeply interested in the *Titanic* disaster for over 35 years. In the process of his research he accumulated over 4,000 index cards with facts and figures, all of which formed the foundation for his best selling *1912 Facts About Titanic*. He speaks regularly on *Titanic* at bookstores, schools, libraries, and the traveling Titanic exhibitions around the country—often accompanied by a large replica of the doomed liner, background graphics, and a large White Star Line flag.

Lee's latest book is *Grey Ghost: The Story of the Aircraft Carrier Hornet* (June 2001) which is both a history of the United States Navy's most decorated warship and a self-guided tour of the Aircraft Carrier *Hornet* Museum in Alameda, California.

A graduate of California Polytechnic State University in San Luis Obispo, California, and a retired United States Army officer, Lee has been in the printing business for more than 25 years and currently lives in San Jose, California, where he works as the production manager for a weekly technical newspaper.

*   *   *

To receive a personally inscribed copy of *1912 Facts About Titanic* or *Grey Ghost: The Story of the Aircraft Carrier Hornet*, or to schedule Lee to speak to your group, email or write to him at P. O. Box 64142, Sunnyvale, California 94088-4142. For more information, see www.factsabouttitanic.com.